Eve's Journey

Feminine Images in
Hebraic Literary Tradition

Nehama Aschkenasy

University of Pennsylvania Press
Philadelphia   1986

Copyright 1986
University of Pennsylvania Press
ALL RIGHTS RESERVED

Library of Congress Cataloging-in-Publication Data

Aschkenasy, Nehama.
  Eve's journey.

  Includes bibliographies and index.
  1. Women in the Bible.   2. Women in Judaism.
3. Women in literature.   4. Hebrew literature,
Modern—History and criticism.   5. Eve (Biblical
figure) in fiction, drama, poetry, etc.   I. Title.
BS1199.W7A78   1986   892.4'09'352042   86-26683
ISBN 0-8122-8033-4

Calligraphy by Renalda Keller

In Memory of My Father
YITZHAK GOTTLIEB
A Talmudist and a Humanist
Who Practiced Our Sages' Dictum
"A Man Is Under the Obligation to
Teach His Daughter Torah"
                              (Sotah 20a)

Contents

Acknowledgments

Thanks are due to the following for permission to quote from their material:

The Jewish Publication Society of America, for quotations from Martin Buber, *For the Sake of Heaven,* translated by Ludwig Lewisohn, copyright © 1953.

Deborah Owen Limited and Amos Oz, for quotations from Amos Oz, *My Michael,* translated by Nicholas de Lange, copyright © 1972; and from "Nomad and Viper" and "Strange Fire" in Amos Oz, *Where the Jackals Howl and Other Stories,* translated by Philip Simpson, copyright © 1980.

Harcourt Brace Jovanovich, Inc., for quotations from "Nomad and Viper" and "Strange Fire" in Amos Oz, *Where the Jackals Howl and Other Stories,* translated by Philip Simpson, copyright © 1980.

Schocken Books, Inc., for quotations from "The Tale of the Scribe," "The Kerchief," "The Lady and the Pedlar," "Agunot," and "The Doctor's Divorce" in S. Y. Agnon, *Twenty One Stories,* edited by Nahum M. Glatzer, copyright © 1970.

Preface

Eve's journey is not a single, clearly delineated chronological progress that leads directly from the biblical Eve to the collective feminine protagonist in modern Hebraic letters. It is many journeys, taken by a variety of female characters. All of them are, perhaps, splinters and fragments of the original Eve; but each and every fictional female figure is also a mirror of her times, a product of her creator's mood and literary imagination, and of his conception of the woman's role in society and in fiction.

Furthermore, Hebraic literature is a massive body of letters, a rich treasury of creative expressions and ingenious stylistic techniques, written over many centuries and in many different locations. Therefore, in my attempts to trace Eve's long and manifold journeys through the ages, I have confined myself to a number of images and to certain literary forms. Any critic's preference is, by definition, somewhat arbitrary, and mine is no different. While the choice of works and figures to be discussed was partly dictated by subjective tastes, the main focus of this study did provide objective criteria for selecting the literary texts.

Before defining the boundaries and limits of the present study, it is important to note that it is not confined to a specific era; instead, it regards the whole historical spectrum of Hebraic letters as a storehouse from which to choose examples and illustrations. The reason for this rather broad perspective is the significance that is given here to the evolution and metamorphosis of a prototype. The present study aims at tracing the migrations of an image or a situation, focusing on the phenomenon of metempsychosis, the Hebraic *gilgul,* not in its metaphysical but in its literary sense. It follows a feminine prototype or a typical, sometimes archetypal, feminine experience from its earliest literary reflection, the Bible, to its later reincarnations. The vast historical body of Hebraic tradition unfolds the evolution of the female image and reveals the various metamorphoses it has experienced through the ages, and the changing cultural conceptions of women and their place in the scheme of things.

Of postbiblical literature, the present study concentrates on the narrative form, both in its prose and poetic genres, and excludes drama and lyrical poetry. As Gershon Shaked rightly maintains, the play form is the only "new" literary genre in Hebraic letters, a genre that has no precedence in earlier times.[1] Though the novel form is also young, it has its roots in the storytelling tradition that started in the Bible itself and continued in the Midrash. Thus, while many biblical female figures are reincarnated in Hebrew drama, I chose not to include a discussion of a dramatic figure, even though she may have originated in an earlier female model, so as not to juxtapose a figure that started in the narrative tradition with one that is seen as a dramatic protagonist.[2] The poetic genre is as old as Hebrew literature itself; nevertheless, a study of feminine images in the tradition of lyrical poetry, and their culmination in the works of several of the prominent modern women poets is outside the boundaries of the present book and would belong in a separate work.

On the other hand, any folk tale, homily, novel, short story, long narrative poem, or dramatic verse that recounts a feminine experience or portrays a feminine image is regarded as a suitable text from which to draw examples. However, a narrative poem or a prose work that recreates a biblical character would not automatically qualify as an example of a stage in Eve's historical odyssey. The mere fact that the writer chooses the biblical Deborah or Ruth, for instance, as the subject of his work is not enough of a reason for discussing this particular work. Such a text will be noted here only if it actually adds a dimension to, or illuminates a certain aspect of the early female figure, or shows an awareness of the feminine predicament that does not exist in the earlier version. Thus Tchernichovsky's poem, "The Dinah Affair" (or "The Dinah Portion"), is of particular significance not because it has the biblical Dinah at its center, but mainly because it gives an antipatriarchal twist to a story rooted in patriarchal tenets, and therefore opens our eyes to the predicament of the biblical Dinah. The same is true of Y. L. Gordon's poem, "The Love of David and Michal," which is discussed in the present study not because of its biblical theme, but because it romanticizes the original story, thus drawing our attention to the decidedly unromantic qualities of the original tale.

If the first principle of selection is the introduction of a new perspective on an ancient female figure, the second is the submerged presence of an early female archetype in a modern fictional creation. In the cluster of works that belong to this category are included all modern texts that revolve around a female protagonist or that address themselves to the woman's question, and where an early female type is embedded in a modern-day, realistically drawn individual. Thus Amos Oz's "Strange Fire," in which the contemporary woman Lily is suddenly revealed as a modern incarnation of the legendary Lilith, is of special interest in the context of the present study.

While the centrality of a female figure is one of the guiding principles in the selection of texts in the present study, another is the accepted status of the literary work as a major artistic achievement, or as a proponent of contemporary literary trends. In short, the standard for isolating a certain work and highlighting it is aesthetic and not ideological; the inherent "sexual politics" of a given work is not enough of a reason for its inclusion in the present discussion. As we know, minor works also reflect social premises and can often serve as important sociological documents. Since the present study focuses on the literary imagination, however, the artistic energy with which the female figure, or the feminine predicament, is infused is of major consideration.

The book starts with a brief historical introduction that traces the evolution of the female "otherness" in Hebraic literature. By definition, this chapter is meant to provide a glancing view of the thread that connects the variety of feminine experiences as depicted in Hebraic letters. This common thread is the role of the "other" that the feminine figure has been relegated to in texts where the male point of view is accepted as the standard and the norm. The following two chapters are arranged in accordance with the two most prevalent and frequent feminine images that populate the male texts: the woman as the deadly seductress and as the formidable giver of life. The next chapter charts the ordeal of the real-life woman in the male-dominant culture, where her precarious legal standing and sexual vulnerability are exploited by the man. The final chapter delineates the variety of female strategies devised by the woman in order to overcome her role in the male's mind as the portentous force of mythic dimensions, on the one hand, and her actual wordly status as the silent, insignificant "second sex," on the other.

I came to the study of female images in Hebraic literature through many routes and a variety of academic and personal interests. As a woman who studied literature before the rise of feminist literary scholarship,

I found myself, in the past decade, going back to familiar texts with a new awareness. On the lecture circuit, I encountered an ever-growing thirst for an exposition of the feminine predicament in the narrative parts of the Hebraic sources. Works that I formerly explicated from a literary perspective, now required a new slant and a new hermeneutical approach. As I reexamined the ancient Judaic works, I found tales of terror that needed to be retold from the perspective of the female victim, side by side with nonsexist enclaves that waited to be recovered and reinterpreted. I also realized that the modern secular and enlightened male writers still draw on old stereotypes, hardened and engraved in the collective Jewish male consciousness, in their creations of contemporary female protagonists. The search for an ancient type in a modern garb proved at once fruitful and illuminating. Consequently, single seminars on women in Judaic sources that I gave to Bible societies and women's groups, ultimately culminated in semester-long courses that I created for a number of college programs in Connecticut.

Since 1980, I have taught courses in images of women in world literature at the University of Connecticut at Stamford. I start each course in "Women in Literature to 1900" with a close reading of the Eve narrative in the Bible, comparing the variety of translations with the Hebrew original. The nonsexist attitudes that this ancient text yields invariably surprise my students, most of whom have never read the biblical text itself, but who are all coming to the old tale with the popular conception that the biblical story pronounces female inferiority and advocates the subjugation of women. Other texts that we study in class also force us to go back to the biblical prototypes. From Chaucer's Proverbs-quoting, misogynic husband of the Wife of Bath, through Milton's vain and stubborn Eve, to Hawthorne's adulterous Hester, cultically sinful yet morally innocent, the literary protagonists reenact and relive biblical attitudes and ambiguities.

The rapid proliferation of works on women in literature in this country, which have aided me in drawing up my courses in women in American, British, and European literature, only illuminated for me the scarcity of studies in English of feminine images in the vast body of Hebraic letters. I hope that *Eve's Journey* will be followed by other explorations of the woman in the Hebraic tradition, covering the many other faces of Eve that the present work could not include.

I was fortunate to have a group of the most distinguished critics and writers read different parts of my manuscript and offer their observations. Among them are Robert Alter, Harold Fisch, Blu Greenberg, David H. Hirsch, and Baruch Levine. Cynthia Ozick read an early version of my discussion of the story of Hannah, and also proposed a change in one of the titles, for which I am grateful. I also wish to thank Mr. Arthur Evans, Associate Director of the University of Pennsylvania Press, for the interest that he took in this project and his determination to see it materialize in book form.

Notes

[1] Gershon Shaked, *The Hebrew Historical Drama in the Renaissance,* in Hebrew (Jerusalem: Mosad Bialik, 1970), 9.

[2] The weaknesses that Shaked has detected in Hebrew historical drama, such as the writers' tendency to stereotype their characters, and their overriding preoccupations with the crises of their own times, that often proved detrimental to the dramatic and theatrical qualities of their works, also contributed to my decision to exclude Hebrew drama from the present study. See Shaked, 153 et passim.

Eve's Journey

The Mutation of
Feminine Otherness:
A Historical Overview

Why does the woman walk in front of the corpse at a funeral, and why was the precept of menstruation given to her? Because she shed the blood of Adam (by bringing death to man). And why was the precept of the dough (hallah) given to her? Because she corrupted Adam, who was the dough of the world. And why was the precept of the Sabbath lights given to her? Because she extinguished the soul of Adam.
  Genesis Rabbah 17, 8

The work of civilization has become increasingly the business of men . . . the woman finds herself forced into the background by the claims of civilization and she adopts a hostile attitude towards it.
  Freud, *Civilization and Its Discontent*

he purpose of the present study is to examine some of the diverse images of the Jewish woman in Hebraic sources, by closely reading representative literary texts and exploring the conception of women reflected in them. The scope of the works discussed here is broad, covering biblical narratives, Midrash commentaries, Kabbalah sources, Hasidic tales, Hebrew literature of the Enlightenment, and contemporary Israeli fiction. This vast historical spectrum is needed if we want to follow an archetypal or prototypical feminine figure as it travels through generations and cultures, often metamorphosing in the process and changing its original essence or meaning. The historical range also helps in uncovering the ancient roots of female predicaments and male biases, and in tracing the changing cultural perceptions of women in Hebraic letters.

The emphasis in this survey is on Hebraic sources, therefore it follows the route that Hebrew literature took from ancient Israel, through the various European countries where the Jews dwelled during their long exilic journey, to the literature of modern Israel, which is the legitimate heir of the Hebraic tradition by virtue of its use of the Hebrew language. Modern Hebrew literature very often denies its debt to the Jewish exilic experience and tries to sever its ties with the European past; nevertheless, by its sheer existence it provides a link in the long historical chain of Hebrew letters. Language is not only a technical medium; it is a realm of cultural symbols and associations that touch depths that the user is often not completely aware of. No matter how much the Hebrew writer attempts, in theory, to define himself by means of the present cultural and geopolitical realities, the genius of the creative minds of the past asserts itself through the language, very often enriching the contemporary imagination, even though the latter professes to be opposed to the basic tenets of the former. Biblical motifs, as well as images created by the rabbinic and Hasidic imagination, often find their way into modern works, sometimes in disguise, thus attesting to the deep roots of the seemingly new and "young" phenomenon of modern Hebrew literature.

American-Jewish literature, another body of creative works that gives testimony to a non-European Jewish experience, will not be

5

discussed in the present study. However, to illustrate the persistence of a literary type and its surprising emergence on a new soil, let us consider the now prevalent stereotype of the American-Jewish young woman, thrice removed from the immigrant experience, that has come to be known as the Jewish American Princess.[1] Contemporary scholars find the roots of this denigrating stereotype of a self-centered, vulgar, and materialistic woman in the particular sociohistorical circumstances of the Jewish-American experience—the erosion of the father's status in the immigrant family, and the awakening of materialism and excessive consumption after years of poverty and deprivation. They also attribute the emergence of this stereotype to general trends in contemporary American culture, including, for example, male writers' inability to cope with a depatriarchalized society.

It is true that this particular stereotype, the Jewish American Princess, is anchored in the Jewish-American experience; significantly, contemporary Israeli writers do not stereotype young women in this fashion. However, the tendency to stereotype women is an age-old tradition, and in attempting to unravel the roots of modern stereotypes we have to go to earlier sources and find how they treat similar feminine figures. While to the unequipped eye contemporary stereotypes are solely the product of present-day social circumstances and biases, cultural roots run deep. The frivolous and materialistic Jewish American Princess sounds very much like the "haughty daughters of Zion" who earn the wrath of the prophet Isaiah. He describes them as they "walk with outstretched necks and ogling eyes, walking and mincing as they go, and making a tinkling with their feet" (Isa. 3:16). And we wonder what happened to the saintly, chaste "daughter of Israel" described, for example, in I. L. Peretz's "Three Gifts." Here the young Jewish girl embodies everything that is exalted and admirable in the Jewish people. Condemned to die by being tied to a horse and dragged through the streets of the city for the crime of inadvertently entering the Gentile quarters, she asks only for pins, so that she can fasten her skirt to her skin and retain her modesty.

Interestingly, in all three sources, the biblical, the shtetl story, and modern American writings, the "daughter of Israel" is the product of the male point of view and is made to epitomize an entire reality. These three images, coming as they are from different literary worlds and historical experiences, can tell us much about cultural attitudes and literary visions. The contemporary writers who have created the unflattering image of the Jewish American Princess are not necessarily expressing the male's derogatory attitude to women; they attempt to criticize a whole life-style and culture, shared by both men and women. In doing this, they follow a tradition in which the feminine figure is made to symbolize an entire reality or a whole race; Jerusalem lying in shambles after the destruction of the first Temple is likened by the biblical poet to a lonely, desolate widow (Lam. 1:1), and the kingdom of Judah, threatened by the Assyrians, is pictured as a young woman who mocks at her assailant: "The virgin, the daughter of Zion, despises thee; the daughter of Jerusalem tosses her head at thee" (Isa. 37:22). Therefore, a horizontal view, that is, a comparison of the literary stereotype with other contemporary feminine images created by male writers, would conclude that the Jewish American Princess is the creation of the misogynist mind. However, a vertical view, that is, a comparison of the modern literary type with earlier sources, would show that the contemporary image is part of a long tradition in which the Jewish daughter is made to be a literary vehicle through which the writer condemns, or celebrates, the entire Jewish people.

When, then, is the feminine literary figure the "other," and when is she made to transcend that otherness and encompass the total reality or the entire human condition? Simone de Beauvoir argues in *The Second Sex* that women have taken a back seat and occupied a secondary position in Western literary tradition, just as in life. Women have played the role of the "other" for men; whether they were put on a pedestal as a symbol of virtue and nobility, or blamed as the originators of death and sin in this world, women were not allowed to epitomize the entire human experience. Beauvoir's thesis generally holds true for the role of women in Jewish literary history, but it fails to exhaust the whole picture.

The theme of "otherness" in Judaic tradition is replete with various meanings. First, there is the concept of the *sitra aḥra,* the 'other side', which applies not to women directly but to the other side in the cosmos and in man, that is, to the realm of darkness and of the antinomian forces that operate in the universe and in the human soul. Does the woman, who has been the sociological "other," come to epitomize the mystical or psychic "other" as well? Many times she does, and the conversion of one form of "otherness" into another, the journey that a literary image is making as it shuttles between the psychic-spiritual sphere and the sociocultural realm, will be made clear as we examine some of the feminine images in Judaic literature.

Secondly, the Jewish exilic experience positioned the Jew as the "other" in the Gentile world and thus created a solidarity between Jewish men and women as both played the role of the stranger, the oppressed minority, in a hostile environment. According to Simone de Beauvoir, the social and cultural otherness of women resulted from the fact that men were the lawmakers and creators of the norms by which women were judged. This was true of the internal relationship between men and women in the Judaic tradition. The men saw themselves as the interpreters of the Mosaic law, and they formulated rules of conduct that applied to the most intimate details of women's life and their physical cycle. Jewish halaka, the Talmudic law, is the product of the male mind and thus it reflects the man's conception of the world. In Jewish halaka women are certainly the "other" since they are being treated and discussed by men, and regarded as part of the male experience. One of the six sections of the Mishnah is titled *Nashim* (Women), which makes it very clear that to the mind of the Talmudic rabbis, women were an object of study and exploration, an entity apart from the male world, the latter being the norm of the human condition. Man experiences life, and woman is one of the objects to be experienced. However, in their status vis-à-vis the outside world, both the Jewish man and the Jewish woman were the social pariah, the other. The Gentile world created the law which the Jew had to follow if he wanted to survive. The social otherness of the Jew was inevitably transformed into a metaphysical otherness, when the Jew came to be regarded in the popular mind as a sorcerer, an evil demon, or a devil that feasts on Christian blood.

The plot thickens when we shift our perspective and observe the image of the Jewish woman as it was perceived through the lenses of the non-Jewish world in European literature of the Middle Ages and later. An interesting evolution in the otherness of the Jew occurred outside Jewish literature, starting in medieval popular lore and culminating in two famous Renaissance plays, Marlowe's *The Jew of Malta* and Shakespeare's *The Merchant of Venice*. The image of the Jew was split into that of the villainous, ugly, and often demonic Jewish father, and his gentle and beautiful daughter.[2] The Jewish daughter helps her Christian lover against her father, who in early sources is an evil magician and in later plays a mean usurer with faint hints of the demonic. By helping her Christian lover outwit her father, and aligning herself with the non-Jewish world (as does Jessica in *The Merchant of Venice*), the Jew's daughter is redeemed from her social and spiritual otherness. She abandons her malevolent father and her cursed race, thus shaking off her universal and metaphysical otherness and becoming part of the mainstream, the norm, represented by the Christian world. Yet if she left one type of otherness behind, the Jew's daughter now entered a literary tradition which, as Katharine Rogers and others have shown, was saturated with the denigration of women and with often unabashed, outright misogyny.[3]

Within the boundaries of Judaic intellectual creativity and literary lore, the image of the woman continued to shuttle between different, and sometimes contradictory, stereotypical configurations. The feminine image took on new meanings and dimensions that often responded to, and reflected, the vicissitudes of Jewish history and the changes in the Jew's fortunes.

The Testimony of the Ancient Documents

Much of feminist scholarship today concerns itself with exposing ancient testimonies to deep-seated sexist attitudes that have long been implanted in the collective human consciousness. Some critics turn to the Bible and early Judaic sources in an attempt to uncover the cultural and mythical roots in which misogyny is embedded. Indeed, the Bible has been accused of having had a major role in promoting and cultivating misogyny and in encouraging the suppression and degradation of women. It has been argued, for example, that the roots of condoning wife battery can be found in the Old Testament account of Eve's sin and her subsequent punishment, a story which helped make women culturally legitimate objects of antagonism.[4] And the Bible's apparent acceptance of the patriarchal system—reflected in both its legal portions and the narratives—has been interpreted as a deliberate strategy on the part of the biblical lawmaker and storyteller to perpetuate male dominance and female subjugation.[5] Biblical language, using masculine pronouns and male metaphors for God, is seen as responsible for the male-sexist bent of monotheism. Some modern feminists argue that social patriarchy and all its accompanying evils were buttressed by monotheism, which they describe—with some justification—as essentially a father religion. They also contend that from a psychological viewpoint, the image of God as a Freudian father figure further conditioned women to submissiveness and self-effacement.

There is no denying that the Bible displays an underlying patriarchal orientation, reflecting a male dominant worldview as well as social system. But it would be simplistic to say that the Bible deliberately promotes male dominion and female subordination. Rather, it reflects an early, primitive socioeconomic reality in which a person's value was determined by his physical strength and his ability to contribute to the family's economy and power. The Bible's legal system is inevitably tied to this premodern, labor-intensive society. Therefore, if many laws, anchored in a patriarchal and patrilineal system, seem as if they discriminate against women, they may have had their origin in necessity rather than a deliberate policy in a society where the survival of the family depended on the number of the males it had.

It is also possible to view the exclusion of women from some of the cultic practices not as a denial of rights but as an exemption from burden, given the hard life of women of childbearing age in biblical and Talmudic times. It is safe to say that biblical law did not create the situation of male supremacy, nor did it openly champion it; it merely responded to a given reality and social structure.

To learn more of the Bible's perception of women and their place in the scheme of things, one has to turn to the stories in which women play a role, whether central or marginal. Again, feminists are right in complaining that the bulk of biblical narratives is centered on men, and that women are usually relegated to a minor position in them. The few "token" prophetesses and extraordinary female characters are an exception and further illuminate the inferior position of the majority of women in the biblical culture, as well as the male writers' lack of interest in women as literary protagonists. Furthermore, the biblical term for sexual relationship, 'to know', puts woman in a position of the "other" in the realm of life's experiences. The phrase "And Adam knew Eve his wife" (Gen. 4:1) suggests that man knows and woman is the known; he experiences, and she is the territory that is explored and acted upon. Before the expulsion from the Garden of Eden they both "knew that they were naked" (Gen. 3:7), but outside the Edenic experience man is the subject, the knower, and woman is the object, the known. The sexual act is the possession of woman by man; man is active and woman is passive in the way they "know" life, that is, understand and experience it.

Still, a close reading of many biblical tales that revolve around women yields mixed results as to the Bible's conception of women. If some tales appear to be imbued with male chauvinistic attitudes, others seem to be free of any sexist bent. Even those stories that throughout the ages have been read as paradigms of female subordination may sometimes reveal a surprisingly unbiased attitude to women and an egalitarian conception of the roles of the sexes. Today's new feminist awareness has lent an added dimension to the reading of many earlier works and uncovered in them voices unheard before. Therefore, a fresh reading that goes beyond the surface layer and that looks for meanings that were never sought before may be applied to the biblical text as well.

A number of studies that challenge the traditional patriarchal reading of the Old Testament have opened up new avenues of approaching the biblical texts that deal with women. These works—coming from both inside and outside the feminist movement—probe suppressions and misconceptions in biblical interpretation, thus offering a fresh view of biblical heritage and forcing us to reconsider unquestioned age-old teachings. Of special interest is the work of Phyllis Trible who applies the "depatriarchalizing" principle in her reading of the biblical stories.[6] For example, when considered with the aid of this principle, the two creation stories in the Book of Genesis reveal an egalitarian approach which views man and woman as complementing each other. Interestingly, the Talmudic sages recognized very early that the phrase "So God created Mankind in his own image, in the image of God he created him; male and female he created them" (Gen. 1:27) refers to the creation of a double-faced, bisexual human, a creature who enfolded within itself both male and female attributes.[7] The second version of the creation story, the one in which the woman is created out of man's rib, can thus be seen as a sequel to the first story. The first story describes the creation of a bisexual being, while the second describes the splitting of that creature into man and woman. Furthermore, after the act of disobedience Adam and Eve are not cursed, but judged, and God's words telling the woman that her husband shall rule over her are not to be taken as a mandate for male supremacy, but as a description of the faulty and perverse nature of human life after the expulsion from Eden.[8] Significantly, a comparison of the Genesis story with the Gilgamesh tale of the initiation of man and the primal woman makes it very clear that, unlike in the latter source, the creation of Eve is a climactic moment in the Genesis story, not an afterthought. In contrast to the Gilgamesh story, the woman in the Genesis narrative is not presented as a negative character but as an agent of civilization.[9]

The nonsexist bent of many of the scriptural stories becomes evident when we compare them with later texts that either recreate these stories or comment on them. The Jewish sages who produced the Midrash attempted to steer many stories, originally free of sexist biases, into the patriarchal orbit. Eve is seen in the Genesis tale as an intellectually curious person whose quest for knowledge ends in the rash act of violating God's law. As a consequence of this act, man and woman are forced to make themselves clothes, till the land, and invent tools—in short, to launch human civilization as we know it. There is no indication in the original story that Adam is perceived as superior to Eve in any way; man and woman are equally culpable in the eyes of God, and equally responsible for the consequences of their deed. However, in the Midrash cited at the opening of the present chapter, Adam is described as far better than Eve—he is the "dough" of the world—and as a victim of woman's pernicious and evil nature. Eve took away the splendor of the crown of creation, Adam, and reduced him to a mere mortal. Eve's female descendants are assumed to be equally destructive, and will constantly have to make amends for corrupting and debasing man's life. If the biblical Eve is the instrument through which civilization comes into being, the midrashic Eve is, to use Freud's words, a retarding element, a force opposed to the progress of civilization.

It is easy to see the metamorphosis of a nonsexist story into a male-biased, and sometimes even misogynist, document, when we observe texts from different periods that treat the same ancient character. Another Old Testament heroine who is obviously depicted through egalitarian, unbiased lenses, and whose story is whipped into the patriarchal mold by the Midrash sages is Hannah, mother of the prophet Samuel. Hannah, the barren woman whose prayers are answered by God, is the central protagonist of I Sam. I; her story launches an important historical narration, the Book of Samuel.

At first sight, Hannah's tale seems to be the prototypical story of maternal yearnings and their eventual gratification. Hannah, one might argue, is not significant in her own right, but only as the begetter of a glorious man. Yet it soon becomes very clear to the careful reader that, though the larger context of this narrative does not require it, the narrator has painstakingly etched a character of great strength and forcefulness and that, within the boundaries of this self-contained tale, it is the single-minded and determined woman, not her famous offspring, who is meant to sustain the reader's interest and sympathy. Ultimately, the tale transcends its initial thrust and becomes a drama of human aspirations and of an individual's iron-willed determination to achieve them. That this individual's particular aspirations take the form of maternal yearnings becomes incidental to the essence of the story. Hannah is dignified, determined and extremely eloquent, and her vision transcends the immediate and the domestic. She maps out her son's future as a man of God even before she is assured that her prayer will be answered. By the force of her language she makes the longed-for child a reality. Hannah's diversified talents seem to be incongruous with her monolithic pursuit of motherhood, and indicate the paucity of opportunities that existed in ancient times for expression of creativity. Only by having a child, by educating him and shaping his life could such a woman find release for all her hidden talents.

Hannah's husband further introduces an egalitarian, nonpatriarchal tone to the story when he says: "Am I not better to thee than ten sons?" (v. 8). In a male-centered economy, where sons were important as a means of strengthening the extended family and a woman's function was, of necessity, that of procreating, one could expect a loving husband to solace his barren wife by reassuring her that she satisfied him in other ways: "You are as good to me as ten sons." Instead, the husband views himself as the loving partner whose duty it is to make his wife happy. He does not define his relationship with his wife in terms of her familial or sexual duties, but in terms of his contribution to her contentment. Erich Fromm's description of love as an active practice rather than a passive experience applies to Hannah's husband: he must actively overcome the prejudices of his culture to be able to address his wife in this manner.[10]

The incongruity between Hannah's great potential and the narrow path that she chooses, motherhood, creates a certain tension in the story that perhaps rings louder in the modern ear, but that was vaguely sensed by the postbiblical sages as well. The midrashim revolving around Hannah prove without doubt that the sages attempted to bring the biblical story into conformity with prevalent sexist attitudes. The Midrash, for instance, elaborates on the husband's meritorious qualities, thus implying that the son's leadership qualities were already revealed in the father and minimizing the mother's forceful presence in the original story. Furthermore, the sages attribute to the barren Hannah the complaint that her breasts have not been put to use.[11] Thus the Midrash steers Hannah's predicament to the orbit of exclusive feminine fate and anchors her need for a child in her uncontrollable biological drives. As the story is reshaped by the rabbinic mind, it becomes an early example of Erik Erikson's theory of women's biological destiny and the tyranny of their biological "empty space."[12]

The validity of the search for an underlying nonsexist attitude in the biblical story might get an additional support when we consider the question of the authorship of the biblical narratives. Biblical scholars suggest that in ancient Israel, as in the neighboring cultures, there was probably a class of professional storytellers who transmitted their stories orally from one generation to the next, before the stories were finally committed to the written word. Behind many of the Old Testament narratives are old legends that were remembered and passed on in an oral tradition through recital and performance. There is also the hypothesis that women, perhaps the "wise women" who appear in some biblical narratives, were the ancient Israelites' "singers of tales."[13] Women as singers are a well-documented phenomenon; they appear in biblical stories as delivering both victory and mourning songs, and some ancient figurines and relics represent women holding tambourines.

If the theory that women were the locus of storytelling in ancient Israel is correct, then new possibilities open up to the literary critic who looks for the muffled voice of the feminine consciousness in the ancient texts. Chaucer's Wife of Bath cries with regret: "By God, if women had written stories," and a similar sentiment is voiced by the chorus in Euripides' *Medea*. Women did not write in ancient times, nor did they take any part in the redacting of the biblical canon. They may have had a hand, however, in one of the early stages of the historical journey of the ancient legend, when the story was still told orally and remembered with the aid of various mnemonic devices. If so, it would make sense to try and uncover those nonsexist voices that are sometimes heard in the biblical text, and be more alert to the faint murmur of unrest and complaint that may be discovered in the ancient story.

The nonsexist enclaves in biblical narratives might be a residue of a very early, even prepatriarchal, social structure, as well as the mark of a female storyteller. As we journey farther away from biblical times and into more modern civilization, however, those nonsexist echoes become fainter. It would be hard to say that the rabbinic Midrash lacks sympathy for women, but its main orientation is clearly patriarchal and male-dominated.

The Midrash sometimes uses a comic technique that is not free of misogyny in its attempts to reclaim the biblical material for the patriarchal domain. A case in point is the rabbis' treatment of the two prophetesses Deborah and Huldah. The tale concerning Deborah in the Book of Judges is imbued with respect towards this female leader. There is no hint in the biblical text that the narrator saw in Deborah an arrogant, ambitious woman who overstepped her feminine boundaries and who might have been seen by her contemporaries as hateful or ludicrous. The biblical episode involving Huldah in II Kings 22, is brief and terse, offering no comment on the fact that the king of Judah consults with a woman prophetess. The narrator's tone is rather matter-of-fact; he is more concerned with the harsh judgment on Jerusalem pronounced by the prophetess than by her sex. The shaken king, too, accepts her unwelcome prediction without reservations and acts accordingly. However, the sages' reading of these two stories singles out nuances of language that they interpret as displaying these two women's arrogance towards the males in the stories. The sages conclude that Deborah and Huldah were named after hateful animals (hornet and weasel, respectively), because they displayed haughtiness and disrespect towards men. Thus the illustrious Deborah is reduced to a detestable hornet, and the courageous Huldah, who was not afraid to chastise the mighty king, is made into a cowering weasel. The comic dehumanization of women that the

Midrash exemplifies in these two cases is a strategy employed by many male writers throughout literary history.

The sages' tactics of bringing the biblical tale back to the patriarchal sphere may be due to the realities of the era in which the Midrash was produced. Historians might explain that in the dark days after the fall of Jerusalem, the rabbis were concerned with creating a regulated, regimented way of life for the Jewish people that would insulate them from outside influences and create an autonomous framework for their lives. In this context, strengthening the family became of uppermost importance; and the only family structure known as viable was the patriarchal. The Talmudic rabbis in general shifted the religious responsibility from the collective to the individual, and transferred the focus of the religious life from the Temple, that was then lying in shambles, to the synagogue and the home; to use Jacob Neusner's phrase, Jewish leaders turned their attention "from politics to piety." The new emphasis on a personalized religious responsibility resulted in the tightening of all areas of Jewish life, and is probably also apparent in the rabbis' attempt to shape every aspect of society and culture in the patriarchal mold; the greater authority given to one person, the father, guaranteed the stability of the family unit, which now became the center of the religious life.

In the Responsa literature which European Jewish scholars produced ceaselessly from the eleventh century onward, the woman continued to be, as she was in Talmudic literature, an object of legal discussion, part of the life experience of man. The premises of the patriarchal structure are taken for granted, and the laws are intended to buttress them. The *Shulḥan 'Aruk,* the sixteenth-century authoritative guide of Jewish law, codifies the marriage laws in great detail. At the same time, it also addresses itself to a subject of no immediate practical significance, the laws of the *sotah,* the unfaithful wife, which were actually abrogated in the first century by Rabbi Johanan ben Zakkai.

An interesting development occurs in Kabbalah, medieval Jewish mysticism, which abounds with sexual and erotic imagery. In Kabbalistic literature, the Talmudic concept of the Shekinah has metamorphosed into the feminine element in God as opposed to the "Holy One," the masculine element in God. In Aggadic Midrash the Shekinah is God's "immanence" or "indwelling" in the world. It is part of God's spirit that resides with his nation, and it accompanies the Jewish nation in exile, *Galut.* Though the word Shekinah in Hebrew is feminine, the rabbinic mind did not conceive of it as the feminine element in God. The Kabbalists, on the other hand, picked up the gender of the noun Shekinah and described it as the celestial bride, engaged in erotic union with the celestial bridegroom. In the symbolic world of the Zohar (The Book of Splendor), which is the most venerated of all Kabbalah documents, the Shekinah is the Queen, the daughter and bride of God. She appears in a variety of names and images, but she always stands for "eternal womanhood."

By introducing the concept of sexual union within the realm of the divinity itself, Kabbalah seems to maintain an attitude to women and sex that is remarkably different from that held by the medieval Christian world and by the non-Jewish mystics. The medieval church accepted St. Paul's misogynistic condemnation of sex and claimed that marriage was a necessary concession to human frailty, but it was inferior to virginity. Non-Jewish mystics also glorified and propagated asceticism. Christian biblical exegesis transformed eroticism into the relation of God and man, most significantly in its treatment of Canticles. In the commentaries of the period, this biblical paean to love symbolizes the love affair between God and his church; some commentaries identify the bride not with the church but with the human soul. At the same time, the implication was that human sexual impulse was base and should be denied or sublimated by being transferred to the religious realm where God and man are seen as engaged in a marital or sexual union.[14] Kabbalah, on the other hand, discovered the mystery of sex within God himself. Thus the sexual union between man and wife was sacred since it was a symbolic realization of the union of God and the Shekinah. Sexuality within the realm of human existence is thus seen as a reflection of the "sacred union" between God and himself. This removal of the barrier of noncorrespondence between the deity and man is seen by Patai as "a stroke of genius of Jewish mysticism."[15] By marrying and procreating the Jew was able to see himself as engaged in *imitatio dei* and fulfilling a divine promise. Therefore, woman was not perceived as representing sexual evil, but as a partner with whom a higher degree of closeness to God was made possible.

Kabbalistic literature seems to be free of the venomous misogyny that pervaded Christian writings of the same periods. Church documents of the times were engaged in a most violent depreciation of women, elaborating on the baneful effects of women's influence and underlining Eve's responsibility for her husband's fall.[16] Yet Kabbalistic writings reveal a paradoxical attitude to women. While the deity enfolded a feminine element in itself, woman and the feminine element were seen as having a demonic quality, too, since the demonic was an offspring of the feminine sphere.[17] This paradox in the imaginative realm of Kabbalah thinking can be attributed to the fact that by its nature, Kabbalah literature was not an attempt to capture the human world in its realistic dimension and, therefore, it did not portray women as real people with realistic human problems. They were the "other" in the world of man, used as symbols of cosmological and psychological forces that govern and trouble man's life. Woman can therefore embody the most sublime, the Shekinah, or the most debased, often represented by the menacing figure of Lilith. In Kabbalistic literature, Lilith is the ghostly paramour of man who joins him at night to generate demonic offspring. The Zohar tells us that after the destruction of the Temple the Shekinah was exiled from Jerusalem and that, therefore, God was forced to accept Lilith as his consort. Lilith and the Shekinah thus represent the two aspects of the Jewish fate, as well as the dual conception of women in their relation to man: the Shekinah is mother, lover, comforter, and the giver of life, and Lilith is the wanton seductress and the death-dealing female fiend.

While a duality of attitudes towards women does exist in early Judaic literature, the nonascetic nature of this tradition and the basically favorable conception of human sexual functions that are consistently expressed in the Bible, rabbinic literature, and Kabbalistic documents created a more positive literary treatment of women than is found in Christian writings of the same periods. Misogyny is undeniably a dominant trait in much of medieval Christian literature, while it is only a faint voice in Judaic records. From a literary point of view, however, medieval Jewish literature divested woman of her human nature and made her represent impersonal abstractions. Shekinah and Lilith are cosmological elements as well as embodiments of the male's psychological needs and anxieties. But the subject and the norm are still man; it is from his vantage point that the symbolic configuration of women is perceived.

A seemingly more realistic approach to women, one that regards the female of the species as a human being functioning in the real world, rather than as a symbolic representation of the male experience, is found in medieval Hebrew poetry. Here women are described as flesh and blood figures, objects of man's desires and romantic feelings. In a manner similar to the European tradition of courtly love poems, some of the Hebrew verses develop the theme of unrequited love, and dwell on the cruel, cold-hearted beauty and her rejected admirer. Much of this poetry is erotic and graphic in nature, describing in minute details the physical attributes of the beautiful woman. The enchanting beauty is put on a pedestal and her body is poetically dismembered by the spellbound young man as he highlights the specific parts of her body that he most admires. Yet what happens in this type of poetry is that the person herself vanishes and, instead, we have a detailed list of physical parts, but not the total human being. The poetic mutilation of the feminine figure is done in the name of love and aesthetic admiration of physical beauty. In this kind of poetry, however, the woman functions as no more than a sex object, a composite of different physical attributes, without a soul of its own.[18]

A popular tradition in the Middle Ages, especially in the Jewish communities of Spain and Italy, was composing poems about women as a form of wedding entertainment. This genre of poems written for weddings included verses that condemned or commended the female sex. The Hebrew playwright and poet Judah Sommo (1572–92) wrote a gallant paean of praise to his noble lady entitled "*Magen Nashim*" ("Shield or Defense of Women").[19] Poets also engaged in exchanging poems which praised or denigrated women; some of these verses appear to be answers to earlier poems on the subject. A poem written by Abraham of Sarteano entitled "*Sone' Nashim*" ("Hater of Women") offers a list of wicked women in history. Eve is the first to be condemned, followed by the daughters of Lot, Dinah "the prostitute" (Jacob's daughter), Delilah, who betrayed Samson, and others. The poet also misrepresents and twists some of the biblical examples to suit his own purposes. He blames the beautiful Tamar, David's daughter who was raped by Amnon, for seducing the man and wreaking havoc on the house of David. This is in contradiction to the biblical story that presents Tamar as an innocent victim, and Amnon as the lustful rapist. Bat-Sheba is condemned for entrapping David by purposely washing on the roof where the king could see her. She is also blamed for all the atrocities committed by David in his attempts to cover up his sin. Non-Jewish women, such as Semiramis and Cleopatra, are also mentioned derogatorily. In short, women are described as sexually voluptuous, wanton, and lascivious. They are also accused of engaging in unnatural sexual acts; one woman is condemned for having sexual relations with a bull, another for seducing her own son, and yet another for seducing her own father.[20]

As a response to this poem, Avigdor of Faro, described as "'*Ozer Nashim*" ("Supporter of Women"), wrote a poem celebrating women's noble attributes, such as courage and wisdom, exemplified by historical figures such as Deborah, Jael, Abigail, and Esther. He condemns the tendency to stereotype women and claims that one prostitute should not be taken as a model of the whole female race.[21]

In post-Talmudic literature, practically until the advent of the Enlightenment, female figures do not appear as full-blown, realistic characters. Three main trends can be detected in the way women are treated and presented in a literature produced exclusively by men. The Responsa literature continues the Talmudic approach in which women are objects of legal discussion. The attitude to women in this type of literature is practical and not disrespectful. As the backbone of the domestic realm, as the sexual partner of man, and as a person whose familial predicament is often the subject of rabbinic discussions, woman plays a role in many halakic documents. Yet the feminine voice is rarely heard, and woman's fate continues to be in man's hands, determined and shaped in accordance with the male's conception of the world and his interpretation of the Judaic law.

In the poetry of the Spanish period woman represents the force of love, and therefore the feminine figure is at the heart of much of the secular poetry of the times; yet the woman's status as the "other" remains unchanged. Whether exalted as a model of beauty and virtue, or condemned as the source of evil or the comic nag, woman is not perceived as epitomizing the total human condition. She is put on a pedestal by the lovesick young man, the admirer of feminine beauty, and she is taken off the pedestal by the self-proclaimed "hater of women"; she is better than man or worse than man, but she is not equal to man. And even when she is put on a pedestal as a paragon of beauty, it is not the person but her various physical attributes that become the object of admiration and the subject of the poetic verses.

In the writings of the Jewish mystics, as well as in many of the tales produced within the Hasidic movement, woman is divested of her human nature and is made to represent impersonal abstractions. She embodies cosmological powers, abstract theological concepts, and forces in the male consciousness. The feminine figure shuttles between the sublime and the debased, but always as the cosmic and psychological "other," and never as the person who experiences spiritual anguish, who is fired by Messianic dreams, and who craves closeness with the creator.

The Mutation of Feminine Otherness in Modern Hebrew Literature

Female figures as life-sized characters confronting everyday situations and functioning in contemporary reality begin to appear in the writings of the Haskalah period. Here the fictional character is modeled after a real-life human being, and is often made to represent the feminine predicament rather than something in man. However, Haskalah literature is imbued with the zeal to revolutionize and modernize Jew-

ish life, and it often uses its fictional characters—both male and female—as a means of illustrating the need for change and reform. Its
tone is generally didactic, often bitterly satiric, aiming at shocking
the reader and stirring him to action. Two polar opposite feminine
images populate Haskalah prose and poetry: one is the contentious
bitch, who appears mainly in the fiction of the period, and the other
is the innocent victim, who also figures in the prose works, but
is mainly the creation of the poetic mind. In the prose works of
Haskalah, which is devoted to exposing the misery of the Jews' economic and cultural existence, the female protagonist is portrayed in
realistic terms, and is meant to represent the backwardness and vul-
garity of Jewish life. The novels of Mendele (1836–1917), the father
of modern Hebrew fiction, which depict the Jewish family in nineteenth-century Russia in the midst of rapid erosion, are saturated
with acrimonious satire and a parodic view of Jewish life. Mendele's
female protagonists further illustrate the crisis in Jewish traditional
values and the need for "enlightenment." Some are downtrodden
and forlorn, neglected or abandoned by a wretched father who has
lost his own self-respect, as is the hunchbacked heroine of *Sefer
Haqabtsanim* (*Fishke the Lame* in English version); others are preyed
upon by evil, corrupt people in a community that no longer protects its orphans and poor, as is the innocent female protagonist
of *Be'emeq Habaka* ("In the Valley of Tears"), who is tricked into a
whorehouse. Mendele's contentious female figures—the nagging
wife, the shrew, and the bitch—are the forerunners of the predatory
Jewish women who would later appear in a modern garb, in the works
of Jewish-American writers. They emasculate the man and usurp that
small shred of patriarchal authority that he was supposed to enjoy in
his own home. Sendrel, the hapless protagonist of *The Travels of Bin-
yomin the Third* (1878), is nicknamed "Sendrel the Housewife" because he wears a skirt, tends to kitchen matters, and is henpecked by
his wife.

The female type that exists in the poetry of the period represents
the other end of the spectrum, the writer's romantic and idealized vision of what the Jew—both man and woman—ought to be.[22] The
tendency to romanticize creates a heroine of a different kind. She is
beautiful, virtuous, and gentle, as is Bat-Shu'a, the protagonist of
Y. L. Gordon's poem "*Qotso Shel Yod*" ("The Point of a Yod," 1884).
Invariably, this kind of fictionalized woman is seen as crushed and
destroyed by the rigidity and irrationality of Jewish law and its interpreters, the contemporary rabbinic authorities. The woman is the
pathetic victim of ancient laws that have lost their relevance and
viability in modern times. But this female figure is a stereotyped im-

age, an instrument in the hands of the writer who has an axe to grind with his fellow Jews. Both kinds of women protagonists, the hateful, loud bitch, and the gentle, appealing victim are threadbare literary figures. As in the case of Haskalah male protagonists, the women exist in the literary work not as individuals who are important in their own right, but as agents of the writer's ideology. Consequently, while Haskalah female protagonists and their predicaments are carved out of authentic situations, the writers' tendency to use them as didactic paradigms and to exaggerate either the characters' virtues or their faults results in one-dimensional, stilted, and undeveloped literary figures.

A writer who freed himself from commitment to Haskalah ideology and whose uniqueness lies in his ability to portray the Jewish shtetl realistically and honestly is S. Y. Agnon. Unlike Haskalah writers, Agnon did not harness his art in the service of an ideology, and his works are free of the zeal to reform that handicapped the art of many of the Haskalah writers. In his attempts to reconstruct Jewish society in the Galician towns, Agnon offers a gallery of feminine portraits that is extremely rich and varied.[23] His female protagonists range from the noble, exalted image of the devoted mother in a story such as "The Kerchief,"[24] to the free-spirited, even promiscuous, modern woman, such as Sonya in the novel *Temol Shilshom* (*"Only Yesterday,"* 1945). Agnon has given us realistically drawn male characters whose authenticity and genuineness are unquestionable. His male protagonists are not just fictional tools that illustrate a point, but believable, multidimensional individuals, created by a shrewd and perceptive observer of life and people. The question is: Can the same statement be made about Agnon's female characters? Was Agnon able to rid himself of the tendency to stereotype women that plagued Hebraic writings in the past?

Many of Agnon's female characters are multifaceted individuals, products of traumatic historical moments who grapple with a rapidly changing society and its conflicting mores. Some are memorable figures, artistically and powerfully etched. Yet, broadly speaking, most of Agnon's heroines maintain the status of the "other" to the male characters in their dramatic function within the context of the short story or novel that they appear in. Protagonists such as the mother in "The Kerchief" and Tehilah in the short story by the same name possess individual characteristics and emerge as authentic flesh-and-blood beings. Yet both are wrapped in a legendary halo and depicted from a nostalgic distance. The mother in "The Kerchief" is portrayed through the eyes of her adoring son who narrates the story from two angles: that of the young child who experiences the events and records them directly and immediately, and that of the adult whose mental, chronological, and geographical distance from the scenes described underlines the remoteness of the mother's image from contemporary reality. The story as a whole reads like a tribute that the adult Agnon pays to the memory of his almost saintly parents and their near-sacred way of life. The mother embodies the perfection of the traditional Jewish woman. She is the loving wife who possesses telepathic powers with which she communicates with her husband when he is away. She is also the ideal mother who teaches her children not by rebuking and scolding them but by serving as a role model of self control and gentility. The story sounds genuine and is free of false sentimentality because Agnon himself defined the boundaries of his short story: the adoring, innocent child and the homesick adult are both forgiven if they tend to idealize and magnify the mother's exalted qualities.

Tehilah is another example of a heroine who is put on a pedestal and endowed with larger-than-life qualities.[25] She is given an authentic personal history as the long-suffering woman who has paid for the follies of others, mainly her own father. Her biography reflects the last chapters in the history of East European Jews: the bitter enmity between Hasidim and Mitnagdim, the loss of faith, and the rejection of Judaism. Yet her main dramatic function is that of the symbolic configuration of everything that is pure and sacred in Judaism. She is a psalm, the distilled essence of Judaism, and the heavenly Jerusalem combined. She provides the narrator with a sudden epiphany, a revelation, that enables him to see the lush beauty and richness of Jerusalem behind the city's shabby, dilapidated exterior. While the mother in "The Kerchief" and Tehilah are given realistic settings and individualized personalities, Gemulah, the female protagonist of the enigmatic "Edo and Enam," serves only as an embodiment of abstractions.[26] Whether she stands for the spirit of artistic inspiration, as a modern incarnation of the mythological Muse, or for the essence of Jewish mysticism, or Judaism in general, she is not a flesh-and-blood woman.

Many other female protagonists that abound in Agnon's works are more realistically drawn and set within the sociohistorical circumstances of a given, clearly defined moment in recent Jewish experience. Three examples would illustrate both the achievements and the limitations of Agnon's treatment of female protagonists in works written in the realistic vein. The tightly structured, tragic novella "Vehaya He'Aqov Lemishor" ("And the Crooked Shall Be Made Straight," 1912) revolves around Menashe Hayim, a pious, somewhat passive man, and his enterprising, ambitious wife Krendel Tcharni, affluent shopkeepers in the nineteenth-century Galician shtetl of Buczacz. Both characters start as stereotypes, yet Agnon's literary genius avoids the trap into which many Haskalah writers fell. While the pushy, nagging wife seems at first more a literary type than a full-blown individual, Agnon, unlike Mendele in similar circumstances, refrains from parodying the woman as she prods and bullies her husband, demanding of him more than he can deliver. Therefore, instead of creating a hackneyed caricature, Agnon offers an insightful look, albeit brief, into the predicament of a woman tragically mismatched with an incompetent, dull man whom she both loves and pities. When they lose their business, the wife drives her husband out of the home and sends him to collect alms in the hope that they will eventually be in a position to retrieve their lost shop and recoup their financial and social standing in the community.

At this point, the story abandons the more interesting protagonist, the restless, unfulfilled woman, and focuses solely on the lackluster husband, an unlikely dramatic protagonist. The narrative now follows the metamorphosis of the hero from a self-respecting, rather dignified individual, to that of a greedy, contemptible beggar. It also subtly traces the process of rebellion that this protagonist undergoes, as he questions his fate and acts in defiance of his former rabbi (he sells the letter of recommendation given to him by his rabbi), and of his earlier piety (while drunk, he uses blasphemous language and wakes up to find that his prized phylacteries were stolen). Menashe Hayim returns home only to find his formerly barren wife remarried and the mother of a newborn baby. The rabbis released the wife from the state of 'aginut and declared her a widow when the letter of recommendation given to her husband by their town's rabbi had been found on the body of a dead beggar.[27]

Menashe Hayim now becomes the pivot of a dramatically enacted spiritual dilemma that characterizes the times; his religious piety and traditional values are pitted against a newly awakened, secular morality rooted in the tradition of Western humanism. If he discloses the tragic mistake, he will ruin the lives of his wife, who cohabits in sin with her new husband, as well as that of her child, who will be declared a bastard, in accordance with Jewish law. If he refrains from revealing his identity, he will betray his former piety and will also have to remain in anonymity for the rest of his life. Our hapless protagonist opts for the latter, and in doing so he rises as a human being who sacrifices his own happiness for the sake of another person, but sinks as a Jew who defies his heritage. The story's power lies in its dramatic presentation of the religious crisis of a whole generation, as well as in its portrayal of the metamorphosis of a weak, indecisive individual into a morally courageous human being. These two aspects are shown through the male protagonist; the heroine who initially catches our attention recedes into the background and is used as the catalyst of the hero's redemption. The woman is at the heart of the hero's dilemma, and his decision regarding her fate finally ennobles him. But it is the male who is seen to face spiritual and psychological crises, while the woman is the literary other who may trigger the chain of events in which the male is the focus of attention, but still remains in the background.

Agnon's tendency to create an intriguing female protagonist, only to abandon her and shift the narrative attention to the male protagonist, is also evident in his *Sippur Pashut* (*A Simple Story,* 1935), written in the tradition of European social realism with forays into the stream-of-consciousness form. In the figure of Bluma, the love interest of the male protagonist, Agnon comes very close to breaking out of the "otherness" in which female figures have been locked in previous literature. Bluma starts as a rather well-known social type prevalent in the European social novel; she is the poor orphan who comes to live with her rich relatives. She is eventually exploited by her relatives, becomes their maid, and is treated accordingly. When the young son of the family inevitably falls in love with the beautiful young girl, he is forbidden by his parents to marry her. Variations of the theme are found in the works of Maupassant, Tolstoy, and others. In this type of story, the poor relative usually resigns herself to her lot and remains loyal to the son of the rich family even when he marries another woman. Sonya, one of Tolstoy's female protagonists in *War and Peace,* remains a spinster and raises the children that her beloved Nikolay fathers with another woman. Unlike her Russian counterpart, Bluma leaves the household of her rich relatives and finds a position with a family that defies the narrow bourgeois morality and hypocritical piety of the Jewish middle class. She also becomes active among Socialist groups, and even somewhat of an early feminist when she states that "not every woman has to get married."

Nevertheless, the crux of *A Simple Story* is its male protagonist and his failure to reach a balance between the demands of traditional society with its custom of fixed marriages, and those of his own heart, which craves the woman of his own choice. The far from "simple" story is the man's story; the narrative centers on him as he reluctantly marries the rich heiress that his parents chose for him, then sinks into depression that culminates in madness, and is finally restored to mental health and to acceptance of his fate. In contrast to the somewhat lackluster male protagonist, Bluma is strong, independent, and infinitely more intriguing. She struggles with the middle-class mores of the times, gradually coming to question them, and becoming more and more reluctant to accept her fate. She is determined to carve out for herself a niche in a world still very traditional and uncompromising, where the nonconformist is quickly expelled. Yet we will never know the degree of success, or failure, that she experiences. At that juncture in the story where Bluma emerges as fully individualized, Agnon recoils from further dealing with her. It seems that the writer has created a female figure that, unexpectedly, transcends the boundaries set by literary conventions. Bluma the fictionalized character has gotten out of hand, and her creator suddenly puts the brakes on his imagination, preferring to deal with a safer, more familiar, subject: his male protagonist. Apparently, Agnon realized that the interest that he aroused in his readers regarding Bluma would remain unsatisfied. In the epilogue to *A Simple Story* he acknowledges that Bluma's story was not exhausted and that it deserves "a book by itself." He there promises his reader that he will "use much ink," and "break many pens" in writing another tale that would do justice to Bluma's history. Yet he never did. Bluma's figure remains an unfulfilled promise that best illustrates Agnon's ability to reach beyond the literary patterns set for female figures, as well as his ultimate failure to act upon his vision.

Bluma's "otherness" is twofold. She is the dramatic other in the sense that she is secondary in importance within the boundaries of Agnon's tale, and is never fully in the limelight. The other aspect of her otherness is the role that she plays in triggering the protagonist's descent into madness. Here Agnon draws on the tradition of associating the female figure with demonic, irrational powers. Even when the woman herself is not evil or fiendish, she can be the force that unleashes the buried demons in man, causing him to succumb to the evil spirits of depression and madness.[28]

Agnon's use of the female figure as an externalization of forces within the man's psyche is again evident in *Only Yesterday,* the novel that commemorates the reality in Palestine of the years of the Second Aliya. The protagonist, Yitshak Kummer, is a young pioneer, *ḥaluts,* who comes to Palestine to fulfill his Zionist dream of tilling the land of Israel. The novel shuttles between two realities, that of Jaffa—a secular, modern center for pioneers, workmen, and bohemians—and Jerusalem, where the pious, "old community" still pursues the old ways of traditional Judaism. Yitshak, who is still imbued with the old-fashioned values of his religious upbringing, finds it very hard to adjust to the free and promiscuous community in Jaffa. His vacillation between the two ways of life and the two conflicting forces in his mind is represented by two female figures. Sonya, a carefree woman, has a brief affair with the innocent Yitshak, but soon tires of him. Shifra, daughter of a pious pillar of the "old community" in Jerusalem, is Sonya's polar opposite; she is chaste and pure, embodying the beauty of the Jewish values of the past. In the depiction of Shifra and her father, Agnon reflects the dual image of traditional Judaism, and resorts to the pattern of "the mean old Jew and his gentle daughter" that prevailed outside Hebraic literature. The father is a venomous, fanatic, and intolerant man, epitomizing the rigidity and irrationality of the religious community. His daughter is virtuous and beautiful, symbolizing the charm of traditional Judaism. As the novel delineates Yitshak's agonizing and painful attempts to assimilate into the secular, licentious community in Jaffa, and his final decision to settle among the pious Jews in Jerusalem and return to his old religious way of life, it becomes clear that the two women are used as embodiments of the hero's conflicts. They are the two poles between which the hero vacillates, but the focal point and the center of interest is the male hero and not the female protagonists.

As the Jewish woman was struggling to free herself from the constrictive norms of shtetl Judaism and take part in the man's cultural and national ambitions, she began to acquire a more significant place in the literature of the early years of our century, either as the male hero's intellectual companion, or as the central protagonist in a novel. A number of works written in this period revolve around a young girl who vacillates between the old world of piety and the new secular values and national aspirations that have pervaded Jewish reality.[29]

Women writers also begin to appear in this period, in the literature that originates in the Zionist movement, and that devotes itself to assessing and evaluating the Zionist enterprise. Interestingly, women writers in the Palestinian period channeled their artistic creativity into the medium of poetry, leaving the broader dimensions offered by the novel form to the men writers of the period. Poets such as Rachel, Yocheved Bat-Miriam, and Lea Goldberg wrote lyrical poetry that offered a view of the world through exclusively feminine lenses. Of the three, Rachel devoted herself to reflecting the pioneer woman who is close to the land and helps till and cultivate the soil. She defined the narrow scope of her vision as a woman who only tells her own story, and whose world is as narrow as that of an ant. Bat-Miriam's poetry is extremely personal, mostly ignoring the Zionist reality and imbued with nostalgia for scenes of her early childhood in a different landscape. The feminine voice is unmistakable; the poetess even refers to her childhood landscape in the feminine pronoun "you" (*'at,* in Hebrew). Goldberg, most versatile of the three poets, also offers poems that are highly personal and introspective, dealing with love, the passage of time, and childhood memories. Though these three poets are different in the lyrical styles and techniques employed in their verses, a common denominator to all three is the attempt to withdraw from the historical moment and from matters of contemporary relevance, to the sphere of the feminine self that would offer them relative mental safety from the political and ideological currents of the times.

The question why the women writers of the Palestinian period chose the poetic medium is of great interest. Aside from personal idiosyncrasies and individual talents, there must have been something in the social ambience of the period that made them divert their talents from prose to poetry. This phenomenon also stands in contrast to trends in English literature, for instance, which abounds with first-rate women novelists, such as Jane Austen, George Eliot, and Virginia Woolf. In *A Room of One's Own* Virginia Woolf discusses the relative prominence of women in the tradition of the English novel.[30] She explains that the epic form and the poetic play represented a patriarchal tradition since they were produced by male writers. When women finally mustered the courage to express their own voice, they had only a man's tradition and a man's way of reflecting the world to learn from; the older forms of literature were hardened and set by the time women began to write. The novel form alone was young enough and lacking in a long masculine tradition for the women writers to feel comfortable with it, and to try to shape it in accordance with their own vision and conception of the world, without having to bow to masculine authority.

As Virginia Woolf reminds us, however, women's novels were very different from men's works written in the same genre. The Brontë sisters, whose life experience was extremely limited, wrote highly personal, lyrical prose, that looked inward rather than outward. Jane Austen's vision was also circumscribed within the domestic sphere and the love problems of her heroines. Only George Eliot successfully merged the domestic with broader historical and social perspectives; still, no woman wrote a novel of the magnitude and breadth of Tolstoy's *War and Peace.*

Hebraic literature had no strong tradition of *belles lettres* of any kind. Any new genre that was experimented with benefited from a sense of freshness and freedom. Hebrew writers, however, more than any European or American writers of the nineteenth and twentieth century, were bound by a sense of commitment to the collective vision, at the expense of the more private, intimate voice of the individual. Novelists like Brenner, Agnon, Kabak and others attempted to encompass social processes of historical significance in their prose works. Thus the woman writer, who felt inadequate or unprepared to handle the momentous events of her times, shied away from the novel form, that came to be associated with the larger perspectives and broader visions. The novel form, as young as it was in Hebraic literary tradition, was already "taken," so to speak, by the masculine voice and used for specific purposes. The question remains as to why women writers did not attempt the genre of social realism that was adopted by their male counterparts. This has probably to do with the social status of women in the Jewish society of the time. Zionism emancipated the Jewish woman and allowed her to feel as an integral part of a historical event, yet between the rhetoric of equality and the actual practice of it there was still a gap.[31] Even those courageous women who left their traditional families in East Europe, sometimes in direct defiance of their families, and came to Palestine to realize the Socialist and Zionist dreams of equality, fraternity, and social justice, could not easily shake off the status of the social other that was their legacy. The Palestinian reality of hard work on the land, Arab riots, and tough economic circumstances, took away from the women's ability to feel like equal partners. The poetic medium offered the woman writer a safe haven and, at the same time, an outlet for her overflowing creative abilities. If she could not plough the land or repel the Arabs with powers equal to men's, she could still be productive in a different way.

The egalitarian utopia of the early Socialist Zionists created a vision of a tough kibbutz woman working the fields alongside the man, and holding a gun while patrolling the kibbutz borders at night. Some women did just this, yet the men's emotional and psychological conception of the woman as marginal was not easily eradicable. In *Ma'agalot* (*Circles*), a novel by David Maletz that explores the interpersonal relations and social conflicts in the *kvutzah,* the role of the female protagonist is pivotal and marginal at the same time.[32] The novel explodes the myth that in a community imbued with the lofty ideas of human brotherhood and social justice there are no personal wars and conflicts of interest. The two male protagonists represent two types of *kvutzah* members as well as two attitudes towards communal life. One protagonist is a seasoned careerist, an aggressive and ambitious man whose sights are set on the most prestigious occupation in the kibbutz. The other is a simple, unassuming man who is a skillful laborer, but otherwise naive and timid, and is constantly kicked around by the more aggressive types. The female protagonist, wife of the latter, is used as a pawn in the power play that takes place.

She is the symbol of the victory of one man over the other, the award won by the stronger man. As the woman moves from her husband to the more dynamic man, and then back to her husband, she reflects the shifting of power from one person to the other.

The conquest of the woman as a sign of victory and the symbol of other forms of success is also apparent in the works of a later novelist, Moshe Shamir. Shamir is intrigued by the character of the winner, the ambitious man who pursues his goals relentlessly and even ruthlessly, either for personal gains or for the sake of an ideal. His protagonists, such as King David in *The Poor Man's Ewe Lamb* (1957), or Jannai Alexander, in *King of Flesh and Blood* (1955), are charismatic men who seize power and women simultaneously. Jannai Alexander, the king of Judea of the Hasmonean dynasty, who ruled Judea in the first century B.C.E., usurps the throne, unlawfully seizes the High Priesthood, and conquers his brother's widow. Winning the woman serves as an "objective correlative" for Jannai's other triumphs, both in terms of the narrative structure of the novel, and in the protagonist's conception of the world.

In the works of the writers of the generations of the War of Independence and those of the Israeli period, women protagonists are still locked in secondary roles. The typical male protagonist in the writings of the war generation is Uri, the central character in Moshe Shamir's *He Walked Through the Fields* (1948). Uri is suffused with a sense of mission, and his love affair with the girl Mikah is of secondary importance, both in Uri's life and in the context of the story. The war protagonists are heroes, aware of the momentous historical events that they help to create. The women represent love and the domestic concerns, which are pale and insignificant in comparison with the larger issues with which the men are consumed.

The male protagonist undergoes radical change in the works of writers of the Israeli period and those who represent the "new wave."[33] The new hero is no longer heroic; he questions the values of the earlier generation and is more concerned with the present moment than with fulfilling a historical mission or helping bring about a Utopian society. The memory of the self-sacrificing pioneers and war heroes ceases to be an inspiration and becomes a burden. The image of the courageous soldier who dies for his country has lost its glory for the modern protagonist, who now wishes to die in his own bed rather than on the battlefield. The new writers voice the fatigue of the modern Israeli who has lived in a state of siege since the inception of modern Israel. They also rebel against the assumption that the Israeli writer has to serve as the mouthpiece of ideologies and give expression to the political and social tensions in the State. Themes of universal concern that tie the predicament of the modern Israeli with that of modern man in general begin to surface in the writings of the period. Nevertheless, the human condition is somehow perceived to be the male condition only. Women represent the healing power of love, and they often personify either the hero's different states of mind or his various alter egos.

In the poetry of Yehuda Amichai, love functions as a haven from stressful realities of dispossession, wars, and untimely death. In Amichai's novel *Not of This Time, Not of This Place* (1963), the female figures stand for the different fragments in the consciousness of the schizophrenic hero, Joel.[34] Ruth, Joel's rejected wife and the daughter of his former army commander, epitomizes Joel's betrayal of the idealistic values of his youth, and the weariness of a whole generation of modern Israelis with the glorious optimism of the early years of the State. Little Ruth, who perished in the Holocaust and whose murder Joel plans to avenge, stands for the protagonist's lost childhood. The mentally sick Mina reflects the decadence, exhaustion, and disintegration of the reality of modern Jerusalem. Einat, who deserts her lover, a Holocaust survivor, and falls into the arms of a cynical, corrupt lawyer, marks, in this journey of the heart that she takes, the deterioration of the modern Israeli society and the erosion of its values. Patricia, the non-Jewish woman with whom Joel is smitten, represents the force of love as well as the protagonist's recoil from his immediate environment, imbued as it is with conflicts and disilllusionments, and from his own personal preoccupations with revenge.

The "feminine condition" has also come to the fore in modern Israeli writings. While it is not possible to speak of a feminist literary movement similar to the one in American and British literatures, some contemporary works highlight the oppression of women in society and in Jewish law. However, in the works of the major women writers of diverse cultural backgrounds, such as the poets Zelda, who writes from within the religious tradition, and Dalia Ravikovitch, whose point of view is secular, as well as in the prose writings of Amalia Kahana-Karmon, the "feminine condition" is dealt with not in its modern sociopolitical sense, but in its psychoemotional aspects. The works of these prominent women writers, especially the poets, focus on personal anguish and dreams of escape. They reveal a marked sexual vulnerability and feminine sensitivity, fear of intrusion and annihilation into nothingness. The reality of a state of siege and the geopolitical constrictions of the State of Israel come through, especially in the poetry of Dalia Ravikovitch, but only as an analogy and reflection of the poet's inner state of mind and sense of entrapment in her feminine existence. Yet the point of view in these writings remains somewhat limited and highly personal and subjective.

Amalia Kahana-Karmon's short stories and her novel, *And the Moon in the Valley of Ajalon* (1971), are written in a lyrical prose that develops its plot through a stream of subjective associations and images in a manner somewhat reminiscent of Virginia Woolf's novels. Kahana-Karmon's female figures are highly sensitive women who reject the crude materialistic values of their environment; they are often victims of crass, insensitive, unloving men. Many of her heroines possess a romantic soul and crave an ideal love relationship, but their search for a pure, perfect love often ends in disillusionment and despair. The bustling, noisy reality of the modern city and the political and military turmoil in Israel are always present in the background, usually as a correlative to the heroines' inner, mental experiences. The geographical landscapes and political developments are internalized, as if they were created or put into motion in order to reflect the heroines' subjective realities. Though her heroines do partake in an essential humanity that is larger than gender, often the feminine sphere seems to be a culture apart. Kahana-Karmon's richly textured prose has made a powerful contribution to modern Hebrew writings; yet the tendency to polarize the world along gender lines has produced a uniform feminine type, one who is often the victim who resorts to a private, marginal existence, away from the mainstream of life.

Paradoxically, the writer who has been able to commute the feminine "otherness" into a universal parable of the human condition is a man, the novelist Amos Oz. Some of Oz's heroines appear to be incarnations of feminine types known to us from earlier literary tradition; thus Lily in the story "Strange Fire" is a modern-day Lilith, roaming the streets of Jerusalem at night on a mission of evil and destruction. Ruth, the mother of the child-narrator of "The Hill of Evil Counsel," is an ironic reversal of her biblical namesake. Hannah, heroine of the novel *My Michael,* is the social "other" who is alienated from her environment, as well as the embodiment of the cosmic "other." She is associated with the *sitra ahra,* the 'other side', the irrational forces in man, as well as with the political "other," the Arab. Yet these women's otherness is not of the background; it is brought to the foreground to epitomize the sense of "otherness" that the modern Israeli feels in his own country, surrounded as it is by hostile forces and barbaric enemies. Geula, the protagonist of "Nomad and Viper," feels entrapped as a single woman, no longer young, in the confining kibbutz community. Her sense of imprisonment in her own body, as well as in an apparently uniform society where she does not fit, is extended to represent the collective sense of confinement within the boundaries of a small country, encircled by savage forces and threatened with violent intrusion. Beyond that, Oz has managed to convert Geula's otherness into an image of the human otherness in the existential sense of man's alienation from the world as well as from himself. Geula, considered the voice of reason and restraint in the kibbutz, surprises herself with her strong attraction to the savage presence and with her sudden, intense awareness of, and response to, the chaotic and irrational. She thus experiences what both Sartre and Camus saw as the essence of the existential "absurd," the unbridgeable gulf between rationality and experience.[35]

The feminine otherness in Oz thus becomes a symbol of man's otherness in a hostile universe. We know that James Joyce chose the Jew as hero of his *Ulysses* not in order to explore the social predicament of the Jew in Dublin but because, for him, the Jew was the ultimate "other" and, as such, he best epitomized the alienation of modern man. Similarly, for Oz the feminine predicament highlights and illuminates the human predicament. It is not that Oz's heroines are seen as integrated into the mainstream, but that, for Oz, every man is the "other." A recurrent stylistic structure in many of Oz's stories is the shifting of the point of view from that of the collective "we," or the "I" who speaks for the whole group, to that of the alienated individual. The collective voice is suspiciously optimistic, overanxious to ascertain the normalcy and sanity of the community. But the voice of the individual—be it the male or the female protagonist—is imbued with a bitter sense of entrapment, of existential boredom and nausea, coupled with a destructive surrender to the irrational and the antinomian. The irrational moments of Oz's female protagonists, or their descent into insanity, are used to underline the inherent irrationality of modern life in general, and of the Israeli reality in particular, behind the facade of normalcy and optimism.

Each of the following chapters concentrates on a particular feminine image or experience and follows its development throughout Judaic literary history. As a female figure or a feminine situation is seen to travel through different texts and modes of thought, we will ask whether the female protagonist who is rooted in an ancient model transcends that model at some point and becomes an individual who represents the human condition. Does the journey of a feminine image lead to a discovery of a more powerful, independent figure under the various garbs that it wore during its historical evolution? We will also explore the relationship between the various feminine figures that are anchored in a shared ancient type. We will examine the features of the older model that are retained in its later incarnations, and how the literary context in which an older type reappears refashions its traits. Another question is whether the writers' conceptions of the feminine situation change through the ages. Does the male writer rid himself of ancient attitudes and biases, or is he still conditioned by age-old values, deeply embedded in the male consciousness?

Notes

[1] On the "Jewish American Princess" see Charlotte Baum, Paula Hyman, and Sonya Michel, *The Jewish Woman in America* (New York: Dial Press, 1976), 236–8, 251–6.

[2] On the ugly Jewish father and his beautiful daughter see Harold Fisch, *The Dual Image: The Figure of the Jew in English and American Literature* (New York: Ktav, 1971), also Hyam Maccoby, "The Delectable Daughter," *Midstream* 16, no. 9 (1970): 50–60. American literature also offers variations of this theme. In William Gilmore's *Pelago* (1838), the Jewish girl Thyrza is in love with Pelago, the eighth-century Spanish hero. She dies in battle, but not before she undergoes conversion. For more examples see Louis Harap, *The Image of the Jew in American Literature* (New York: Jewish Publication Society, 1974). On the dual image of the Jewish woman in non-Jewish literature see Livia Bitton Jackson, *Madonna or Courtesan? The Jewish Woman in Christian Literature* (New York: Seabury Press, 1982).

[3] Katharine M. Rogers, *The Troublesome Helpmate: A History of Misogyny in Literature* (Seattle: University of Washington Press, 1973).

[4] See, for instance, Terry Davidson, *Conjugal Crime: Understanding and Changing Wifebeating Pattern* (New York: Hawthorne Books, 1978), 95–99.

[5] See Kate Millet, *Sexual Politics* (Garden City, N.Y.: Doubleday, 1970), 51–54. For a discussion of Freud's diagnosis of father-religion as an Oedipal trap and its implications for the modern feminist, see Naomi R. Goldenberg, *Changing of the Gods* (Boston: Beacon Press, 1979). On the subordinate status of women in ancient Israel see Roland de Vaux, *Ancient Israel: Its Life and Institutions,* trans. John McHugh (Toronto: McGraw-Hill of Canada, 1961), 20 ff.; and Anthony Phillips, "Some Aspects of Family Law in Pre-Exilic Israel," *Vetus Testamentum* 23 (1973): 350.

[6] Phyllis Trible, *God and the Rhetoric of Sexuality* (Philadelphia: Fortress Press, 1978). Another study that challenges the traditional patriarchal reading of the Bible is John H. Otwell, *And Sarah Laughed: The Status of Women in the Old Testament* (Philadelphia: Westminster Press, 1977). Among the growing number of studies that have appeared in recent years that either explore the theoretical validity of feminist hermeneutics or offer a nonsexist reading of biblical texts are Rosemary Ruether, *Sexism and God Talk: Toward a Feminist Theology* (Boston: Beacon Press, 1983); Phyllis Trible, *Texts of Terror*

(Philadelphia: Fortress Press, 1984); Letty M. Russell, ed., *Feminist Interpretation of the Bible* (Philadelphia: Westminster Press, 1985).

[7] This is how the Bavli, Eruvin 18b, and Genesis Rabbah 18:1 explain the Genesis phrase "male and female he created them." The Kabbalistic work the Zohar also tells us that when Adam was sent down to the world, the female was attached to him; afterwards, God sawed her off from him. See Curt Leviant, ed., *Masterpieces of Hebrew Literature* (New York: Ktav, 1969), 462. Phyllis Trible, in "Depatriarchalizing in Biblical Interpretation," *Journal of American Academy of Religion* 41, no. 1 (1973):35, 37–38, proposes the theory, similar to traditional Jewish interpretations, that the first human was androgynous until the separation of female and male. Trible modifies this view in *God and the Rhetoric of Sexuality* and suggests that the first creature was sexually undifferentiated (141). Searching for mythic symbols of androgyny, Carolyn Heilbrun, in *Towards a Recognition of Androgyny* (New York: Knopf, 1973), indicates that the stories of creation in Genesis suggest that the original human pair was opposite-sex twins and that Jewish tradition, "committed to the superiority and dominance of the male, changed the story" (35). It seems, however, that the Judaic texts perpetuated the idea of a double-faced original creature, as seen in the Talmudic and Kabbalistic accounts of creation. Furthermore, the medieval commentator Rashi quotes the Talmudic legend about a dual-faced original human in his interpretation of Gen. 1:27. As we know, for generations of traditional Bible students Rashi's commentary was inseparable from the biblical text itself, and therefore, the egalitarian conception enfolded in the first Genesis version of the creation of man was, to them, a familiar idea.

[8] For similar conclusions see also Clarence J. Vos, *Women in Old Testament Worship* (Delft: Judels and Brinkman, n.d.).

[9] A comparison of the biblical account of the creation of woman and the Gilgamesh story is offered in J. S. Bailey, "Initiation and the Primal Woman in Gilgamesh and Genesis 2–3," *Journal of Biblical Literature* 89 (1970): 137–50.

[10] For a detailed analysis of the nonsexist language and concepts in this tale see Nehama Aschkenasy, "A Non-Sexist Reading of the Bible," *Midstream* 27, no. 6 (1981):51–55.

[11] Berakot, 31b.

[12] Erik H. Erikson, "Womanhood and the Inner Space," in *Identity: Youth and Crisis* (New York: Norton, 1968), 261–94.

[13] This hypothesis is proposed by Edward F. Campbell, *The Book of Ruth: Translated with Introduction and Notes,* the Anchor Bible (New York: Doubleday, 1975), 21.

[14] See Joan M. Ferrante, *Woman as Image in Medieval Literature* (New York: Columbia University Press, 1975), 28.

[15] Raphael Patai, *The Hebrew Goddess* (New York: Ktav, 1967), 181.

[16] See Rogers, *The Troublesome Helpmate,* 14.

[17] See Gershom G. Scholem, *Major Trends in Jewish Mysticism* (New York: Schocken, 1974), 37, 38.

[18] See "A Mouth As Round," in *The Penguin Book of Hebrew Verse,* ed. T. Carmi (Middlesex, England: Penguin), 360.

[19] In *Saḥut Bediḥuta deKiddushin,* ed. Hayim Schirmann (Jerusalem: Tarshish, 1946), 149–67.

[20] In Abraham Neubauer and Moshe Shteinshneider, *Shebaḥ haNashim uGenutan,* ed. A. M. Habberman (Jerusalem: Ben Uri, 1968).

[21] Ibid.

[22] On the difference between Haskalah prose, which aimed at a realistic portrayal of Jewish life, and its poetry, devoted to an idealized vision of the Jew as he should be, see Simon Halkin, *Modern Hebrew Literature* (New York: Schocken, 1970), 34–53.

[23] Baruch Kurzweil, the pioneer in Agnon criticism, illuminates Agnon's place in the history of modern Hebrew literature as the first writer whose treatment of the shtetl reality was free of any didactic purpose or reformist zeal. Agnon approached the shtetl from a geographical and chronological distance with the view to reconstruct objectively a world that was disintegrating rapidly and was soon to disappear completely. See *Essays on Agnon's Stories,* in Hebrew (Tel Aviv: Schocken, 1963), 9–17.

[24] In S. Y. Agnon, *Twenty-One Stories,* trans. I. M. Lask (New York: Schocken, 1970), 45–59.

[25] S. Y. Agnon, "Tehilah," in *Israeli Stories,* ed. Joel Blocker and trans. Walter Lever (New York: Schocken, 1970), 22–64.

[26] S. Y. Agnon, "Edo and Enam," in *Two Tales,* trans. Walter Lever (New York: Schocken, 1966), 143–233.

[27] In this tale, Agnon has given a shtetl setting to the "Enoch Arden" motif. A close parallelism exists between the plotline of Agnon's tale and that of Tennyson's poem "Enoch Arden," where the protagonist, thought to be dead, returns home only to find his wife nursing a child by a second husband. See Nehama Aschkenasy, "Biblical Substructures in the Tragic Form: Hardy, *The Mayor of Casterbridge;* Agnon, 'And the Crooked Shall be Made Straight'," in David Hirsch and Nehama Aschkenasy, eds., *Biblical Patterns in Modern Literature* (Chico, Calif.: Scholars Press, 1984), 85–94.

[28] The role of the protagonist's mother in triggering his descent into madness is discussed in Chapter Three, "The Empty Vessel: Woman as Mother."

[29] Among them are Isaiah Bershadsky's *Neged haZerem* ("Upstream," 1901), A. A. Kabak's *Levadah* ("Alone," 1905), M. Smilansky's *Hadassah* (1911), and M. J. Berdichewscky's *Miriam* (1921). The latter, named after its female heroine, in the European tradition of Tolstoy, Flaubert, and Zola, fails to create a fully-fledged, convincing female character and disintegrates into an episodic, unfocused story of fragmented scenes from Jewish life. See Dan Miron's introduction to the new edition of the story (Tel Aviv: Yahdav, 1971).

[30] Virginia Woolf, *A Room of One's Own* (1929; rpt. New York: Harcourt Brace Jovanovich, 1957).

[31] On the paradoxical psychology of equality, underlying socialist Zionism, and the cult of manhood, with which the pioneers' thinking, as well as modern Israelis' attitude, is imbued, see Lesley Hazleton, *Israeli Women: The*

Reality Behind the Myth (New York: Simon and Schuster, 1977), 91–111, 137–61 et passim.

[32] It appeared in English as *Young Hearts* (New York, 1950).

[33] See Gershon Shaked, *A New Wave in Israeli Writings,* in Hebrew (Tel Aviv: Poalim, 1974).

[34] Trans. Shlomo Katz (New York: Harper and Row, 1948).

[35] "The Hill of Evil Counsel," in Lelchuk and Shaked, eds., *Eight Great Hebrew Short Novels* (New York: Meridian, 1983), 269–317. "Nomad and Viper," and "Strange Fire" are in *Where the Jackals Howl,* trans. Nicholas de Lange (New York: Harcourt, 1981). *My Michael* (New York: Knopf, 1972) was translated by Nicholas de Lange with the writer's collaboration.

Evil, Sex, and the Demonic

For the lips of a strange woman drip honey,
and her mouth is smoother than oil.
But her end is bitter than wormwood,
sharp as a two-edged sword.
Her feet go down to death,
her steps take hold of She'ol.
  Prov. 5:3−5

*T*he ancient tale revolving around a female figure that had the greatest influence on the literary treatment of women in earlier times is undoubtedly the Genesis story of Eve's defiance of God's command and the subsequent expulsion of the primeval couple from the Garden of Eden. The first female became the prototype of all women and her story a paradigm of female existence. The most complete poetic treatment of the Eve story as the original precedence foreshadowing future feminine experience, as well as the best example of the sexist slant that the story received, is found in Milton's epic *Paradise Lost.* In this poem Eve emerges as childishly irresponsible, susceptible to flattery, and predisposed to evil. Her vicious and jealous nature is revealed when she vacillates between offering the fruit to Adam and withholding it from him. If her mental capacities have indeed been augmented as a result of eating from the Tree of Knowledge, so she reasons, then by sharing the fruit with Adam she runs the risk of making him as wise as she has become. If God's threat was real, however, and she has become mortal as a result of her violation of His command, then by keeping the fruit away from her mate she would enable him to survive her and marry another woman.[1] By contrast, Adam's motives for tasting from the forbidden fruit are purely noble: he would rather die than live without Eve. Many of the characteristics attributed to Eve by Milton, and the various details that he adds to the biblical story, such as the motivation of the characters and their attitudes before and after the act of disobedience, are already found in the Midrash, in the form of short dramatic fables and exegetical homilies scattered in various Aggadic texts.

In the many transformations that the prototypical figure of Eve has experienced in her journey both in Judaic literature and outside it, three main strands are consistently manifest: First, Eve has become closely associated with evil, since she is the one who first surrendered to temptation and violated God's law. Her story is thus seen as a parable of the moral weakness and the strong proclivity for evil that characterize the female of the human species. Her corruptibility is matched by a tendency for insubordination, a shameless defiance of moral norms, and the power to seduce man and introduce evil into his life.

Second, in many exegetical documents, both Jewish and Christian, which elaborate on the story of Eve's original act of transgression, there is an identification of the woman with carnal desires.[2] Woman is seen as primarily a sexual being whose moral weakness is coupled with sexual power which she puts to evil use. Woman's sexuality is for her the weapon with which she gains mastery over man and eventually destroys him. From the object of male lust woman has become the cause of it, and the story of Eve is seen as the introduction of sinful sex into the realm of human life. In her struggle for dominion, woman uses her erotic appeal to bring man down to her bestial level. The female has thus come to represent that part of the human composite that is more physical than spiritual and is more defenseless against the weaknesses of the flesh.

Third, in the biblical story it is only Eve, and not Adam, who has dealings with the serpent; therefore, in her many literary incarnations Eve was described as having a special affinity with the devil. And since she was the harbinger of death, Eve, as the eternal woman, was believed to have a demonic side to her being. This close association with the devil and the ability to bring man unto death through her wiles and manipulations are interconnected, and are manifest in many of Eve's literary descendants. In sum, the three traits of the biblical Eve that were assumed to prefigure the essence of womanhood are a proclivity for evil, a destructive sexuality, and a demonic-deadly power.

Eve and the "Strange Woman" in the Bible and Midrash

In our attempt to trace a development from ancient tales that have gained through the ages the power of archetypal myths, to modern stories that have incorporated in them early feminine prototypes, we have to start with the biblical text itself. Our reading should be free of the preconceived notions implanted in our collective consciousness with regard to the Genesis story of Eve. Is Eve in the Genesis story (chapters 1, 2, and 3) an evil, sexual or demonic being? How has she come to be perceived in this way, and how did this literary figure evolve through the various phases of Hebraic literary history?

The biblical narrator is reticent with regard to the serpent's motives in approaching the female rather than the male in the Garden of Eden. Is it because he saw that Eve was less intelligent and more susceptible to temptation? Our storyteller prefers not to make any comment here, yet he does explain very clearly what brings Eve to eat from the forbidden fruit. Scriptural style is known for its terseness and economy of language; it also rarely delves into the protagonists' inner deliberations. Therefore, the brief but condensed sentence that divulges Eve's reasons for picking the fruit and eating it is extremely meaningful. Eve saw that the tree "was good for food, and that it was pleasant to the eyes, and a tree to be desired to make one wise" (Gen. 3:6). To Eve's mind, the fruit is endowed with all the gifts that life has to offer: it pleases the palate and satisfies hunger ("good for food"), it provides aesthetic pleasure ("pleasant to the eyes"), and it increases one's intellectual abilities ("to make one wise"). In one brief second, Eve has a vision of the total range of the human experience, and by eating from the Tree she expresses a lust for life in all its manifestations. The act of violating God's order is not described by the biblical author as the surrender to temptation of a silly, empty-headed person, but as the daring attempt of a curious person with an appetite for life to encompass the whole spectrum of life's possibilities. To the extent that Eve enters into a pact with the devil (though we should remember that the serpent in this story is no more than an animal), she takes on a Faustian dimension. Eve can be seen as epitomizing the human condition in her tragic eagerness to make the most of the limitations of existence and taste as much of life as she can. In her thirst to exhaust the whole gamut of the human existence, and in the price that she pays for it, Eve is the precursor of the tragic Dr. Faustus who made a pact with the devil and paid dearly for it.

The Genesis narrator is surprisingly silent about Adam's motives for eating the fruit. However, this narrative vacuum is consistent with the characterization of Adam throughout the story as a passive, acted-upon character. He has no part in choosing his mate, and Eve comes to life when he is asleep. The polarity created in this story between Adam and Eve is not between good and evil, morality and sinfulness, but rather between a passive, lackluster personality on the one hand, and an intellectually curious, aggressive individual, on the other.[3] Interestingly, when Adam tries to shake off his responsibility for the violation of God's law, he excuses himself by claiming that Eve "gave" him the fruit, using the verb from the stem *ntn*, which implies the mechanical way in which he acted. Eve, on the other hand, uses the unusual, richly connotative verb from the stem *ns'*, when she explains that she was deceived, or seduced, by the serpent. The difference in vocabulary implies the difference in verbal abilities as well as intellectual maturity between the man and the woman. To the narrator of this story, Eve, in her prelapsarian state, is not the "other" to man; rather, she occupies center stage as the character around which the dramatic story revolves. The change in Eve's position comes only after the couple's expulsion from the Garden of Eden, when Adam becomes the active partner and Eve recedes into the background and turns into the passive helpmate: "And Adam knew Eve his wife" (Gen. 4:1).

Is Eve seen in this story as a sexual being, connected with things of the flesh? There is no hint here that Eve is a sexual threat to the man, or that she uses her erotic appeal to persuade man to eat from the fruit. Furthermore, while Milton sees in Eve's sudden burst of hunger a decisive factor in her impulse to eat from the fruit, the biblical narrator makes it clear that Eve was motivated by a complex set of inner drives, anchored not only in her physical, but also in her intellectual nature.

The connotations of sexuality with which the Genesis story has been burdened throughout generations of exegetical endeavors are due most probably to the prominence of the stem *yd'*, to know, that serves as a leitmotif in this tale. The forbidden tree is associated with morality in general, but not specifically with sex; it is described as "the tree of the knowledge of good and evil." In fact, many commentators regard the phrase "knowledge of good and evil" as not restricted to moral awareness only, but as denoting a "full possession of mental and physical powers."[4] The verb 'to know' becomes linked with the sexual element and with the physical differences between male and female only after Adam and Eve have sinned, when they suddenly "knew that they were naked." The culmination of the sexual meaning of the stem *yd'*, 'to know', comes only when the narrator uses it to indicate the first sexual intercourse between Adam and Eve after their expulsion from the Garden of Eden.

Furthermore, since the Genesis text gives no hint that it conceives of the serpent as more than an animal, albeit an unusual one, Eve's relationship with the serpent is not seen as an affiliation with a Satanic power. Unlike the serpent in the Miltonic epic, who is Satan in disguise, and the serpent in the midrashic version, who stands for Satan and the "evil inclination," the Genesis serpent never transcends his concrete existence as one of the animals in the primeval garden. Therefore, within the boundaries of the biblical text, Eve's dealings with the serpent carry no demonic connotations.

Eve's special link with death and her supposedly deadly powers are also not an integral part of the original tale. While both Adam and Eve become mortal as a consequence of their transgression, it is the nature of Eve as life-giver that is emphasized in the aftermath of her sinful act. Immediately after God's harsh words to Adam that end with "for dust thou art and unto dust shalt thou return," there comes a surprisingly conciliatory tone: "And Adam called his wife's name Eve, because she was the mother of all living" (Gen. 3:20). This is an affirmation of life and of Eve's role as a life force and mother.

A selection from the Aggadic Midrash will clearly exemplify how the rabbinic exegetes and storytellers picked up some of the strains of the biblical story, while at the same time they tried to suppress other elements of the ancient story that did not conform to their patriarchal norms.

The rabbinic sages offer a different etymology to Eve's Hebrew name, *Ḥawwa*, from the one given by the biblical text itself. By relating Eve's name to the Aramaic word *ḥiwya* which means serpent, the rabbis tighten the link between the woman and the serpent. *Ḥawwa* thus means "Female Serpent," and in naming her so Adam implied, according to the Midrash, that Eve functioned as his serpent, or seducer.[5] But the harshest judgment of Eve as a figure closely linked with the devil is pronounced in the statement: "As soon as Eve was created, Satan was created with her."[6] If the serpent represents Satan, then this rabbinic saying seems to suggest that the serpent started as a simple animal and took on demonic powers only when Eve came into being. Yet in spite of this devastating commentary that not only puts woman in one league with the devil but actually sees in her the origin of cosmic evil, most of the midrashic stories revolving around Eve are of a very different kind. Generally, the image of Eve in the rabbinic tales is not that of a dangerously evil creature, but rather that of a silly and childish female. The rabbis filled the narrative lacuna in the Genesis text regarding the serpent's motivation for approaching Eve rather than Adam, by reconstructing the serpent's inner deliberations that conclude with his observation tht women are light-minded and therefore he would fare better if he used his cunning on Eve.[7] In spite of this derogatory remark against women in general, it is significant to note that the serpent's reasons for allying himself with the woman are not based on the fact that he has found in Eve an evil soul mate, but on his assumption that Eve, as a woman, is silly and can be easily manipulated.

Another tale, found in three different versions, again illuminates the rabbis' attempts to reduce the stature of Eve to that of an empty-minded, jealous housewife. What follows is a summary of this parable:

This is a parable of Adam and Eve. Adam is like a husband who filled a cask with figs and nuts. Before fastening the top, he put a scorpion in it. He said to his wife: "My daughter, you have free access to everything in the house, except for this cask, since it has a scorpion in it." After he left, an old neighbor came in to borrow some vinegar. She asked the wife: "How does your husband treat you?" The wife answered: "He treats me with every kindness, save that he does not permit me to approach this cask which contains a scorpion." "It contains all his finery," the old woman said, "he wishes to marry another woman and give it to her." What did the wife do? She inserted her hand into the cask, and the scorpion bit her. When her husband came home he heard her crying out with pain. She told him that the scorpion bit her and he said: "Did I not tell you that you can have anything in the house except this cask?"[8]

The main impetus behind this story is clearly the wish to convert the biblical conflict between Adam and Eve to a domestic squabble, and to diminish Eve's figure to that of a silly woman. The near-heroic dimension that the Genesis Eve gains when her motives are elaborated upon is nonexistent here. Instead, we have a wife who is patronized by her husband ("my daughter"), distrusted by him, and who finally pays for her excessive curiosity. A faint misogynist echo is heard in the punishment that the woman gets; being bitten by a scorpion is a penalty too harsh for the crime. Yet if the hapless woman in this tale is excessively curious, she is far from being evil incarnate.

Unlike the biblical narrator who uses a somber tone to describe Eve's downfall, the Aggadic voice is frequently comic. Eve is described as the stereotypically comic nag who gets her husband to surrender to her will not through her cunning manipulations but by pestering and badgering him. Eve prevailed upon Adam to take the fateful step by crying and weeping over him.[9] A derogatorily comic assessment of the nature of women in general is presented by the following homily:

Said He (God): "I will not create her from Adam's head, lest she be swell-headed; nor from the eye, lest she be a coquette; nor from the ear, lest she be an eavesdropper; nor from the mouth, lest she be a gossip; nor from the heart, lest she be prone to jealousy; nor from the hand, lest she be light-fingered; nor from the foot, lest she be a gadabout; but from the modest part of man, for even when he stands naked, that part is covered." And as he created each limb He ordered her, "Be a modest woman." Yet in spite of all this . . . "I did not create her from the head, yet she is swell-headed . . . ; nor from the eye, yet she is a coquette . . . ; nor from the ear, yet she is an eavesdropper . . . ; nor from the heart, yet she is prone to jealousy . . . ; nor from the hand, yet she is light-fingered . . . ; nor from the foot, yet she is a gadabout."[10]

Chaucer's Jankin the Clerk, the misogynist husband of the Wife of Bath in the *Canterbury Tales,* who knew more proverbs about women "than there are blades of grass or herbs in the world," was undoubtedly reading a similar text when he recited to his wife the comic foibles of women.[11]

While the rabbis' overall attitude to Eve and women in general is more condescending that condemning, their greatest disgust is reserved for the serpent. The serpent is described as the basest of animals, whose physical repulsiveness is matched by his moral corruption. In the midrashic homilies the serpent becomes the prototypical slanderer and informer, as well as money lender and ususrer.[12] The Midrash introduces the erotic dimension to the biblical story by attributing to the serpent sexual lust. One midrash tells us that the serpent wanted to kill Adam and marry Eve.[13] The Zohar picks up the theme of the serpent's lust by going one step further and suggesting that the serpent not only desired Eve but actually had sexual relations with her that produced Cain.[14]

The biblical Eve, then, may be seen as epitomizing the human predicament in her wish to transcend her limitations and expand her horizons. The midrashic Eve, on the other hand, is a mundane housewife, frivolous and jealous, who needs man's wise guidance and often tries his immense patience. A different version of feminine evil, closely linked with death and damnation, is incorporated in the image of the "strange woman" (or "stranger woman" as suggested by the Anchor Bible edition), who is a frequent subject of discussion in Proverbs. In fact, it is the "strange woman," rather than Eve, who plays the role of the sexual, moral, and cosmic "other." She is a wanton seductress who introduces the innocent young man to "stolen waters" (8:17) and to a moral and spiritual nether land that can only lead to death and damnation. But the "strange woman" is not meant by the teacher in Proverbs to epitomize the entire feminine realm; she is only one aspect of womanhood. Nevertheless, in the figure of the dangerous temptress and adulteress, Proverbs embodies all the elements of potential feminine evil that are muted in the Eve story in Genesis. Proverbs not only sermonizes about the dangers of the "strange woman" but actually creates dramatic scenes in which the stereotypical image comes to life as an individual and is seen as trying to entrap the gullible young man:

For at the window of my house / I looked out through my lattice,
And beheld among the simple ones / I discerned . . . a young man
void of understanding.
Passing through the street near her corner / and he went the way to
her house.

In the twilight, in the evening / in the blackness of the dark night.

*And, beheld, there met him a woman / with the attire of a harlot, and
wily of heart.*

She is noisy and ungovernable / her feet do not remain in the house.

*Now she is outside, now in the streets / and she lies in wait at every
corner.*

*So she caught hold of him, and kissed him / and with an impudent
face said to him:*

I have had to sacrifice peace offerings / this day I paid my vows.

*So I came out to meet thee / diligently to seek thy face, and I found
thee.*

*I have decked my bed with coverings / with tapestry of the yarn of
Egypt.*

I have perfumed my bed / with myrrh, aloes, and cinnamon.

*Come, let us take our fill of love till morning / let us delight ourselves
with love.*

For my husband is not at home / he is gone on a long journey.

*He has taken a bag of money with him / and will come home at the
full moon.*

*With her much fair speech she causes him to yield / with the
smoothness of her lips she seduces him.*

*He goes after her at once / as an ox goes to the slaughter / and as a
man in chains to the chastisement of a fool.*

*Till a dart strike through his liver / as a bird hastens to the snare /
and knows not that it is for his life.*

. . . .

*Her house is the way to She'ol / going down to the chambers of
death.*

(Prov. 7:6–27)

This is a powerful dramatic scene that portrays the "strange woman"
luring the young man into her house and seducing him as an archetypal human situation. The woman and the young man are not
named, nor are they anchored in a specific period or place. The in-
structor of Proverbs means to create a recurrent human drama, in
which man and woman enact a typical experience. The woman appears as the sexual seductress, the evil influence, and the agent of
death and hell; the man, as her foolish victim. Yet in spite of the archetypal power of this scene in Proverbs, the "strange woman" is not
meant to represent womanhood in general. The balanced and fair-
minded conception of women in Proverbs is exemplified in the admirable feminine figure that stands for Wisdom. The woman Wisdom is
the antithesis of the woman Folly, and the "strange woman" is one of

the variations of the woman Folly. Moreover, the "strange woman" is not described as a threat to all men, but to the foolish, inexperienced young man. If he succumbs to her, he might be harmed socially and financially, and eventually find himself at death's door. The tone of this poem is rather practical, cautioning the young man against getting involved with the promiscuous woman, not so much for moral reasons alone as for pragmatic reasons. The poet of Proverbs seems to vacillate between giving this seduction scene universal symbolism, on the one hand, and keeping it within the boundaries of a particular human threat that can be avoided, on the other. At the imaginative-poetic level, the scene seems to reenact an archetypal human drama; at the didactic level, the teacher gives the scene a hypothetical quality, regarding it merely as a pedagogical device that dramatizes to the young man the evils of a particular kind of woman. To mitigate the somberness of the picture and its ability to release in man a primordial fear of women, the narrator employs a comic tone in his description of the restless, corrupt woman: "She is noisy and ungovernable / her feet do not remain in the house. Now is she outside, now in the streets / and she lies in wait at every corner." [15]

But if the biblical poet ultimately refrains from depicting the wanton seductress as the eternal woman, this feminine image reemerges as a universal female symbol in the literature produced by the Essenes, the Jewish sect that lived around Christ's time. This group, which advocated self-denial, extreme physical purity, and—in some cases—even celibacy, left its legacy (so some scholars believe) in the famous Qumran scrolls. One scroll fragment from the Qumran cave exhorts men to beware the wiles of the immoral temptress, who "lies in wait" for a gullible young man, and seeks out "a righteous man" in order to lead them astray. The men who act sinfully are exonerated, and the blame falls on the wanton woman whose eyes "glance hither and thither," and who "displays herself" in such a seductive way that even a "perfect man" stumbles when he comes under her influence. [16]

Unlike the teacher of Proverbs, who balances the scenes of the "strange woman" with the idealized image of the "woman of valor" (31 : 10–31), the delectable "wife of your youth" (5 : 18), and the exalted Wisdom as a female figure, the Essenes focused only on the evil of women. The dead sea scrolls reveal the Essenes' abhorrence of sexuality and their misogynic contempt for the female flesh. In fact, there is a close similarity between St. Paul's disparagement of the married state and his disgust of sexual relations and the Qumran fragments that deal with women and sexuality. While St. Paul anchors his theological distrust of women and condemnation of sex in the story of the Fall, it is obvious that he reads more into the story of

Genesis than it really contains.[17] It is very possible that his misogyny was fueled not so much by the Genesis story as by the ideas and modes of thinking represented in the Qumran writings, of which the poem on the wanton woman is an example.

The image of the woman as the deadly seductress who leads man to death and hell is twofold. In Proverbs and the Qumran poem the female figure is an actual flesh-and-blood human being who plays the role of the agent of sin and damnation. But the converse aspect of the same image is that of the diabolic female as a phantasmic figure, existing only in the man's heightened imagination, or that of a chimerical figure who looks like a woman but is actually the devil in disguise. The image of the female seductress as the human embodiment of the devil appears in various midrashic tales. The following story is told in two versions:

> Rabbi Meir used to mock at sinners. One day Satan appeared in the likeness of a woman on the other side of the river. As there was no ferry boat, he seized the rope bridge, and went across. When he was halfway, Satan vanished, saying, "If they had not called out from heaven 'beware of Rabbi Meir and his Torah', I would not have assessed your blood at two farthings." [18]

A similar story is told of Rabbi Akiba. Satan appeared to him in the form of a beautiful woman on top of a palm tree. The rabbi began to climb the tree, but when he was halfway, Satan vanished, making the same remark as he did after the attempted seduction of Rabbi Meir. In both cases, the rabbis learned to be more understanding towards sinners.

Aside from the obvious moral message of this type of story, which teaches tolerance and recognizes the power of temptation, these two tales are not without their comic side, especially when they describe the two dignified rabbis overcome by uncontrollable lust and acting impulsively and irrationally, rushing to seize the spectral figures and returning empty-handed. However, the implications of these two stories regarding the Talmudic conception of the nature of women are far-reaching. The interchangeability of Satan and woman is disturbing. In the cases of Rabbi Meir and Rabbi Akiba the devil impersonated a woman; when can a man be sure that the beautiful woman that he desires is not really the devil masquerading as a woman? On the other hand, if the feminine body is used by the devil as a tool of temptation, the real-life woman is exonerated, and the blame for succumbing to sin is put either on the tempter, Satan, or on the male's strong sexual drives and stimulated imagination.

Indeed, while the Midrash establishes the affinity between woman and the serpent-devil on a number of occasions, it also offers a tale that reverses the Genesis account of the corruption of the woman by the serpent. The following is a summary of the story about Rabbi Akiba's daughter and a snake:

> From Rabbi Akiba we learn that Israel is free from planetary influence. For Rabbi Akiba had a daughter. Now astrologers told him that on the day she enters the bridal chamber a snake will bite her and she will die. He was very worried about this. On the day of her wedding she took a brooch and stuck it into the wall and by chance it penetrated into the eye of a serpent. The following morning, when she took it out, the snake came trailing after it. "What did you do?" her father asked her. "A poor man came to our door in the evening," she replied, "and everybody was busy at the banquet, and there was none to attend to him. So I took the portion which was given to me and gave it to him." "You have done a good deed," said Rabbi Akiba to his daughter. Thereupon Rabbi Akiba went out and lectured: "But charity delivereth from death" and not merely from unnatural death but from death itself.[19]

The tale about a young woman who is in mortal danger of a snake reenacts the biblical drama of Eve and at the same time introduces a twist to the ancient narrative by suggesting the other route that it could have taken. Rabbi Akiba's daughter defeats both the snake and the deadly prediction by performing a good deed, while Eve is overpowered by the snake and by death itself when she violates God's law. While the main thrust of this Talmudic legend is moral and didactic, in its fictional dimension it refashions the earlier text by giving a domestic setting and a historical reality to its characters. It also redeems the Genesis tale by presenting the woman as a positive force, capable of thwarting cosmic evil. In a way, the essence of this tale stands in opposition to the general tendency of the Midrash to enlarge Eve's culpability and her frivolous surrender to evil. It also seems that this tale seeks to sever the mythic ties that connect the female with the serpent. In many ancient cultures, woman was conceived of as having a special relationship with serpents; snakes were frequently a sexual symbol. The myth of serpents in young girls' vaginas combined man's terror of woman's sexuality with his age-old fear of snakes.[20] It is true that the main purpose of this Talmudic story is to exemplify the didactic principle that "charity delivers from death"; it therefore diverts the thematic focus from its underlying redemptive view of womanhood, to the universal moral lesson that it wishes to teach. Nevertheless, the woman's innate goodness is seen as triumphing over cosmic powers and their evil agent, the snake.

Lilith in Person and in Disguise: Woman as Obstacle to Redemption

The culmination of the perceived link between woman and the devil appears in the Kabbalistic figure of Lilith, the winged she-demon who joins men at night and bears them demonic offspring. As we have seen, unlike in Christian Bible exegesis, the figure of Eve in Judaic tradition did not take on the aspect of cosmic evil. It seems that the character of Lilith, instead, came to assume the role of the sexual, demonic, and deadly feminine image. Interestingly, an illustration in a sixteenth century Italian translation of Josephus' *Jewish Antiquities* depicts Lilith with the face of a woman and the body of a snake lurking behind the trees in the garden and spying on Adam and Eve.[21] This drawing seems to capture the specific roles that Lilith and Eve came to play in the popular mind. It transfers the affinity with the serpent from Eve to Lilith by envisioning the latter as the devil's tool, and thus absolves Eve of the stigma of being the serpent's original soul mate. Adam and Eve are seen in this illustration as the innocent couple, while the figure of Lilith is merged with that of the serpent, representing the jealous, evil force that preys on the unsuspecting victims, planning to convert their paradisal idyll into catastrophe.

The Talmud does not dwell much on Lilith, though it mentions her several times as a demon. The main story comes in a late midrashic work, *Alpha Beta diBen Sira*. Lilith was Adam's first wife who, like him, stemmed from *'adamah,* 'earth'. However, when Adam wanted to subjugate her to his will, she refused and fled from the Garden of Eden. Jealous of her successor, Eve, she became especially dangerous to infants newly born to Eve's descendants.

Lilith became an important protagonist in the Zohar's conception of the cosmic drama of good and evil. The Zohar tells us that Lilith roams the universe at night, when the moon is on the wane, seducing men and then afflicting them with sickness.[22] Lilith is also a threat to women, especially at childbirth. By becoming the enemy of women Lilith is thus relegated in Kabbalistic thinking to a limited role; she is not the epitome of womanhood, but only one aspect of the male conception of feminity. Lilith's antithesis in the Kabbalistic picture of cosmic structure is Matronit, the daughter in the mystical holy tetrad. Together, Matronit and Lilith embody the many contradictory aspects attributed to womanhood by man. Matronit is an affirmation of life, the mother and bride, while Lilith threatens life; she stands for the dark forces in the cosmos and in man's psyche in her role as seductress and killer.

The evolutionary line that leads from the Genesis Eve through the "strange woman" of Proverbs and the Talmudic "Satan in disguise" to Lilith of the Kabbalistic mind exemplifies the transmutation of the female figure in the male consciousness. Woman is seen as introducing man to the concept of sin and of the violation of moral order; she then proceeds to seduce man and attempts to pull him down to hell, She'ol, metaphorically and physically. Yet man, the Subject, the "I" who experiences the world, is engaged in an eternal struggle to recapture his original purity and innocence and redeem his faulty earthly existence. Now the female becomes an obstacle to redemption, an impediment in man's progress towards the salvation of his private soul, as well as in his attempts to bring about cosmic redemption. Within this frame of thinking, the figure of Lilith has gained an additional dimension; she becomes linked with man's failed attempts to bring about the Messiah.

Lilith reappears in the various versions of the story of Joseph Della Reina, the Kabbalist who was thwarted in his attempts to bring an end to Satan's power and hasten the arrival of the Messiah. In a story that was widespread in Safed, Joseph Della Reina had to overcome Samael and his permanent female partner, Lilith, before bringing about redemption. Joseph succeeded in overpowering these two archdemons, but erred later when he burned incense before Satan, which caused his undoing. After his failure, Joseph never recovered from his fallen state and sank further into evil, becoming an ally of Satan and the lover of Lilith. Lilith dominated him completely and even brought to his bed the wife of the King of Greece.[23]

The emergence of Lilith as demon and as representative of that element in womanhood that would forever try to stop man from precipitating the process of personal and cosmic salvation is a double-edged sword. On the one hand, it might signify the shifting of male fear of women from womankind in general to one aspect of femininity, that which belongs to the exotic and occult. On the other hand, the figure of Lilith as the rebellious, independent first mate of Adam had all the ingredients to become prominent in legendary lore as well as an attractive subject to writers drawn to the mystical and demonic. But if Lilith had feminine form, perhaps many flesh-and-blood women are really Lilith in disguise? The literary and imaginative preoccupation with Lilith thus enhanced the identification of the female with the demonic.

The role of Lilith as the universal and psychological impediment to salvation, a force representing at once the moral and cosmic "other side" as well as the dark side in the human soul, was picked up by the Hasidic imaginative genius and attributed to woman in general, not necessarily to Lilith, and sometimes even to actual historical figures. In the Hasidic tale, the demonic woman is very often man's dark double, a projection of his evil inclination, *yeṣer haraʿ*, as well as of his fears and anxieties regarding evil both in the human nature and in the universe.

The motif of the woman as the devil in disguise that appears in the Aggadic tales on Rabbi Akiba and Rabbi Meir reemerges in the Hasidic tales with some variation. Martin Buber reconstructs the story that the great Hasidic rabbi, known as the Yehudi (Yaʿakov Yitzhak of Pshysḥa), tells the Zaddik, his teacher, about an incident in which the devil entered into a real-life woman and tried to seduce him:

> In the house there lived, too, . . . a married daughter . . . One night, while I was studying by the light of the candle, she came into the room. She stood still and looked at me silently . . . as though she wanted to throw herself down before me and did not dare. She was in her night garment and her feet were naked. I perceived that she was beautiful, a thing I had not known hitherto. A compulsion went out from her humility. I admired her beauty and felt a burning compassion for her humanity. Simultaneously that compulsion attacked me and now it used the forces of both my admiration and my pity. Suddenly, I was aware that I was looking at her naked feet. "Do not compel me!" I cried. The woman apparently did not understand me. She came nearer. And so I leaped out of the open window and ran a long distance through the March night. A long time thereafter . . . the woman came to see me and with tears begged me to forgive her, something had come upon her on that occasion which she had never understood. "I know," I consoled her, "the master of all compulsion incarnated himself in you. Thus he had first to compel you to become his vestiture." [24]

The story recreates an archetypal male-female situation. The setting is the dead of the night, the conventional hour of temptation, and the actors are the saintly man and the beautiful seductress in her nightly attire. The man's last-minute escape is a reenactment of the Joseph episode in the Bible. In addition, the man is seen as momentarily transfixed by the woman's naked feet which, in Hebraic sources, especially in biblical exegesis and Kabbalistic literature, carry sexual and erotic connotations. The word *regel*, 'leg' or 'foot', is often interpreted as a euphemism for intercourse, and a woman's exposed leg is meant to represent the nakedness of her body.[25] Thus this nocturnal scene is weighted with traditional symbols and associations that endow this particular incident with universal symbolism. Interestingly, though, the woman protagonist who plays the role of the temptress is not blamed. She is seen as temporarily possessed by the "master of all compulsion," the evil inclination or Satan, and doing his will unconsciously. The woman here is not a demon, but she unwittingly serves as the devil's agent. If the story does not condemn the woman as evil or diabolical, it nevertheless views the feminine body as the devil's instrument, which can cause the downfall of the great man.

As a response to this story, the Yehudi's rabbi then recounts an incident that happened to him:

"Once upon a time," said the Rabbi, "when in my youth, I had a similar experience, I found that one need not leap out of the window. On an icy winter evening . . . I lost my way. Suddenly I saw in the forest the illuminated windows of a house. In the house there was no one except a young woman. Until then I had looked upon no woman except the one to whom I had been wedded and from whom I separated myself because I saw upon her forehead not the symbol of the divine but a strange sign. After I separated myself from her, she did wander forth among the strangers. The woman in the house in the forest gave me food to eat and mulled wine to drink. Then she sat down beside me and asked me whither I had come and what my plans were and, finally, what I had dreamed about the night before. I was frightened by the magic which her eyes and her voice exerted upon me. The fright pierced to the very bottom of my soul, where hitherto there had been nothing but the fear of God and a shy attempt to love Him. When now this terror touched the bottom of my soul, love shot up like a flame and grasped the whole power of my being. Nothing remained without me; all the passionate power which rested within me was devoured by this flame. At that moment I looked up. There was no woman, no house, no forest. I stood on the road that leads straight to Lisensk."[26]

The Zaddik's tale interweaves the image of the "strange woman" of Proverbs with other traditional motifs. Like the "strange woman," the female in this Hasidic tale lures the young man into her house with the promise of food and wine and then proceeds to seduce him. The man is on a journey to Lisensk, to see the great Hasidic master

Rabbi Elimelech. The journey is geographical as well as mental. The delay in the man's progress is seen as caused by inner forces since the woman and her seductive paraphernalia turn out to be a projection of the young man's agitated and sexually aroused psyche. When the young man solves his inner conflict, when the power of the love of God overcomes his bodily urges, the woman and her house vanish. In other words, the feminine figure here is not a reality but a mental image, an embodiment of the young man's own "evil inclination," reminiscent of the phantasmic females who try to ensnare the two Talmudic rabbis. In both Hasidic tales, the female figures share much in common with the legendary Lilith in that they appear at night, exert a pernicious, magic power over the young man, and are warded off only when their potential victims are aided by the power of their faith.

Furthermore, in line with the general tendency of the Hasidic tale to convert the demonic from a cosmic reality to an inner, psychological force, these two stories shift the focus of interest from the images of temptation to the man who creates these corporeal feminine figures out of his inner anxieties and stimulated imagination.[27] Nevertheless, the women in these tales are divested of any realistic dimension and are viewed only in their relation to man, and in their role as an obstacle on man's road to salvation. The idea that getting rid of the woman is a step on the man's way to redemption, a necessary act in the process of the cleansing of the self, is implied in the Zaddik's dismissal of his wife. In the Zaddik's story, the wife is seen as unworthy of the man, who observed a Cain-like sign on her forehead. However, this narrative element links up with an ascetic, self-denying motif that runs through some Hasidic stories in which the legitimate, real-life wife of the rabbi is conceived of not as a "helpmate" but as an enemy, an instrument of the *sitra ahra*.

The culmination of the motif of the woman as the creator of a psychic and cosmic disharmony that hinders the arrival of the Messiah appears in the story entitled by Buber "A Seder That Went Wrong."[28] The protagonists in this story are the historical figures of the Yehudi and his wife Schoendel. In many other stories, Schoendel plays the role of the stereotypical comic nag, the contentious wife who pesters her husband with her poisonous tongue and long tirades; in the present story, however, Schoendel is given an additional role. The event narrated in this story is tied to Napoleon's invasion of Russia, viewed at the time by some Hasidic leaders as the beginning of redemption. The defeat of the Emperor who emancipated the Jews and who was regarded by many European Jews as a friend signified to the Hasidic mind another failed opportunity to bring about a Messianic era. Significantly, the day before Napoleon set forth from Paris on his Russian campaign that ended in disaster was Pesach. The night of the Seder was designated by the Seer of Lublin as the time when a concerted effort on the part of that generation's great rabbis would hasten the arrival of redemption. On the Pesach Eve, during the Seder, all the rabbis and their disciples and followers were to concentrate with their entire soul on salvation, *ge'ulah*. They also had to conduct the details of the ceremony according to the Seer's specific instructions, so that all their actions were to be in synchrony. However, in the middle of the Seder in Lublin the rabbi suddenly cried: "It has failed, the Seder is disturbed," and then he whispered "Pshysha," and "all is lost." It turned out that it was Schoendel, the Yehudi's wife, who disrupted the coordinated efforts and wreaked havoc on the cosmic harmony that was needed for the era of redemption to materialize. As the family members were preparing to take their seats at the Seder table, Schoendel flew into a rage and demanded to sit at the Yehudi's side, the place that was customarily her mother-in-law's. This potentially comic domestic squabble turned into a nightmare when Schoendel appeared to be possessed by an evil spirit. She tore the cushions and covers from the seats around the table and shrieked in irrational fury. This incident took up much time and this lost time could not be retrieved. The Seder in Pshysha was out of tune with the Seders in the other rabbis' tables, and this discordant note was enough to destroy the perfect harmony that the Seer of Lublin wished to achieve.

Schoendel is a real flesh-and-blood person who is temporarily possessed by the forces of evil that fight the rabbis' efforts to hasten the arrival of the Jewish and universal "end of days." Thus, if the woman is not a demon herself, she becomes the seat of a demon, if only for a short while, and through her the devil's work is done. The historical Schoendel is blamed for a cosmic accident, and with her, womanhood is condemned as a disruptive, unredeemable element, that by its nature is opposed to universal harmony. Interestingly, Schoendel is not viewed as a witch possessing magic powers but as the cantankerous shrew that she has always been; this time, however, her actions have repercussions beyond the domestic.

The same Schoendel appears in a disturbing dream that the Yehudi recounts. As in the case of the dreams of Rabbi Nahman of Bratslav, we do not know whether the rabbi is retelling an actual dream, or whether he uses the dream element as a literary device that would allow him to free his story of the rules of rationality and consistency.[29] It is clear, however, that by using the dream as a framework for his story the rabbi is employing the confessional tone, and that he is aware of the fact that the protagonists of the dream are projections of his inner fears and anxieties and have a psychological, but not necessarily realistic, validity. In that dream a staff turns into a snake and is then transformed into a doll with naked feet.[30] The doll's head identifies itself first as Foegele, the Yehudi's dead first wife, and then as Schoendel, his second wife. The dream strings together the elements of man's subconscious fear of woman, and the close affinity, almost interchangeability, between snake and woman.

Schoendel, the Yehudi's second wife who appears in the Hasidic legends recreated by Buber in *Gog uMagog,* is a protean figure of many dimensions and various literary functions. In some stories she is depicted realistically as the typical nag, a neurotic, discontented woman who turns the life of the saintly Yehudi into hell. In this chain of stories, there is even a comic element to the narrative, in line with the satirical tone with which the stereotypical nag is generally treated in literature. However, in other stories, Schoendel is divested of her human traits and becomes associated with the demonic, with the dark forces in the cosmos, which constantly attempt to defeat the Yehudi in his strivings to attain redemption.

If one aspect of the association of the female with the demonic views woman as the devil's vassal who is forced to do his bidding, the other aspect is that of the demon who appears like a real woman. The theme of the demon in a woman's form is dominant in the narrative yarn spun around the two saintly Hasidic brothers, Rabbi Elimelech and Rabbi Zusha.[31] In this tale, the two brothers are still in their "exilic" period, that time in their lives when they wandered around the countryside as part of preparing themselves for their future role as Hasidic leaders. The two brothers stopped at a country house owned by two young Jewish sisters. The young women invited them in and offered them food. The brothers were afraid to touch the food since, though the women claimed to be devoutly Jewish, their wanton demeanor and appearance belied their claims. In the middle of the night, when the brothers got up to meditate, as was their custom, they were suddenly seized by a sense of impurity and lewd desire. When they peered into the women's room they saw them leading animals into the room and taking off their harnesses, at which point the animals turned into men. The sisters then had sexual relations with the men, after which they transformed them again into animals. The brothers realized that the women were witches whose purpose was to reduce men to animals and engage in unnatural sexual acts with them. The rest of the story describes the brothers' struggle to free themselves from the witches' power and rescue the other men from the animal bodies in which they were imprisoned. The main interest of this story, which belongs to the literature of demonology, lies in the fact that this incident is part of the trials and tribulations that the saintly brothers had experienced before they became known as worthy of leadership in the Hasidic community. These women are not real figures, but neither are they perceived as solely the projection of the rabbis' imagination. They belong to the twilight zone of fantasy, where the rabbis' stimulated erotic desires become embodied in the female figure, as well as to the realm of the folktale, where man encounters evil in the form of a demonic witch or a fiendish sorcerer. The destruction of the sexually seductive and depraved female figures signifies the holy brothers' spiritual fortitude and their mental readiness to confront and defeat the powers of evil in themselves and in the universe.

Modern Incarnations of Eve and Lilith

From a prominent demon in East European Jewish folklore, Lilith progressed to become a favorite subject of Western writers such as Robert Browning, Dante Gabriel Rossetti, and Anatole France. In the era of Jewish Enlightenment she was revived by I. L. Peretz, whose protagonist (in "The Miracles That Failed") describes his fallen state as a result of Lilith's pernicious influence: "Lilith, the queen of Hell, enticed and snared me with her spells; / I chanted her praises to the strains of my golden harp—and one by one its strings snapped."[32]

In many modern works, however, Lilith is not named but appears in disguise and is often blended with other images of evil females from earlier Judaic sources. Selected examples from twentieth-century Hebrew works will illustrate how contemporary writers have incorporated into their women protagonists various figures of deadly and demonic females with which Judaic literary documents are replete. Very often it seems that behind the facade of a contemporary literary creation lies an earlier female model that attempts to assert its presence by means such as physical appearance, character traits, and, especially, its status vis-à-vis the male protagonist. When it turns out that the female protagonist is not conceived of as a separate entity but as a symbol of something in man, or when she functions as a catalyst for man, either as temptation or as inspiration, it is either because she is patterned after an earlier female example or because she has become assimilated with previous literary reflections of women.

In "The Lady and the Pedlar" (1943)[33] S. Y. Agnon weaves together some strands of the "strange woman" with those of the murderous, batlike Lilith, in the figure of Helene, the blue-eyed lady of the title. The plot line of the story, with its subtle tension between the two protagonists and bloody resolution, reenacts three archetypal situations. On one level, "The Lady and the Pedlar" is a morbid gothic fable, modeled after familiar European folk tales that depict the confrontation of a human with a demon, which in this story is a bloodsucking female vampire. The human meets a demon in disguise, is enticed into friendship and trust towards the evil supernatural spirit, and then manages a last minute escape. The story dramatizes man's fear of the supernatural and his nagging suspicion that the world is populated by diabolical forces, inimical to him.

On another level, the story is a parable of the precariousness of Jewish life in exile, in the midst of hostile strangers. Joseph is the archetypal "wandering Jew," a homeless nomad who knocks at strangers' doors in search of temporary shelter and dubious rest. Helene, the beautiful Gentile lady who lets him in on a stormy night and allows him to stay a while in her home, is the world community at whose pleasure the uprooted Jew finds momentary peace. Joseph the guest moves quickly up the ladder, as he is promoted from handyman to companion, and then to lover. But the idyllic relationship is short-lived, since the lady, having fed and clothed the Jew, now desires his blood. When her bloodthirsty attack fails, Joseph, the eternal wanderer, is on the road again, in search of another temporary, insecure haven. Helene's name evokes the Hellenic world and, by extension, all foreign cultures and powers which the Jewish world had to contend with during its long history. The story celebrates the Jew's survivability in the face of universal hostility. Joseph's trade stands for the Jew's lack of roots and attachment to one geographical place; but it is also a strategy for survival. Joseph's attempts at assimilation are unsuccessful. He is ready to give up his tradition and values and is led into believing that he has been accepted by the lady's countrymen. But this is an illusion only; what the lady really wants is to fatten the Jew in order to devour him when the time comes.

Beyond the obvious allegorical juxtaposition of the exiled Jewish nation and the Gentile world which welcomes it and then tries to destroy it, Agnon's tale reveals man's age-old ambiguity towards women, and reenacts the typical confrontation between the gullible man and the murderous female. Again the man is seen as knocking on the woman's door. The woman stands for home and stability, but also for entrapment and danger. She lures the man indoors with promise of warmth, food, and sex, but she offers only death and destruction. Joseph's name is especially significant, since it evokes the biblical Joseph, the ancient example of a young man who escapes the treacherous seductress.[34] The protagonist's name also brings to mind the figure of Joseph Della Reina, whose journey to salvation was interrupted. The alluring, bewitching Helene is the eternal woman as well as an incarnation of Lilith. Helene's name means light in Greek, but she stands for the darkness of the night, the hour when she attacks men and sucks their blood. In Ashkenazi folklore, the figure of Lilith coalesced with the popular image of Helen of Troy. Thus the lady Helene of the story is an amalgam consisting of the "strange woman" of Proverbs whose house leads to She'ol, the mythological Helen, whose radiant beauty brought death and devastation, and the wicked, predatory Lilith, who cohabits with men at night and then destroys them.

Death and erotic attraction are closely related in this story. The woman's sexual promise turns into a deadly trap. Furthermore, the erotic relations between man and woman are seen as dehumanizing and demoralizing for man. When Joseph finally moves from the storage room to the lady's bedroom, he rids himself of his former squeamishness at the sight of Helene brutally slaughtering animals and becomes dehumanized himself. Unbridled sexual appetite finds its correlative in coarse, bestial eating habits, when man is reduced to a predator and loses his human sensitivity:

> And the pedlar stayed with the lady. Not in the old cowshed and not in the room of the old things that were no longer in use, but in the room of the lady he lived and in the bed of her husband he slept, and she served him, as if he were her lord. Every day she prepared him a meal of everything she had in the house and in the fields, every good bird and every fat bird. And if she roasted him meat in butter, he did not turn away from it. At first he shuddered, when he saw her wring the head of a bird, then he ate and even sucked the bone, in the manner of frivolous people who in the beginning do not intend to commit any offense and then commit every offense in the world with pleasure (173).

Joseph's ascent from servant to lover is a journey down on the human scale; the lady's sexual partner becomes as bestial as the lady herself. In a nightmare that reveals Joseph's anxieties and fear of the woman, the lady is seen as a growling bitch who attacks him and sucks his blood. The bitch as a female fiend is a Kabbalistic image and further ties Helene with the demon Lilith.[35] In this macabre vision Agnon portrays the eternal male-female sexual dependency as that between victim and vampire. Eros and death are closely connected, and any surrender to the former brings man to the threshold of the latter. In the sexual battle, man is viewed as the victim, rather than the victimizer, and the woman is seen as the domineering partner who feeds on the male and sucks out his vitality and life. The sexual act is pictured as a cannibalist act in which the woman devours the man: "And she, too, kissed him again and said: 'Joseph, when you first showed yourself to me, I wanted to set my bitch on you, and now I am myself biting you like a mad bitch, in such a manner that I fear you will not get away alive out of my hands, oh my sweet carcass mine!'" (174).

In its particular national symbolism, the story seems to represent the unholy union of the Jewish man with the non-Jewish woman; therefore the biblical precedence of Samson and Delilah is evoked. In the context of sexual symbolism however, both the victimized Samson and the treacherous Delilah, as well as the gullible Joseph and the fiendish Helene are seen as reenacting an archetypal male-female situation:

> He who has dealings with women knows that every love that is not unconditional must come to naught at the end. And even a man who loves a woman as Samson loved Delilah—in the end she makes fun of him, in the end she annoys him until his soul is weary to death (175).

The Lilith stature of Helene and the other Kabbalistic elements in the story lend an added meaning to the journey of Joseph the pedlar. Like his earlier namesake Joseph Della Reina, the wandering Joseph seeks redemption, but is distracted by Helene who offers him the momentary salvation of sex in exchange for eternal damnation and death.

The story shuttles between its national symbolism and sexual vision; in its ending, the national and the sexual coalesce. Joseph the Jew escapes by the skin of his teeth and is now again on the roads of history, looking for another temporary refuge. Joseph the man, having successfully foiled the attempts of the female vampire to feast on his body, continues his restless search for home and woman.

It is impossible to see Helene and Joseph as individuals; the allegorical framework of the story and the archetypal dimension of its protagonists are undeniable. By contrast, in "Agunot" (1908), the first story published under the pen name Agnon, the writer has endowed his characters with a realistic and psychological authenticity.[36] Dinah, its woman protagonist, reenacts Eve's sin and, like her ancient prototype, pays dearly for it. Like the biblical Eve, Dinah commits an act of transgression which breaks the idyllic harmony of her surroundings; in both cases, the violation exemplifies the human condition and is seen as inevitable. Yet Dinah comes to life as an individual in a way that the primordial Eve never does, and her rebellious act and subsequent agony not only elicit the reader's sympathy, but are made credible within the social and psychological circumstances of the story.

"Agunot" is replete with midrashic, Kabbalistic, and Hasidic motifs that portray the universe as well as the human soul as a battlefield where the forces of good and evil, light and darkness are engaged in eternal combat. Its folktale quality is enhanced by the theme of the star-crossed lovers and the tragic coincidences and errors that dominate human life.

The protagonist's name, Dinah, evokes the figure of Jacob's daughter, the protagonist of a famous episode in the Book of Genesis. In the scriptural story itself, Dinah, who was raped by Shekhem the Hivvite, is seen as a victim, yet the Midrash holds her responsible for what happened to her. Similarly, there is an ambivalence in our story regarding Dinah's guilt; she is at once a sinner and a victim of circumstances beyond her control.

Dinah is the only daughter of the wealthy Ahiezer who has settled in Jerusalem with the hope of rebuilding the city's ruins and restoring its old glory. But when he takes for his daughter a bridegroom from Poland, thus slighting all the young Jerusalem scholars, a discordant note enters into Ahiezer's grand plans, and the forces of evil are set in motion. Ahiezer decides to build an academy and a synagogue in honor of his son-in-law, and hires a gifted craftsman, Ben Uri, to build and decorate the ark for the synagogue. Dinah falls in love with the artist Ben Uri, but the latter becomes so immersed in his sacred work, that he hardly notices the beautiful young woman. Dinah sees in the ark a rival for Ben Uri's attention, and in a rash moment of uncontrollable jealousy, the rejected woman pushes the ark into the garden where it lies among the roses. Ben Uri is blamed for Dinah's action and is banished from Jerusalem by the enraged community and its rabbi. The desecrated ark disappears and the mood of *'aginut*, separation and alienation, now sets in. The soul of each of the story's protagonists is now in limbo, suspended between a sense of terrible guilt and the impossibility of rectifying the damage. Ahiezer, Dinah, and the rabbi (to whom Dinah discloses her secret but who prefers to keep it silent) have each committed a transgression and will never again find peace for their tormented souls. Ben Uri has disappeared, but his apparition haunts the rabbi. Dinah's husband, who never consummated the marriage because of his attachment to the girl he left in Poland as well as his wife's past, divorces Dinah and returns to the

Diaspora. Ahiezer and his daughter also leave Jerusalem. At the end of the story, Jerusalem the city is like an *'agunah;* is it once again a deserted city whose hopes for restoration have been shattered.

The story shuttles between the optimistic mood of love and renewal that characterizes the Song of Songs, and the fatalistic spirit of melancholy and resignation that dominate Ecclesiastes, while at its core is a reenactment of the Eve episode in Genesis. In the opening lines, God talks to the feminine figure that represents the congregation of Israel in language taken from the Song of Songs, and is answered with another quote from Canticles. And the garden where the beautiful, virginal Dinah walks, with its doves fluttering about her, is the Canticles garden of love. However, soon after Dinah's desecration of the ark and the expulsion of Ben Uri, the language formula is patterned after that of Ecclesiastes: "Day ebbed and the sun set" (38), "month comes and month goes" (40, 41), and so forth.

The opening lines of the story quote a homily that pictures God as weaving a resplendent prayer shawl out of the good deeds of the people of Israel. But when the people of Israel deviate from the right path, the thread breaks and the shawl is damaged. This mystical vision of cosmic harmony that can be ruined as a result of human action is enhanced by other Kabbalistic themes such as the correspondence between divine love and human love and the eternal struggle between the forces of good and evil in the universe. The midrash conceives of the bond between God and His congregation as that between lover and his beloved; and Agnon's own tale is supposed to illustrate the idea behind this midrash on the level of human love and its brutal disruption by the forces of evil. The story abounds with images of evil: when the shawl is blemished "evil spirits hover around it" (30), and when Sire Ahiezer makes the unforgivable mistake of looking for a son-in-law in Poland rather than in Jerusalem, it is because "the evil one interrupted . . ." (32). Dinah commits her rash act when she is under the influence of "the evil one" (35).

The Genesis spirit is introduced in the opening lines, when the sinful people of Israel are filled with shame "and they knew they are naked" (30), which is the phrase used by the biblical narrator to describe Adam and Eve's feelings after they have eaten from the forbidden fruit. And the garden where Dinah roams happily before her evil deed, and where the defiled ark falls, can be seen as the Garden of Eden, scene of the primordial transgression.

The homily that serves as a motto for the story has far-reaching implications. The vision of God as lover and His nation as His beloved can be, and has been throughout the ages, wrongly interpreted.

If the ideal form of love is that between God and man, which is fundamentally spiritual love, than any other kind of love, the carnal union between man and woman is debased and wrong. Indeed, this distorted notion of human sexuality dominates Agnon's male protagonists in other stories. This is also what afflicts Ben Uri who becomes so consumed with the holy work that he is performing that he ignores the young woman who pines after him. The love song that he should be singing to the woman turns into a sacred song, and the spirit of earthly love is replaced by the spirit of holy devotion:

> But as Ben Uri pursued his work, he cleaved more and more to it, until both eyes and heart passed into the Ark; no part of him was free of it. Memory of Dinah fled him; it was as though she did not exist. Not many days passed before he stopped singing altogether; his voice rang out no more (33–34).

Ben Uri's "cleaving" to his holy work proves how wrong and misguided the young man's self denial is. In the Genesis text, a verb from the same root is used to indicate the physical and spiritual union between man and woman: "That is why a man leaves his father and his mother, and cleaves to his wife, and they become one flesh" (Gen. 2:24). Ben Uri, however, transposes his passion to "cleave" from the flesh-and-blood woman to the symbol of spiritual devotion, the Ark.

The two different narrative viewpoints that are evident in the entire story are clearly manifest here. The pious storyteller, who is fully within the tradition of religious devotion, is not aware that Ben Uri's total immersion in his sacred task is excessive and wrong. He uses the verb "to cleave" as part of his general tendency to describe reality with the aid of the biblical idiom. However, the more enlightened and somewhat rebellious voice that is often heard in the story is cognizant of the disparity between the meaning of the verb and Ben Uri's ascetic interpretation of it. This second narrative angle sympathizes with the lovesick, rejected Dinah, who refuses to accept the pious man's rigidity and sublimation of his human emotions and carnal desires.

Ben Uri is so successful in transcending his physical and emotional being that when his work is done he feels empty; instead of elation he experiences depression. He then goes out for a walk "among the trees in the garden," a phrase which again brings to mind the Genesis garden. At the same time, Dinah is overcome by her longings for him and goes into his room: "Her robe clung to her flesh; fear was in her countenance" (34). Dinah is now guided by the urges of her flesh, and she seems to be afraid of her own body and of what she might do. The scene in which Dinah pushes the Ark down the window is reminiscent of the midrashic reconstruction of the Genesis scene in which Eve is induced by the devil to violate God's order:

> Dinah stood in Ben Uri's chamber, and the Ark of God stood at the open window, where Ben Uri had worked. She stood near the Ark, and examined it. The evil one came, and poured a potion of vengeance into her heart. He pointed at the Ark and said, "It is not for nought that Ben Uri takes no thought of you; it is the Ark that separates you twain" (35).

At this moment, the "evil one" pushed Dinah against the Ark; the Ark "teetered and fell through the open window."[37]

The two conflicting narrative voices again assert themselves here. The secular, psychologically oriented approach views Dinah's act as motivated by jealousy and rebelliousness. But from the viewpoint of the pious narrator, Dinah's act is a result of the temptation of the devil, the *sitra ahra*. Like the female characters in the Hasidic tales, Dinah becomes possessed by the devil and is forced to do his bidding. In the aftermath of her evil deed, Dinah feels like a sinner: "Her sin weighs heavily upon her"; yet on the other hand, it seems that the Jerusalem air approves of what she has done and rewards her with a sensual experience that evokes for Dinah the figure of Ben Uri: "The wind . . . played around her hair and through her ears, whispering sweet melodies, like the songs Ben Uri had sung" (35).

After Ben Uri's unjustified banishment, the forces of darkness and evil take over. Dinah becomes possessed by a spirit of depression and melancholy, which in the Hasidic context is a sin in itself. Though Ben Uri has vanished, his spirit lingers on, but now it is merged with the evil spirit (40). And the rabbi who condemned Ben Uri will be forever roaming the limbo sphere, between life and death.

Agnon's story thus provides a particular illustration of the homily that it quotes at the beginning. It creates human drama in which harmony, both personal and cosmic, is broken as a result of an evil human act; the divine shawl has been damaged because the people of Israel pulled out a thread. However, the exact identity of the wrongful act that is responsible for the shattering of harmony is open to interpretation. From the angle of the simpleminded, pious narrator, immersed in the traditional conception of cosmic order which clearly defines right and wrong, the evil act is actually a series of events: Dinah's and Ben Uri's attraction to each other when Dinah is betrothed to another man, the desecration of the Ark, and Ben Uri's unjustified banishment. But to the more enlightened narrator, who employs the linguistic and imagistic formulas of the old documents,

but not always agrees with their values, the wrongful acts are the social and religious norms that make it impossible for Dinah to choose
her own mate, Dinah's unfulfilled desires, and Ben Uri's suppression
of his own humanity.

On the surface, Agnon's story, which is couched in the traditional
idiom of piety and devotion, seems to repeat the Hasidic formula. It
presents woman as the agent of the devil, destroying the life and
work of a great man, and thus delaying both personal and national
redemption. But the young Agnon has inserted in this very early
story a romantic, rebellious, and basically secular voice that questions the traditional conception of good and evil. Dinah comes to life
as a victim of circumstances, as well as of an oppressive, though well-
meaning, patriarchy. Her burst of jealousy is seen not only as psychologically inevitable, but as justified. Her "illicit" passion for the
craftsman Ben Uri and her attempts at physical closeness to the ascetic young man are condoned. Agnon thus gives us a glimpse of the
other side of the coin: the conception of woman as evil is subterfuge
for feminine oppression; behind the image of the woman as victimizer there is the real woman as victim. Interestingly, the story's
title implies a similar idea. The state of *'aginut* is seen here as a spiritual condition of alienation, of people yearning for what is forbidden,
and of the inability of any protagonist to find either his or her true
match, or to restore harmony and rectify the damage. *'Aginut* is thus
a mystical state of broken harmony. Yet in its narrow, halakic meaning, the state of *'aginut* applies to a woman who has been deserted by
her husband without being divorced by him, and who finds herself
in a limbo state where she has no married life, yet is not free to remarry. This is an example of female oppression, a predicament experienced by women only. Agnon has exercised poetic license in his use
of the term *'aginut* in the spiritual sense of separation and existential
loneliness. In this story, *'aginut* is a mental state shared by both men
and women, yet behind the abstract state of *'aginut* looms the real
woman, whose predicament is not shared by men.[38]

While Dinah's voice of rebellion is muffled and framed in the traditional language of sin and evil, Agnon has introduced in this tale a
new voice that questions the conception of femininity as creator of
cosmic chaos, and directs towards a more realistic assessment of the
predicament of the real woman in a patriarchal environment. The exalted feminine images with which the story is laced, the Shekinah as
a lovely woman dressed in black and mourning the devastation that
has occurred, the feminine nature of the city of Jerusalem, and the
collective people of Israel incarnated in the Canticles' lovesick woman
searching for her beloved, God, also help dilute the harsh impact

of the affinity between woman and evil that lies at the heart of the tale.

The saintly Tehilah, the protagonist of Agnon's story by the same name (written in 1950), serves as a redemptive counterpoint to the concept of feminine evil. It seems, however, that the woman's ability to divorce herself completely and absolutely from evil hinges on her sexless and ageless existence. When the first-person narrator of the tale meets Tehilah for the first time, walking vigorously through the narrow alleys of the Old City, she is a legendary figure, over one hundred years old, whose beauty and agility belie her years. For the narrator, Tehilah functions as an epiphany, an illumination, a catalyst that deepens and widens his vision. If he might flinch from the decay and filth that he observes, looking at Jerusalem through Tehilah's lenses, he is able to discern the pristine beauty and everlasting glory behind the city's shabby exterior.

As in many other Agnon stories, the city of Jerusalem here is not merely a backdrop for the human drama that occurs, but an active participant. In "Agunot," Jerusalem is one of the tale's protagonists, the ultimate *'agunah,* left destitute and empty after Ahiezer's attempts to redeem her and restore her ancient glory have failed. In "Tehilah," the fusion of city with the woman reinforces the old woman's mythic dimension as well as the ancient city's feminine nature. In fact, Tehilah and her polar opposite, the old *rabbanit,* embody the dual nature of the city: The radiant, benevolent, and pure Tehilah stands for the heavenly Jerusalem (*Yerushalayim shel ma'alah*), while the cantankerous, selfish, and fault-finding *rabbanit* represents the earthly Jerusalem (*Yerushalayim shel matah*). At the same time, Tehilah herself epitomizes the sum total of the city's tragic history and changing fortunes, as well as its magnetic essence. Like Jerusalem in its halcyon years, Tehilah was courted and wooed by many when she first came to settle here as a wealthy widow. As the years went by, Tehilah, like Jerusalem, has lost her glamor and wealth; and in the present time of the story, Tehilah, as well as the city itself, is regarded by many as just another impoverished old woman.

Tehilah becomes the locus of a number of feminine images that populate early Judaic texts. The close identification between the city and the female protagonist, whereby the city and the woman mirror each other, is a culmination of a long tradition, starting with the biblical images of the defeated Jerusalem as a mournful widow, and the unfaithful city as a whoring female. Furthermore, in her innate sagacity and ability to perceive harmony where others see only chaos, Tehilah is a latter-day incarnation of the biblical "wise woman." The admirable Tehilah practices in her everyday life, and manifests in every facet of her being, the Kabbalistic and Hasidic ideas of the sacredness of the word and of time. She employs the language of praise only, and thus confirms the truthfulness of her name, which means 'praise' (as well as 'a psalm' and 'a prayer') in Hebrew. And she sees every minute that passes without the performance of a good deed or giving praise to God, as abuse of the gift of life. Tehilah is, therefore, the epitome and essence of the biblical book of Psalms, the ancient collection of sacred hymns incarnated in the female body, reminiscent of the Kabbalistic image of the Torah as a beautiful woman.

Nevertheless, as our storyteller's curiosity about Tehilah is gradually being satisfied and the larger-than-life mythic character becomes anchored in human time, a different aspect of Tehilah's existence is revealed. Though herself a nucleus of total innocence and sanctity, Tehilah was propelled, very early in her life, into an orbit of sinful acts and passionate vendettas. In fact, Tehilah's biography is a chain of calamitous events, triggered by a wrong act committed by Tehilah's father on behalf of his daughter. The rapid succession of disasters that marks Tehilah's life—the tragic deaths of her two sons, her husband's untimely demise, and her daughter's conversion to Christianity—is a result of the hotheaded decision made by Tehilah's father to break his daughter's engagement to a young man who turned out to be a Hasid. While the woman herself had no part in the breach of contract, she was nevertheless pivotal in this drama of Jewish feuds and follies. Therefore, though herself guiltless, Tehilah carried the seeds of suffering and destruction, planted in her by the family patriarch, and unwittingly brought tragedy to those close to her. In spite of herself, Tehilah became the carrier of bad luck, the focus of avenging spirits, and the center of a widening circle of misfortunes.

Tehilah's nature is twofold and dialectical. In her mythic dimension, Tehilah possesses magic powers of durability and invincibility. Like Jerusalem, the city that has survived the ravages of time and hostile invaders, Tehilah seems to have conquered Time itself. She has outlived not only her own generation, but that of her grandchildren, and she is the one who decides when her time to die has come. With the hypnotic force of her gaze, she makes the British officer return the chair that he took away from a frail old woman in front of the Western Wall. Nevertheless, though Tehilah has succeeded in commuting her tragedy into triumph by living to be very old and enjoying the gift of life, the fact remains that her story is a paradigm of woman's powerlessness and victimization. By surrendering to male authority, Tehilah has become a center of bad luck and a conductor of evil. Though the role of the transporter of evil has been imposed on her by outside forces, and stands in contradiction to the very essence of her luminescent being, Tehilah sees herself as responsible for the disruption of cosmic harmony, and plans to make amends in the world to come.

As in "Agunot," Agnon's treatment of the theme of feminine evil in this tale is fraught with ambiguities, although unlike Dinah, the protagonist of the former, Tehilah is completely innocent of the evil that she has caused. Indeed, Tehilah stands out as one of the most admirable female figures in Hebraic letters. Agnon has introduced here a new twist to the traditional affinity between woman and evil, and made us turn from the mythic figure to the frail woman and question this literary convention that has always fertilized the male imagination.

A writer of a younger generation, Amos Oz, has strung together elements of the Eve tale, the Lilith myth, and the Proverbs verses on seduction in his story "Strange Fire" (1964).[39] Though she resides in modern Jerusalem and ostensibly leads a normal life as the mother of a young woman about to be married, Lily, the heroine of this story, is an enigmatic, even diabolical character. The story's title, *'Esh Zarah* ("Strange Fire"), evokes in its sound the Proverbs image of *'ishah zarah* ('strange woman') and thus ties Lily with the prototypical seductress. But the term *'esh zarah* is cultic, denoting an improper form of worship which is offensive to God and modeled after the pagan altar. And indeed, behind the facade of normal life in the modern city and the ordinary people who roam its streets, lies a hidden, dark, and alien reality, a certain "strange fire."

The quote from Berdichewscky's story "Hiding in the Thunder," that serves as a motto for Oz's story, pictures night as a primordial force which brings out the beast in man, his carnal desires, which can lead man to his grave. The story itself starts in an everyday, ordinary reality, when two scholars, both rather uninspiring and lackluster, walk home from a party meeting. The question of good and evil enters their conversation in an academic, abstract fashion, yet through them Oz subtly introduces the theme of the story: "Apparently degeneracy and purity are absolute opposites, whereas in fact one draws the other out, one makes the other possible" (108).

Even before the perverse Lily comes into the scene, the streets of Jerusalem at night are portrayed as the physical and moral battleground of the forces of good and evil, represented by the "birds of the day" and the "birds of the night." Oz's language abounds with intimations of evil that lurks behind the normal, ordinary reality, and that is let loose at night. Lily Dannenberg is also a nocturnal creature and, while she is named after a white flower, her entire being evokes the darkness of the night, *Lailah*. Lily is a modern incarnation of the mythic Lilith, roaming the streets of Jerusalem on a mission of ruin and corruption. Like her legendary namesake, she is a threat to a young man (her future son-in-law), and to a young woman about to be married (her own daughter).

Two planes of existence manifest themselves in the story. One is the reality of modern Jerusalem with its scholars, students, and young couples planning their future life. The other plane is the sphere of evil, chaos, and madness that takes over the streets of Jerusalem at night. Lily is the link between the two planes. She is a middle-aged, divorced woman, the mother of Dinah, and the former wife of the scholar Yosef Yarden. She is both an integral part of the Jerusalem community, and the social "other." She thinks in the German language and finds the Hebrew inadequate for expressing the profundities of existence. In her role as the sexual temptress of the young protagonist, Yair, she is also the psychological "other," and her affinity with the mysterious forces of darkness make her the cosmic "other" as well.

Lily arranges to meet Yosef Yarden, her longtime friend and former husband, to discuss with him the details of the upcoming wedding of her daughter to Yarden's son, the young student Yair. The hidden tension between Lily and the respectable elderly scholar is revealed when Lily deliberately leaves her home before Yosef arrives at her door. Knowing that he is on his way to her, Lily goes to Yosef's home, lures the bewildered young man, Yair, to the street, and after a long walk, in which she tells him his father's secret, Lily seduces Yair.

The subtle conflict between the three male protagonists, on the one hand, and the vicious Lily, who possesses an inner "strange fire," on the other, is mirrored in the war between the forces of darkness and the forces of light, the "birds of darkness" and the "birds of light," that takes place in the kingdom of the night (115). Lily herself is also a bird of the night whose true province is the dark, mystical, and demonic ambience of the blackened streets. Her affinity with Lilith is made clear when she is called the "Queen of Sheba" by the taxi driver. As we know, the images of the Queen of Sheba and Lilith merged in the popular imagination; several early legends contended that the Queen of Sheba was actually Lilith who came to seduce King Solomon.⁴⁰ Lily also sees herself in the role of the evil serpent, lurking among the trees in the garden: "Pity I'm not there among the trees in the garden, secretly watching him, enjoying the expression on his face" (118). We know that Lily is not entirely human when she plays a vicious game with the street cat, gaining its trust and then cruelly hitting its belly.

As the social other, Lily is reminiscent of other Oz female protagonists (such as Hannah in *My Michael*) who are contemptuous of the ordinary people who surround them and their dull, humdrum existence. But in Lily the domestic and the demonic merge. Her attempts to escape what she sees as a confining, provincial environment are not depicted without sympathy; and the taxi driver's admiration for Lily is seen as well-founded. Yet Oz's general ambivalence towards his female protagonists is evident in this story, too. While the narrative voice is not without a note of compassion towards the woman's sense of social and psychological estrangement, Lily's otherness inevitably becomes tied up with the demonic. When Lily seduces her future son-in-law she is the moral corrupter as well as the Satanic killer. She also turns into an owl, the bird Lilith, one of those night creatures who are messengers from the subterranean sphere of chaos and madness (113).

Yair is not the only man who experiences the "strange fire" while under Lily's influence. It seems that Lily's presence in Jerusalem induces irrational conduct in all the men around her. At the same time that Yair unwillingly succumbs to Lily's feminine and hypnotic charms, the sedate scholar Elhanan Kleinberger, universally known as the zealous admirer of the Hebrew language and the defender of its honor, resorts to his hidden passion, which is composing love poetry in the German language (134). The height of Kleinberger's guilt-ridden moment of vision coincides with the climax of lust that seizes Lily and her victim Yair, and is reflected in the image of the bird who suddenly screeches with "malicious joy" (134). Kleinberger now surrenders completely to the spirit of the "strange fire" that overcomes him; he despairs of creating his own magic words and, appropriately, settles down to read a study of demons and ghosts in ancient ritual.

Lily is thus not only a restless, uprooted woman, the social "other," who converts her frustrated sensuality and voracious appetite for life into a deadly weapon. She also embodies the black and abysmal side of life and of the human psyche. Her role is that of the catalyst that releases the subterranean forces of chaos and madness in her surrounding. The female is the keeper of the pagan "strange fire" which, according to ancient Jewish legend, was the reason why God killed the two sons of the high priest Aaron in the desert.

In her birdlike qualities and her ability to turn reality into nightmare, Lily represents the archetypal Feminine in its negative and death-dealing aspect. While the birdlike character of woman in ancient art pointed primarily to her correlation with the heavens, it later developed into a negative image. Erich Neumann describes a Hellenistic relief whose characteristics are also shared by the goddess Lilith, representing a siren with wings and a bird's claws: "This nude female creature appears as an incubus riding on a likewise nude and evidently dreaming man; she belongs, as the Dionysian symbols of the relief show, to the domain of the mysteries. She is an enchanting, seducing, orgiastic, and nightmarish form of the Feminine, whose ambivalent character for man's ego begins where the excessive power and fascination of the numinous becomes a disintegrator of consciousness, and hence is experienced as negative and destructive."[41] Neumann's description explains Lily's archetypal origins and her role as the embodiment of the male's primordial fear of the female.

The last chapter of the story abandons the human protagonists and shifts its focus to the Biblical Zoo, as the entire Jerusalem night now dissolves into bestiality and savagery. The whole universe becomes the domain of Lily-Lilith, surrendering to the cosmic "otherness," and returning to primordial chaos.

The conception of the female as a destructive force of cosmic magnitude is again exemplified in A. B. Yehoshua's enigmatic, Kafkaesque short story "The Evening Journey of Yatir."[42] The story, imbued with biblical and Kabbalistic motifs, recreates the Eve story of Genesis, but gives it a terrifying, demonic twist. Yatir is a small, God-forsaken village, nestled among heavy rocks and towering mountains, and overlooking the deep abyss. The bleakness of the surrounding terrain and the mercilessness of the stormy winds are exacerbated by the villagers' sense of geographical and existential loneliness. The express train that passes by the village never stops there, and the residents' lives are centered around that one fleeting moment, every evening, when the train passes by with maddening speed. Life in the village is seen as an anxious state of waiting for that moment of epiphany that would never happen, when the train would acknowledge the existence of this anguished community and stop at its station.

The town's name, Yatir, which means superfluous, unnecessary, epitomizes its inhabitants' sense of being the universal outcast. The young girl Zivah, whose name means 'light' or 'splendor', devises a plan to alleviate the existential ennui that plagues the town and saps its people's vitality. She suggests to the story's narrator, a young man who pines after her, to direct the train away from its regular route and into the town's old, defective tracks, thus causing it to derail and roll down the mountain. She implies that she will give herself to the young man after the planned disaster occurs. Zivah manages to secure the enthusiastic consent of the village secretary and the railroad supervisor to her plan, overriding the desperate objections of the old stationmaster.

The story's timeless, placeless quality lends itself to an allegorical interpretation. It may be read as a political parable of modern Israel which, like the fictional Yatir, was founded by idealists and social visionaries who hoped to create a "new life" in this remote part of the world. Yatir has been painfully and laboriously carved out of the stubborn, unyielding terrain, yet as soon as it was founded, a sense of total isolation and estrangement settled on its inhabitants. They feel outside the normal track of time and history, and they only come to life when a cataclysmic event takes place. The disastrous derailment thus stands for the cataclysm of war which, according to Yehoshua, is the only experience that can jolt the villagers-Israelis out of their existential apathy and give meaning to their bored lives.

The rhetorical language with which the pioneer origins of the village is depicted would lend credence to a political interpretation that directs us to the author's pacifist stand and his conception of the constant military flare-ups on Israel's borders as sought-after crises, a form of a collective death-wish. But while this layer of meaning undoubtedly exists in the story, it fails to account for the many metaphysical and mystical images and structures that underlie it. As in other of Yehoshua's stories (such as "Facing the Forests"), the sociopolitical dimension is but one aspect of the total meaning. In the broader allegorical aspect of the story it depicts the human condition of existential alienation by tying together images taken from early Judaic sources, and offering a new reading to the biblical tale of the primordial woman as the creator of chaos. Zivah's name implies splendor and brightness, but it also evokes the phrase *ziv haShekinah*, the splendor of the face of the Shekinah, and evokes the mystical vision of an encounter between man and God. Zivah is the initiator of evil and is successful in luring the male protagonists into her conspiracy. The two authority figures, Bardon and Addon Kanaoth, take on a metaphysical quality by virtue of their names alone. Bardon is *bar-addon*, the 'son of the master', or God, and Addon Kanaoth is the jealous master, God himself. The new mythology created by Yehoshua in this story exposes the biblical tale as naive and simplistic. The divine figures do not forbid, but condone; they do not command, but comply. The world returns to primordial chaos as the woman now becomes master of its fate. Zivah's figure is a throwback to the Kabbalistic vision of the feminine as powerful and demonic, and to even earlier images of the Female as cosmic threat. Yatir is a grotesque version of the Garden of Eden; it seems sleepy and calm, yet it is restless and anxiety-stricken. Like the biblical Adam, the story's narrator is a passive accomplice. Zivah enacts the role of the "strange woman" of Proverbs as well; she lures the young man with sexual promise, and her face wears "a strange expression." The ancient Eve lays the blame on the serpent, "the serpent beguiled me," while Zivah names the innocent stationmaster as the culprit and promises to turn him in. Zivah, as the eternal woman, awakens the town into life and activity, but she accomplishes this through death and destruction. The motif of the bridge, which evokes the mystical and Hasidic metaphor of this world as a bridge to the next, is also employed ironically in this story. Zivah's metaphysical yearnings do not lead to a mystical union with God, but to the abyss, She'ol.

Zivah is closely associated with the time element. Yatir's existential ennui stems from its status as the pariah of time and history. Zivah corrects this by causing the disaster and thus putting the time-forgotten village back into the realm of human time. Ironically, by derailing the train, Yatir comes back to the "normal" track of time and history. Zivah's special affinity with time is also anchored in her femininity: in midrashic and Kabbalistic metaphorical world woman is linked with time.[43] Furthermore, the element of light implied in Zivah's name also summons earlier Judaic sources that identify woman with fire, candle, and light.[44] Yet in spite of her name, Zivah, like Oz's Lily, is a night creature, and her face is described as "enveloped in darkness." Yehoshua's story offers no counterpart to the biblical serpent; but Zivah herself assumes the role of serpent, though she falsely accuses the innocent Ardity of beguiling her. In the texts discussed previously we have seen the woman as the serpent's agent, and the female body as merging with that of a snake, or in the process of metamorphosing into a snake; in Yehoshua's story the woman is female in her corporeal shape, but a serpent in her dramatic function. The impact of this story lies in its recreation of motifs and narrative structures from earlier Judaic sources in which woman is pivotal, only to reverse them, or to bring to light their suppressed elements and steer them to shocking conclusions.

The cluster of images associated with the female figures discussed in the present chapter, night, abyss, the menacing depth, sorcery, snakes, destruction, and the unconscious, portray woman as the force that strives to bring man and civilization back to primordial chaos. It further identifies the feminine as the irrational and the disintegrator of the male consciousness. These images belong to the archetypal image of the Feminine as the goddess of disastrous floods, nocturnal darkness, and the negative unconscious. They are also linked to the symbol group of the "Terrible Mother," and reveal the male's fear of women.[45] Indeed, the power of the woman as the sexual seductress is only equalled, in man's mind, to the female's mysterious reproductive abilities. Therefore, our next chapter discusses the diverse and ambiguous images of the woman as mother in some of the Hebraic texts.

Notes

[1] *Paradise Lost,* Book 9. The appropriate lines are found in the Nonesuch Library edition (Glasgow: The University Press, 1952), 271–73.

[2] See Rogers, *The Troublesome Helpmate,* 3–23, and Ferrante, *Woman as Image,* 17–35. Midrashic sources also introduce sexual elements into the Genesis story. The tree of knowledge is described as having power to increase desire, and it is also suggested that the serpent desired Eve and therefore wanted to get Adam out of the way. Woman in general is condemned by the Midrash as immodest and voluptuous, especially in connection with the story of Creation. See Genesis Rabbah, 17, 18; Sotah, 19b; Abot deRabbi Nathan, 1.

[3] On the personality differences between Adam and Eve, see Phyllis Trible, "Depatriarchalizing in Biblical Interpretation," op. cit.

[4] E. S. Speiser, *Genesis: A New Translation with Introduction and Commentary,* the Anchor Bible (Garden City, N.Y.: Doubleday, 1982), 26.

[5] See U. Cassuto, *A Commentary on the Book of Genesis,* part 1, trans. Israel Abrahams (Jerusalem: Magnes, 1972), 170–1.

[6] Genesis Rabbah 17.

[7] Genesis Rabbah 19.

[8] Abot deRabbi Nathan 1. A similar version is found in Genesis Rabbah 19.

[9] Genesis Rabbah 19.

[10] Genesis Rabbah 18.

[11] The Prologue of the Wife of Bath's Tale," ll. 710–803.

[12] Shemot Rabbah 31:a–b.

[13] Sotah 9a and 9b.

[14] The Zohar 3, 76b.

[15] The full impact of this seduction scene was not lost on the twentieth-century novelist James Joyce, who recreated it in an episode in *A Portrait of the Artist as a Young Man* (New York: Viking, 1968), 182–3. In this episode Davin, the peasant friend of the protagonist Stephen Dedalus, passes at night by the house of an unnamed peasant woman. The young woman, who is pregnant and half-undressed, tries to lure the young man to spend the night in her house, telling him that her husband left for the night. The feverish Davin reacts to a subconscious male fear of the wanton adulteress, and escapes. While this Joycean episode seems to belong to the lore of the Irish land, its imaginative vitality is due to the scene from Proverbs incorporated in it. The threat of death is not implied in the Joycean scene itself, but it un-

derlies it, especially if one remembers the warning that closes the seduction scene in Proverbs: "Her house is on the way to She'ol / going down to the chambers of death" (5:5). See Nehama Aschkenasy, "Biblical Females in a Joycean Episode," *Modern Language Studies* 15, no. 5 (1985):28–39.

[16] This scroll fragment from Cave 4 was first published by J. Allegro in *Palestine Exploration Quarterly,* 1964, 53–55. The "strange woman" also figures in the book of Sirach, or Ben Sira, composed in the second century B.C.E. See Warren C. Trenchard, *Ben Sira's View of Women: A Literary Analysis* (Chico, Calif.: Scholars Press, 1982), 118–28.

[17] On St. Paul's misogyny see Rogers, *The Troublesome Helpmate,* 8–11 et passim.

[18] Kiddushin 81a.

[19] Sabbath, 156b. On the other aspects of this tale see Jonah Fraenkel, *Studies in the Spiritual World of the Aggadic Tale,* in Hebrew (Tel Aviv: Hakibbutz Hameuchad, 1981), 13–16.

[20] On the serpent as a sexual symbol and the mythic affinity between woman and snake see: Wolfgang Lederer, *The Fear of Women* (New York: Harcourt, 1968), 22, 47–49, 57, 164–5.

[21] Reproduced in Saul Liptzin, "The Rehabilitation of Lilith," *Dor leDor* 5, no. 2 (1976–7):68.

[22] The Zohar 1, 19b. See also "Lilith," in Gershom Scholem, *Kabbalah* (New York: Quadrangle, 1974), 356–61.

[23] See entry "Joseph Della Reina" in *Encyclopedia Judaica,* vol. 10 (Jerusalem: Keter, 1974), 239–40.

[24] In *For the Sake of Heaven* (in Hebrew *Gog uMagog*), translated from the German by Ludwig Lewisohn (Philadelphia: Jewish Publication Society, 1953), 58–59.

The controversy between Gershom G. Scholem and Martin Buber regarding the latter's interpretation of the nature of Hasidism, and Scholem's reservations about Buber's methods in collecting and recounting the Hasidic tales, need not concern us here. Buber's reconstructed tales are literary masterpieces, and even if he gave a personal slant to the original Hasidic stories, there is no doubt about their essential authenticity. See Gershom G. Scholem, "Martin Buber's Interpretation of Hasidism," in Judah Goldin, ed., *The Jewish Expression* (New Haven: Yale University Press, 1976), 397–418.

[25] See entry *"regel"* in Jacob Nacht, *Simlei 'Ishah (The Symbolism of the Woman)* (Tel Aviv: Hotsa'at va'ad talmidav va-ḥanikhav shel ha-meḥaber, 1959).

[26] *For the Sake of Heaven,* 59–60.

[27] Gershom Scholem shows how the concepts of exile and deliverance were converted by the Hasidic mind into terms denoting personal-psychological processes; see *Major Trends in Jewish Mysticism* (New York: Schocken, 1974), 286, 305.

[28] *For the Sake of Heaven,* 270–7.

[29] On this aspect of Reb Nahman's dreams, see Joseph Dan, *HaSippur HaHasidi* (Jerusalem: Keter, 1975), 179 ff.

[30] *For the Sake of Heaven,* 123–24.

[31] Quoted in Joseph Dan, op. cit., 229–35.

[32] I. L. Peretz, *In This World and the Next,* trans. Moshe Spiegel (New York: Yoseloff, 1958).

[33] *Twenty-One Stories,* 169–81. All page references are to this edition.

[34] Baruch Kurzweil was the first to draw our attention to the biblical underpinnings of "The Lady and the Pedlar," focusing on the national meaning of the confrontation between the biblical Joseph, the prototype of the Jew in exile, and the Gentile woman. See *Essays on Agnon's Stories,* 121–9. Arnold Band illuminates the analogy between this story and the Joseph Della Reina tale and highlights the story's national-religious significance. See *Nostalgia and Nightmare* (Los Angeles: University of California Press, 1968), 399–402.

[35] The bitch is the female "sitra aḥra." Also, the dog belongs to Lilith's entourage. See Nacht, 129–30. It seems that the scene in which the lady turns into a bitch, in the pedlar's nightmare, denotes an upper displacement of the male's subconscious fear of teeth in the vagina.

[36] In *Twenty-One Stories,* 30–44. All page references are to this edition.

[37] The translator of this story, Baruch Hochman, renders the text as follows: "At that moment Dinah lifted her arms and smote the Ark. The Ark teetered, and fell through the open window." In the Schocken Hebrew editions of 1953 and 1971, however, Dinah knocks over the Ark inadvertently when she is pushed against it by the "evil one." The scene is thus reminiscent of the midrashic tale where the serpent pushes Eve against the forbidden tree. Arnold Band, in his summary of the story, also maintains that Dinah "pushed the ark" (*Nostalgia and Nightmare,* 61). It seems that the translator read the verb from the stem *dḥp,* to push, as *daḥpah* (sounding *daḥfah*), which means "she pushed." However, the correct reading of this verb should be *deḥapah* (sounding *deḥafah*), which means "he [the 'evil one'] pushed her."

[38] For a slightly different interpretation of the story, see Hillel Barzel, *Agnon's Love Stories,* in Hebrew (Ramat Gan: Bar Ilan University, 1975). Barzel sees only one narrative viewpoint in the story and argues that the pious narrator himself absolves Dinah of her sin, since he maintains that she was driven to sin by Satan.

[39] In Amos Oz, *Where the Jackals Howl,* trans. Nicholas de Lange (New York: Harcourt Brace Jovanovich, 1981), 107–36. All page references are to this edition.

[40] Scholem, *Kabbalah,* 358.

[41] Erich Neumann, *The Great Mother: An Analysis of the Archetype,* trans. Ralph Manheim (Princeton, N.J.: Princeton University Press, 1970), 146.

[42] In *'Ad Horef,* in Hebrew (Tel Aviv: Hakibbutz Hameuchad, 1975), 9–30.

[43] See Nacht, op. cit., 33–34.

[44] Nacht, 168.

[45] See Neumann, op. cit., 187 et passim.

The Empty Vessel: Woman as Mother

The very existence of the inner productive space exposes women early to a specific sense of loneliness, to a fear of being left empty or deprived of treasures, of remaining un-fulfilled and of drying up.

Erik H. Erikson, "Womanhood and the Inner Space," in *Identity: Youth and Crisis,* 1968

Vis-à-vis the upper realms, she [Shekinah/Malkhut, the feminine element in the deity] is the bottom link in the chain of divine emanations, and serves as a receptacle to the radiation that comes from above; yet vis-à-vis the lower world, Shekinah is first and foremost, the mother of the world and its leader.

From Y. Tishbi's Introduction to the chapter "Sheki-nah," in *Mishnat HaZohar,* vol. 1, p. 120

. . . Beside the fecundated womb and the protecting cave of the earth and mountain gapes the abyss of hell . . . the devouring womb of the grave and of death. . . . For this woman who generates . . . all living things on earth is the same who takes them back into herself.

Erich Neumann, *The Great Mother,* p. 149

*F*rom ancient formulations of the nature of the female as mother, saturated with awe, superstition, and mystery, to the modern, scientific conceptions of motherhood, claiming to be based on observations and research, the woman's biological function as the bearer of children has often been reflected in the image of the empty vessel waiting to be filled and fulfilled by and through the male impregnator. The noun for 'female' in Hebrew, *neqebah,* creates the mental image of an orifice, an empty hole or cave. As Erich Neumann tells us, while the experience of the body as vessel is universally human and not limited to woman, the most central, archetypal symbol of the essence of femininity has always been the vessel: "The basic symbolic equation woman=body=vessel corresponds to what is perhaps mankind's—man's as well as woman's—most elementary experience of the Feminine." [1]

Biblical language, portraying God as "opening" or "closing" the woman's womb, also reinforced the picture of the woman's womb as an empty cave which, when "closed," the woman is sterile, and when "opened," the woman becomes fertile. [2] In the mystics' symbolical configuration of the Sefirot, the spiritual elements that comprise the deity, the Shekinah, or Malkhut, is visualized as the receptive female who possesses no light or shade of her own until she receives the radiation that flows from the upper "Sefirot." The Zohar plays on the motif of the female as an empty vessel in various ways: the Shekinah is likened to a woman who is empty until impregnated by man, or to a dry well (a feminine noun in Hebrew) ready to be filled with water; she is also envisioned as various female animals that become "full" when they carry an embryo, or to the moon (a feminine image), which has no immanent light of its own, but receives its light from the sun (the male). [3]

If the Shekinah is a hollow entity, an empty container passively waiting to be nourished by the upper realms, in her relationship with the lower world she is the all-powerful giver of life, bountiful, fertile, and loving. And as the Supernal Mother, the Shekinah has its corresponding reality in the earthly, human mother. Yet as illustrated by Neumann, just as the archetypal Feminine has the power of causing positive transformation, such as from hunger to satiety and from thirst to appeasement, she can also cause deprivation and diminution. The other side of the protecting mother is the clinging mother who will release nothing from her dominion.[4] The archetype of the Great Mother is thus ambivalent; by releasing the fetus from her dark womb she gives him life, but her inner space can become a snare and a prison, and the shelter might become a state of fixation and stagnation.[5] Furthermore, "the release from darkness to light characterizes the way of life and also the way of consciousness. On the other hand, the Great Mother in her function of fixation and not releasing what aspires towards independence . . . is dangerous."[6] The mother is seen as the giver of physical life as well as psychic life, leading the child from the state of lack of consciousness to consciousness. By depriving the child of her bounty, however, she can lead him towards physical death or towards madness, a psychic-spiritual death.[7]

The ambivalence of the mother figure is thus related to the image of the empty inner space of the feminine anatomy. Another biological trait of the female has been seen, in modern times, as the reason for feminine inadequacy and for the dual nature of the mother. Freud, borrowing from Aristotle the conception of the woman as a "defective male," regarded the female body as that of a castrated male, and anchored the totality of the woman's psychic life in her "penis envy." Because of the predominance of envy in their mental life, Freud argued, women are especially prone to neurosis,[8] and they have "little sense of justice."[9] Later in life, so Freud explained, the wish for a penis is replaced by a wish for a child; the child takes the place of the missing organ. At the same time, the woman as mother exerts extreme influence, and holds tremendous power over her male child, which can easily turn into domination and destruction. The infant's absolute dependence on his mother is intensified by the little boy's Oedipal complex, which causes him to fall in love with her; yet the mother's unwillingness to release her son, and her wish to make up for her sexual inadequacy by holding on to him ultimately cause an ambivalence of emotions on the part of the male child towards the mother.[10]

Erik Erikson's theory of motherhood also hinges on the woman's biologically-determined fate stemming from her anatomic "inner space." Erikson believes that the fear of being left empty is at the center of the woman's need to be pregnant and give birth to children, and that, very early in life, little girls' awareness of their inner "empty space" determines their spatial conceptions, and is reflected in their tendency to create enclosed structures and to envision sheltered, domestic situations. Thus the woman's "inner space" is for a woman a source of anguish, stemming from her fear of being left empty or dried up, as well as the center of potential fulfillment, when her "inner space" harbors a fetus.[11]

Our discussion of the figure of the mother as filtered through the Hebraic mind will concentrate on two principal aspects: images of emptiness and fulfillment that are related to women in their capacity as progenitors, and the twofold image of motherhood, the "positive" and the "negative" elements, to use Erich Neumann's words, in the literary reflections of motherhood.

The biblical tales abound with dramas of barren women who plead to God for a child, and even strike a "bargain" with God in order to induce Him to "open" their wombs. Indeed, of the four matriarchs, three were infertile and became pregnant only after great heartbreak and effort. Other great men's mothers, such as Samson's and Samuel's, were also barren before they gave birth to their illustrious sons. As a literary device, the mother's inability to conceive heightens the anticipation of the birth of an unusual man and adds a miraculous element to it. But in the several stories about the sterile women, the female protagonists' characters are often illuminated, too. Interestingly, the three matriarchs who were greatly loved by their husbands—Sarah, Rebecca, and Rachel—became pregnant only after suffering the agony of barrenness, while Leah, who was not loved by Jacob, was fecund, and gave her husband six sons and a daughter.

The biblical story often creates the impression that the woman's wish for a child surpasses any reasonable emotional need, and is almost irrational in its force and magnitude, anchored in an uncontrollable psychic drive. Some of the biblical incidents may conform to Erikson's modern paradigm of the tyranny of the woman's biological constitution, presenting women like Rachel and Hannah as almost undergoing character transformation when gripped by the misery of barrenness. The gentle and beautiful Rachel becomes hysterical when she says to Jacob: "Give me children, or else I die" (Gen. 29:1). And the noble Hannah, who never stoops to the base level of her husband's other wife and refrains from responding to her provocations, seems like a drunk to Eli the priest, when she prays to God in the "bitterness" of her "soul" (1 Sam. 1:10, 13). As we know, lack of children was the greatest calamity that could befall a couple in the ancient Middle East, since more children, especially males, meant more manpower, and therefore greater social status as well as security to both parents in their old age.[12] Yet the stories about sterility are women's stories, since in the polygynous system the husband could always take another wife who was fertile. In the stories about Rachel and Hannah, the women's need for a child is not seen as stemming from their concern for sheer survival. Both women are greatly loved by their husbands and are assured of material security even if their husbands passed away leaving them childless. Elkanah, Hannah's husband, makes this point clear to his wife when he gives her a symbolical "double portion" (or: "worthy portion") during the festivities at the Temple in Shiloh. It seems, then, that these two women need children neither because they are starved for love, nor because they are looking for the security that would come with giving birth to heirs, but simply because they are women, and their need for a child is biological; their maternal yearnings are seen as almost a physical pain, the cure for which will only come with the woman's pregnancy.

Yet when we read the stories more closely, other reasons and motivations are indicated as driving the women towards motherhood, reasons that have little to do with strong, uncontrollable maternal urges. In the case of Rachel, the Bible simply points out that Rachel "envied her sister" (Gen. 30:1). Hannah's case is more complicated, since the biblical narrator portrays her as a woman of great inner beauty who possessed manifold gifts, such as language abilities, far-sighted vision, and personal charm (indicated in her name, that is related, in Hebrew, to the noun *hen,* 'charm'). We cannot assume that it is jealousy of her husband's other wife that makes Hannah yearn for a child. Hannah's many talents may point to the woman's need of a channel through which she could exercise her abilities. Hannah may have desired a child so that she could teach and educate him, giving expression to her energies that otherwise would have gone to waste. Moreover, the biblical text shows in many ways that Hannah transcends her feminine predicament, and that she views the attainment of a child as a challenge to her tenacity, and as proof of her ability to persuade God with her language and with the vision of her unborn son as a man of God.

Hannah's rhetorical powers are amply illustrated in this tale. In her plea to God the woman's language displays both humble deference and strong determination. While using the conditional, tentative "if," and referring to herself as God's "handmaid," Hannah seems to be resolved not to leave God empty-handed. In fact, she actually wills her child into being by proceeding to describe the kind of life that she maps out for him. In language, at least, the child has already come into being: "I will give him to the Lord all the days of his life, and no razor shall come upon his head" (1 Sam. 1:11). Later, in her confrontation with Eli the priest, Hannah once again proves that she possesses passionate eloquence. Eli is so impressed with the woman's words that he immediately changes his initial attitude to her and sends her away with a blessing. Hannah's powerful command of language is demonstrated again later when, reluctantly, she brings her son to Shiloh to serve God. The play on the root *s'l*, 'ask', (vv. 27, 28), subtly suggests the tragedy of the woman who "asked," or "borrowed" a child from God, and who now has to make good on her promise to let God "borrow" the child from her. Indeed, the midrashic sages themselves responded to Hannah's vision and eloquence by elevating her to the position of a prophetess.

That a woman with Hannah's talents would center her total being on producing an offspring is a reflection of women's circumscribed existence in ancient times. George Eliot's complaint in the "Prelude" to her novel *Middlemarch* may apply to Hannah's situation as well: "Many Theresas have been born who found for themselves no epic life wherein there was a constant unfolding of far-resonant action; perhaps a life of mistakes, the offspring of a certain spiritual grandeur ill-matched with the meanness of opportunity."[13] In contrast to the explicitness of the nineteenth-century woman writer, we have the reticence and perhaps only partial awareness of the biblical narrator. However, while Hannah's choice of motherhood is not presented in our story as a "mistake," the artistic creation of a remarkable woman (not required by the context) who identifies totally with "the common yearning of womanhood," to quote George Eliot again, adds a disturbing note, however muted, to our story.

Hannah's vision for her son can also be seen as the woman's attempts at vicarious fulfillment, whereby she will experience through her offspring the opportunity denied her. Yet Hannah's son is not viewed as merely an instrument to appease and fill the woman's empty "inner space." By the force of her will Hannah carves for her son a place in the history of the Hebrew nation. In turn, the biblical narrator himself finds for Hannah a spot outside the biological and domestic spheres, and positions her at the center of a story that launches an important historical narration, the Book of Samuel. Furthermore, the psalm that is attributed to Hannah with the happy conclusion of her story, the "Song of Hannah," is not a "woman's song," nor is it a paean to motherhood; the singer is a human being who rejoices in her salvation and warns man against excessive pride. The barren woman who is remembered by God is only one example of the principle by which God governs His world. The breadth of perspective offered in this psalm suggests that Hannah has not viewed her plight strictly in biological-feminine terms, and that she feels that it is not just her "inner space" that has been redeemed, but her dignity and pride as a human being.

The need for children may lie in base motives, such as feminine jealousy and rivalry in the case of Rachel, as well as in sublime ones, the wish to educate and exercise unused spiritual talents, as in the case of Hannah. In the story of the matriarch Rebecca, the need for a child seems to be anchored in the woman's sense of responsibility to a spiritual legacy, that of the Abrahamic family. We know Rebecca as cunning and independent, and her husband Isaac as somewhat passive and lackluster; when she turns to him to plead with God for progeny, she indicates that the need is not hers alone, but also that of Isaac, as the only heir to the Abrahamic promise.

If barrenness was a cause of great misery for a woman, fruitfulness did not necessarily guarantee her happiness. Elkanah's second wife, Peninah, emerges as a bitter, unfulfilled woman in spite of her fecundity. The fact that she "provoked" the infertile Hannah and made her "fret" may point to an inner misery that found its outlet in nastiness towards the vulnerable Hannah. The Midrash elaborates on the terse biblical language by telling us how Peninah teased Hannah: "She (Peninah) used to rise early in the morning and ask Hannah: 'Aren't you washing your sons and getting them ready for school?' And in the afternoon she used to say: 'Hannah, aren't you going out to welcome your children from school.'"[14] Peninah might be viewed as the stereotypical bitch, the product of the male's misogynist conception of the nature of women. On the other hand, she might be used by an enlightened narrator (or perhaps by a female storyteller) as an example of the evils of polygyny and an indication that a woman's contentment is not anchored in her procreative abilities alone. It is clear, however, that Peninah uses her children as leverage against her rival and as a means to enhance her status in the patriarchal family.

Another example of a woman whose fertility does not result in happiness if that of Leah, Jacob's unloved wife, who was blessed with sons, but was unable to gain her husband's love. Robert Alter alerts us to the "little name-speeches she [Leah] makes after the birth of each son,"[15] which reflect her hopes and diminishing expectations. The births of the children do not seem to be for Leah a source of physical or emotional satisfaction, only a hope that she will finally find in Jacob a loving companion, instead of the reluctant husband that he has been. When her first son is born she optimistically exclaims: "Now therefore my husband will love me." That this did not happen we learn from the second speech that accompanies the name-giving of Leah's second son. Now she no longer expects Jacob to love her, but she hopes that he will at least not hate her: "Because the Lord has heard that I was hated, he has therefore given me this son also." When Leah's third son is born, she has given up any hope of an emotional response on the part of Jacob, but she expects that, as the father of three sons, Jacob, by necessity, will have to spend more time in her tent: "Now this time will my husband be joined to me." When Judah comes to the world, Leah ignores her husband altogether and simply thanks God for giving her a fourth son (Gen. 29:31–35). At this point, Leah seems to despair of ever gaining Jacob's attention and seems resigned to finding solace in her sons; thus the sons are seen as a forced substitute for the man, not as a source of the greatest feminine joy. After a pause, Leah bears Jacob two more sons, and her expectations are revived; both sons' names mirror her renewed hope for the only reward that seems to matter to her: "Now will my husband dwell with me" (Gen. 30:20).

The agony of the unloved but fertile Leah clearly points to the narrator's awareness that the woman Leah had needs that transcended her physical nature. She repeatedly expresses her wish for Jacob's company, and makes it clear that her maternal happiness is secondary to sharing her life with the man that she obviously loves.

The biblical narrator manifests a sober, unsentimental attitude towards motherhood. He avoids panegyrizing it as a sublime state and perceives it as a means for the woman in a male-dominated society to express herself and, very often, to promote her own standing in the tension-filled polygynous family. But if the woman's maternal instincts are not celebrated as always noble and selfless, neither are they demeaned as rooted in blind biological drives only, nor is the woman herself reduced to a procreating automaton.

Motherhood and History: The Ancient Ruth and her Modern Namesake

A series of stories, which Harold Fisch has called "the Ruth corpus,"[16] revolve around women who cunningly get a man to impregnate them, and culminate in the tale of Ruth. In these stories, the theme of the woman's uncontrollable physical need to be with child is shown to evolve from a primitive, almost bestial instinct, into a more sophisticated, cultured attitude that transcends the sheer physical drive, and embodies historical awareness and responsibility.[17] Fisch discusses the two literary precursors of the Ruth drama, the Genesis stories of Lot and his daughters (chapter 19) and Judah and Tamar (chapter 38), and delineates the cultural progress evidenced in them. The "corpus" starts with a barbaric cave-people tale, in which the two daughters of Lot make their father drink wine and then lie with him, after which they both conceive; it moves to the somewhat more civilized ambience of the tale of Judah and Tamar in which Judah's widowed daughter-in-law uses guile in order to conceive from Judah, and climaxes in the cleaned-up tale of Ruth's successful efforts to make Boaz recognize his familial responsibilities and "redeem" her. Fisch persuasively suggests that while Boaz redeems Ruth, and the newborn son redeems Naomi, Ruth herself "is the redeemer of the unnamed ancestress who lay with her father," and that "the story of Ruth looks back to these earlier paradigms," by offering a tale of "salvation history," purged of the unseemly elements of the two previous tales, and "looking forward to what is to be disclosed of the house of David."[18]

The progress from barbarism to civilization, from a primitive conception of the individual and his immediate survival, to an attitude weighted with historical responsibility, where the individual is able to transcend his time and place and correct the past as well as lay the ground for a redemptive future, is paralleled by a similar evolution in the conception of feminine biological fate. Lot's unnamed daughters act out of instinctive, animalistic drive for procreation when they lie with their father, using his seed in order to conceive. Appropriately, their dwelling place is now the cave, the "earth womb," to use Erich Neumann's words,[19] that may subconsciously remind the two young women of their own inner caves that wait to be fructified. Fisch points out that the biblical text refrains from any judgmental comment regarding the daughters' deed; a possible reason is that the women are seen as driven by physical urges beyond their control, and act out of a bestial instinct for survival that recognizes no morality or human custom. Terrorized by their fear of remaining "empty," as Erikson would say, a state pictorially epitomized for them by the dark cave where they dwell, the daughters find themselves in the grip of their feminine instinct that temporarily takes over and makes them retreat to blind impulse, just as their own culture has regressed to primeval chaos.

Tamar, Judah's daughter-in-law, uses a more complicated ruse in her attempts to become pregnant. The Judah-Tamar tale takes place in a more civilized agrarian community that observes customs and laws; moreover, the man that Tamar lures is not her own father, and thus the theme of incest is less prominent. Like some of the enterprising biblical females before her, Tamar cunningly plans the entrapment of the man in a scheme that involves role-playing and costume-donning, when she dresses as a harlot and goes to meet Judah. Tamar is also motivated by the fear of remaining empty, enhanced by the fact that her second husband purposely avoided impregnating her. Appropriately, Tamar lies with Judah during the sheep-shearing festivities, a seasonal celebration that heightens the woman's sense of loneliness and lack of fertility.

The seasonal barley feast is at the center of the Ruth story and lends it a setting that is regulated by the natural cycles, in a community that depends on the bounty of nature and celebrates it. Thus Ruth, the childless widow, and Naomi, bereaved of her husband and sons, are starkly contrasted, in their destitution, with the natural abundance that they encounter when they arrive in Bethlehem "at the beginning of barley harvest."[20] Naomi, the older woman, who is more acutely aware of her deprivation, immediately harps on the fullness-emptiness theme, which becomes a central motif in the story: "I was full when I went away, But empty Yahweh has brought me back" (Ruth 1:21).[21] Ruth picks up this theme, partly out of her own sense of emptiness, and partly in sympathy with her mother-in-law's feelings. Later, when Boaz promises to help Ruth, after discovering that she has slept at his feet all night, he ceremoniously measures out a significant portion of barley, tells Ruth to hold her apron up, and pours the produce into Ruth's apron. Ruth returns "full," both figuratively and physically: she has received a definite pledge of redemption, and her bulging apron serves as evidence and as promise of things to come. When Ruth comes home, she quotes Boaz, and adds words that Boaz probably did not say to her, but that would comfort a woman who complained about her "emptiness": "For he said, 'You shall not go empty / To your mother-in-law'" (3:17).[22]

Ruth's actions are not seen as anchored in her reproductive needs alone, nor in blind biological drives that have to be appeased. Boaz commends her for "not going after the young men" (3:10) and looking for a redeemer instead.[23] Ruth not only wants redemption for her unfulfilled femininity, but she wants it to be done within the laws and customs of the faith that she has adopted. It is not only material and biological survival to which she aspires, but also becoming an integral part of the Israelite community and being accepted into an illustrious family in a religiously sanctioned manner. The sexual elements of the story are suppressed, and the narrator is purposely ambiguous about what really happens at the threshing floor. The language describing the events at the threshing floor is elliptical and euphemistic; the verb *skb,* 'to lie down', occurs several times, and Naomi's instructions to Ruth to "uncover" Boaz's legs are filled with erotic innuendos, especially because of the sexual connotations of the noun *regel,* 'leg', in Hebrew. Boaz is called a *moda',* which indicates that he is an acquaintance or a relative. But the word literally means a 'knower', with the verb 'to know', which in Hebrew suggests sexual intercourse, underscoring Naomi's intentions to have Ruth instill in Boaz a sense of sexual guilt as well as sexual responsibility.[24] But while the language is suggestive, it is at the same time ambivalent and nongraphic, in contrast with Judah's language in the Genesis episode, when the man bluntly and graphically says to the woman: "let me come in to thee" (Gen. 38 : 16). The Ruth story thus "redeems" the antecedent tales about Ruth's and Boaz's ancestors, where the sexual improprieties are essential parts of the drama, by remaining silent on the matter of erotic seduction and highlighting, instead, the dialogue between the two people, which is dignified and laced with the language of faith, propriety, and redemption. If the Ruth tale "redeems" the preceding tales, the Ruth narrator, be it male or female, "redeems" the primitive, sexually prejudiced approach of the earlier storytellers, who saw in the woman only a physical being, tyrannized by her reproductive organs and insensitive to moral and sexual taboos.

Ruth the Moabitess mends the past and looks towards a glorious future, putting her faith in the Israelite civilization, and finding for herself a niche within its religious and ethical structure. The inner emptiness that she senses and that she is successful in defeating, is not biological, but rather cultural. She comes from a morally loose, corrupt society, and in order to learn the customs of her adopted people, she has to shed many of her old ways. For instance, when Boaz meets Ruth for the first time, he requests that she cling to his girls (2 : 8); yet when Ruth repeats his words to her mother-in-law, she says that Boaz instructed her to stay close to his young men. Naomi redirects the young Moabitess by suggesting that she go out to the field with Boaz's young women (2 : 22). The Israelite culture, with its socially conscious customs—one of which is the levirate marriage, intended to perpetuate the dead man's name and at the same time redeem his widow—is a new normative framework within which Ruth finds fulfillment and a sense of completeness. The theme of fullness that runs through the dialogues is first related to nature and to the woman's physical need, but is then converted into a spiritual and historical concept; thus Boaz wishes Ruth "full" payment from God (2 : 12). Ruth herself provides a link in the Israelites' historic journey towards redemption, by becoming the ancestress of David, and thus "fills" and completes the generational chain.

If the ancient Ruth becomes an inextricable part of Jewish history, her modern incarnation in the fictional person of Amos Oz's Ruth, the protagonist of "The Hill of Evil Counsel" (1974), escapes from history, and by doing so, betrays her country and people.[25] The backdrop of Oz's novella is the Jewish community of Jerusalem in what was then Palestine, during the waning years of the British mandate. Oz depicts the treacherous mother through the eyes of her small son, Hillel. Ruth, a dreamy, romantic woman, is completely removed from the social and political reality around her, which is rife with tension and imbued with nationalistic sentiments. She is still immersed in the Polish culture and landscape of her childhood, and is unable to lift herself out of her nostalgic visions and identify with the explosive reality of a new country about to be born. Hillel's father, Hans, is a gentle, peace-loving veterinarian, who, though not carried away in the general hysteria, is a man with strong national sentiments.

While the historical moment of the story—the volatile last days of British rule and the rise of patriotism and the mood of national rebirth—is realistically depicted, the modern family takes on a biblical dimension as intimations of another era, or perhaps another life, seep through. Hillel, the impressionable boy, sees himself as the young man from the family of shepherds who became king of Israel, and Ruth the mother evokes memories of biblical women (300). Within the biblical substructure of the story, the mother's figure shuttles between that of the model of evil, treachery, and foreignness, the biblical Jezebel, and the paradigm of loyalty and commitment, the ancient Ruth. The lodger Mitya, who laces his language with biblical rhetoric, sees in Ruth a modern incarnation of the vain Jezebel, but her son Hillel maintains that she is not Jezebel, and by envisioning himself as the king of Israel, he implicitly assigns to his mother the role of the ancient progenitor of the admirable king, the faithful Ruth. We know that Hillel is associated with no other than King David, the founder of the royal dynasty, when his father playfully calls him "King Hillel the First" (279).

In spite of the son's conception of his mother as a modern version of a biblical model, it soon becomes clear that the contemporary Ruth is the direct opposite of her early namesake. In an ironic reversal of the idyllic old tale, the latter-day Ruth betrays her son and her husband, as well as her people and their historic memory, by running away with the lecherous British admiral. The story is imbued with an inner tension: it is anchored in the spirit of rising hopes, as the new Zionist aspirations evoke the ancient Israelite optimism and anticipation of a glorious future, yet at its center is a tale of betrayal, when the unfaithful Ruth casts her lot with a dying civilization, represented by the corrupt, old British admiral. The ancient Ruth left an immoral, decaying society and tied her destiny with that of a young, future-oriented society. But the modern Ruth, who finds herself in a similar situation in Jerusalem of the prestatehood years, prefers to turn her back on the emerging society and regress in time, as well as in morality, by leaving Jerusalem with the embodiment of a fading kingdom.

The mother figure becomes a focus of great hopes and terrible disillusionment for the boy Hillel. While the child faithfully records his mother's sense of alienation from her immediate environment and her longings for the Polish culture that ejected her, he fails to understand the full implications of his adored mother's state of mind. Ruth's historical memory does not coincide with that of her people; for her, the glory and beauty of foregone years are exemplified in the past of the Polish people, in whose culture she grew up. The landscapes that she evokes with tears of longing are those of European castles and forests, not the pastoral biblical scenes that run through her son's mind.

Some of the structural elements of Oz's story reinforce the ironic analogy between the ancient tale and the modern drama. Just as the ancient Ruth's acceptance into the Israelite society happens during the period of the harvest celebration, so the contemporary Ruth's betrayal occurs during the May ball at the house of the British High Commissioner. While the story of Ruth is a spring story and Ruth the Moabitess is forever associated, in the Hebraic memory, with the spring season, Hillel's mother's beautiful smile is "autumnal" (389).[26] The ancient Ruth is a foreigner who embraces the Israelite culture, while the modern Ruth is a Jewish woman, who yearns for foreign men and alien landscapes. The two tales are positioned on the two extreme ends of Western civiliation. The old tale of Ruth marks the beginnings of civilized society, and portrays a community of benevolent patriarchy where people are bound by moral and social codes. Oz's tale, on the other hand, is dialectically imbued with a sense of an ending, when family and morality collapse, as well as with a tentative hope for rebirth. It is when Ruth the Moabitess is integrated into the Israelite society that the Davidic dynasty is heralded; it is when Hillel's mother expels herself from her family and environment that the air is cleansed of the hidden yearning for foreignness and the new Israeli reality finally establishes itself. The novella thus starts on a realistic note, then dissolves into nightmare when the father, Hans, realizes at the ball that his wife has disappeared, and finally returns to the normalcy of real life, however painful and incomplete, when the mother removes herself from the scene.

The son's attitude to his mother is ambivalent. She remains a unique figure of charm and beauty, and at the same time a source of great anguish and a model of betrayal. There is a sympathetic identification between the son and his mother which finds its ultimate expression during the time of the ball. The son, who spends the night with two women acquaintances, goes through an erotic experience as he is lying in a strange bed and watches the two women, as if through a mist, dancing in a seductive manner. The son's strange, sexually heightened episode occurs simultaneously with his mother's own dreamy and bizzare adventure, when, in a moment of sensual abandon, she is swept away by the lecherous admiral.

The mother's annoyance with the political situation around her does not necessarily discredit her in her son's eyes, in spite of his own complete identification with the ideals of political independence, since he is already aware of the duality of the historical experience. Hillel believes in the Judaic historical promise when, at the end of the third grade, he writes a letter to the High Commissioner telling him that the land belongs to the Jewish people, both according to the Bible and according to justice (279). At the same time, Hillel is aware of history's terrifying face, exemplified to him in the grotesquely smiling skeleton of a Turkish soldier that he once discovered (291). But the mother's national disloyalty is tied to her defection from her son and husband, and when she leaves, Hillel's world is diminished and atrophied, losing its former luster to everyday banality. Paradoxically, while Ruth the mother betrays the biblical spirit, she also embodies it.[27] The life into which Hillel, his father, and their male friends settle after she leaves is devoid of the impassioned biblical spirit. Even Mitya the lodger who, for the boy, was the incarnation of a fanatic ancient prophet, calms down, gets a job, and retreats from biblical rhetoric. It is the mother Ruth who held the biblical promise, and with her betrayal, modern life has shrunk, has become less "biblical," yet perhaps, more "normal."[28] Oz perceives the mother's departure from the scene as almost necessary for the return of equilibrium and balance.

The paradoxical nature of the modern Ruth stands in opposition to the clearly defined message embodied in the ancient Ruth. The biblical Ruth is not seen as a mother, since the tale ends when she gives birth to a son. But she is perceived as an ancestress, a founder of a dynasty, thus enfolding in her maternal function not only a biological reality, but a historical role. The contemporary Ruth removes herself from her people's history and their future, and is seen as a mother only, but as such she manifests the "negative" aspects of motherhood. The mother's desertion of the family at the point in history where the larger family, the nation, is in the process of reclaiming and redeeming the mother country is an ironic, disillusioned reflection of motherhood and its historical function. Oz's female protagonist reveals the other face of the mother and leaves behind gnawing questions about the validity of historical promise, the wisdom of attempting to recapture biblical times, and the genuineness of the motherhood mystique.[29]

Sons and Mothers: The Dialectical Relationship

The early sources pay tribute to motherhood, yet the maternal bond is not seen as stronger than the paternal one. God's compassionate feelings for his nation are likened to those of a father for his sons; God is also seen metaphorically as a father eagle protecting its young. Several biblical stories, however, portray the extent of maternal devotion and the agony of the bereaved mother. In one such tale, the woman Rizpah, whose sons had been hanged by the Givonim, sat by her dead sons' bodies from the beginning of the harvest season to its end, protecting them from the birds and the beasts (II Sam. 21:9, 10). Another mother, the Shunamite woman, pursued the prophet Elisha and pressed him to revive her dead son; the prophet performed the miracle in gratitude to this lady's past generosity to him (II Kings 4:20–38).

The sorrow of the Judaic exilic experience is epitomized in the prophet Jeremiah's vision of the eternal mother, Rachel, mourning over her dispersed children: "A voice was heard in Ramah, lamentation, and bitter weeping / Rachel weeping for her children / She refused to be comforted for her children, because they are not" (Jer. 31:14). Though in this particular scene Rachel weeps over the Israelite tribes who were deported more than a century before the times of Jeremiah, the prophet's memorable verses, evoking the ancient matriarch who died at childbirth, have become emblematic of the historic agony of the whole Jewish people. Nevertheless, in the same context, the prophet creates another metaphorical drama in which God, as father, remembers the exiled tribes of Israel, and refers to the tribe of Ephraim as "my dear son" and "darling child" (Jer. 31:19).

The Midrash offers various stories with a clearly pedagogical message concerning the respect due to both father and mother. Not surprisingly, the tales invariably illustrate their didactic teachings in stories about sons, not about daughters, who are seen as paying homage to their parents. The Midrash recounts the great lengths to which some of the noted rabbis went in order to honor their mothers. R. Tarfon used to crouch at his old mother's bed, so she could step on her son's back when she climbed, or descended from, her bed.[30] Another rabbi used to stand up whenever his mother's footsteps were heard, claiming that his mother deserved the same show of respect as the Shekinah herself.[31]

In several such tales, however, the son is described as patiently catering to a mother who is often demented, erratic, and irrational. The Midrash sages purposely created extreme situations in order to impress upon their students the importance of honoring both parents; therefore, the son is invariably a famous and much-revered personage, and the mother often an irrational woman who embarrasses her son and yet is greatly respected by him. The rabbis hold up as a paragon of filial patience a certain person by the name of Dama whose deranged mother beat him with her shoe while he was presiding over a council meeting. When she dropped the shoe, her son picked it up and gave it to her, so as not to upset her.[32]

Beyond the didactic end of these tales, which calls for larger-than-life characters and modes of behavior, there is still the question as to why it is only the mothers who are depicted as trying their illustrious sons' patience beyond belief. Of course, the message to honor one's parents is much clearer when the child is a man, and an important man at that, and the parent is a mother who has become less than human and lost her mind. Nevertheless, it is equally clear that the two faces of motherhood, imprinted in the male child's subconscious, underlie these tales about mothers and sons. Characteristically, while these tales ostensibly intend to put the mother on a pedestal, they actually extol the dutiful sons rather than their female progenitors.

The mother is often seen as ferocious and capable of betraying her innate maternal instincts of love and compassion for her offspring. The mother who eats her own son and the one who would see her sons die rather than betray their religion are extreme cases which serve to illustrate the harshness of Jewish fate that drives mothers to act against their own natural instincts. Thus, when the biblical poet bewails the fact that during the siege of Jerusalem "hands of compassionate women have boiled their own children" (Lam. 4:10), he exemplifies, in the most vivid and graphic fashion, the terrible starvation that Jerusalem suffered. A later poet, glorifying the Jewish martyrs of Mainz in the eleventh century who chose to commit mass suicide rather than convert, describes how the mothers bound their sons so that they would not shudder when they were slaughtered by their fathers.[33] And in the famous story of Hannah and her sons, the mother encourages her male offspring to die as martyrs and urges her youngest one to join his martyred brothers and not listen to the tyrant's pleadings and promises.[34]

The mothers who sacrifice their sons are exalted images, meant to exemplify both the dire circumstances in which the women find themselves, as they share in the bitter fate of their nation, and the women's great devotion to their faith. At the same time, the ability of the male narrator to create visions of fierce mothers, associated with death rather than with life, implies his own fear of the mother figure and his awareness that the giver of life is not always inextricably connected with the forces of life, but that she sometimes acts, albeit often unwillingly, as the agent of death. In the midrashic tale about the death of Beruria's and Rabbi Meir's sons, the narrator implies that Beruria, the mother, is much stronger and more ready to accept her sons' death than is the children's father. While Beruria herself is still shocked by the sudden death of both her sons, she devises a scheme to keep her husband in ignorance until the end of the Sabbath. She then gradually breaks the news to him in a dialogue that reveals not only her erudition and intelligence, but also her ability to accept the fact of death as part of life.[35]

The mother's religious devotion, her ability to transcend physical and material considerations, is a theme that runs through many Hebraic documents, and is dialectic in its implications. This motif stands in opposition to the view of the woman's reproductive abilities as indicative of the female's closeness to things of the flesh, and, instead, emphasizes the mother as a spiritual being, capable of rising above her physical nature and identifying with higher ideals. At the same time, the mother's piety often involves sacrificing not only herself, but also her sons. This theme is exemplified in Bialik's poem "My Mother of Blessed Memory," in which the poet reconstructs, in verse, a tale narrated by a Hasidic rabbi.[36] The poem is enveloped in a legendary aura, and the son's voice is unwavering, even simplistic, in its piety. The widowed mother is viewed as a saintly figure, tested beyond belief by life's hard realities and spiritually triumphing over her dreary existence. The mother finds herself on the Sabbath eve with "neither candle nor food" for her family. By miracle, she discovers some coins, and now she asks herself whether to purchase candles, the lighting of which is an essential part of the ritual of welcoming the Sabbath, or to buy bread, which is needed for the ritual, but which will also serve as a meal for her deprived children. The mother opts for the purest symbol of spirituality, and returns home with two candles. Since she cries bitterly while lighting the candles, a tear lands on one of them and extinguishes it. It now seems to the woman, and to her onlooking son as well, that the Sabbath has been blinded by God, indicating to them that He has scorned the widow's meager gift. Then a second miracle happens, and another of the mother's burning tears, which falls on the extinguished candle, rekindles it, and the whole house is now flooded with "splendor of the Genesis light." This is not a regular light but that mystical radiance which, as the Zohar tells us, permeated the universe during the six days of creation, but was then withdrawn by God and treasured up for the righteous in the world to come. The saintly mother, who deprives herself and her own children of bread in order to be able to welcome the Sabbath properly, is now rewarded by God with an illumination from the divine light reserved only for the select few. Whether the secular poet himself believes in the value of the mother's sacrifice or not is immaterial. Bialik is purposely quoting a Hasidic rabbi in order to give authenticity to the tale, and at the same time remove himself from the scene. The son's view of his mother in this poem, a mixture of compassion and awe, is completely positive. The pitiable, unfortunate widow challenges God when she says: "If your handmaid has sinned / what is the sin that your Sabbath committed?" and is answered by the "double light" that illuminates her dilapidated home.

Another poem by Bialik that also positions the young son as the observer of his widowed mother's struggle with poverty is "My Song."[37] Unlike the previous poem which is filled with a legendary and mystical flavor, "My Song" is autobiographical and imbued with the unrelieved realism of destitution and poverty. No miracle happens here, and yet the poet–narrator, who explores the origins of his poetic genius, finds them in the dark scenes of his miserable childhood. The opening lines of the poem present the father as an emaciated figure who feels guilty because of his inability to perform his paternal duty to provide for his family. During the wretched Sabbath meal, the father and his children suddenly hear a cricket joining in their feeble attempts at reciting the liturgical verses. The cricket, "the bard of poverty," is seen by the poet as the source of the grief and sorrow with which his poetry is saturated. The poet then goes on to trace the source of the "sighs" with which his poetry is filled. He reconstructs the domestic misery in the period after his father's death, when the burden of providing for the family has fallen on the shoulders of his frail mother. The son watches his mother get up very early in the morning and knead the dough for her children's morning bread, sighing and crying softly as she works. His heart tells him that his mother's tears fell into the dough, and when he eats the freshly baked bread, he swallows with it his mother's sighs and tears, which now seep into his bones and become part of his very being.

If the father remains a figure of wretchedness and misery only, the weak, but fiercely struggling mother is seen as infusing into her son the power of poetry, albeit poetry imbued with sorrow and grief. The father has escaped through death, yet the mother has remained to support her children and to fight the battles of life.[38] The warm bread, soaked with the mother's tears, becomes a symbol not only of nourishment but also of the spiritual and mental powers with which she endows her son. The mother's powerlessness becomes a potent source of poetic creativity through which the son redeems his mother's destitution, and commutes her frailty into strength. While both parents are viewed by their son with pity and great love, it is the mother who, at least in her son's mind, rises above the physical misery of her existence and is converted into the spiritual force of poetry, which transcends time and place.

The mother's figure as both a redemptive force in her son's spiritual progress, as well as a catalyst of maturation in his emergence from the Oedipal state, is at the heart of Agnon's short story "The Kerchief" (1932).[39] This nostalgic evocation of childhood innocence and of the visions of a lost world of harmony and wholeness is filtered through the eyes of two narrators: the young son, who records the events in his family as they occur, and the adult writer, removed geographically and chronologically, as well as spiritually, from the idyllic haunts of his early years. For the admiring child, the beloved parents become mythic figures that represent God and his nation. The father's departure from his family is seen as God's desertion of his nation, and the mother's painful waiting is likened to that of the desolate Jerusalem as described in Lamentations. For the young son, reared in a pious culture that harbors dreams of redemption, the figure of the Messiah, of whom he has read in the Talmudic legends, is a pivotal image which merges with that of the father. It is when the father is absent from home, and the family conducts itself as if it is commemorating the destruction of the Temple, that the child's dreams about the Messiah intensify. In one of his nocturnal visions, the child is brought to the city of Rome where, according to the Talmudic legend, the Messiah sits among the poor and waits for the moment of redemption when he will reveal himself to his people. The child sees a beggar, described in the very same language, and in the same position, that the ancient legend depicts the beggar-Messiah sitting among other beggars and bandaging his sores. For the young boy, immersed as he is in the folktales and legends of his people, the beggar is no other than the Messiah. Yet the boy is overcome by a squeamish sense of revulsion, and instead of helping the beggar, he averts his eyes from him. Suddenly, "there grew a great mountain with all kinds of thorns and thistles upon it, and evil beasts grazing there" (48). The boy sees the mountain with the evil beasts as punishment for his inability to help the Messiah and thus bring about redemption. Since he is still at a stage where fantasy and reality are sometimes fused, the boy is now intent on correcting the wrong which he committed in his dream.

With the father's return from the fair another image attracts the son's imagination, that of the silk kerchief which the father gives as a gift to his wife. While the Messiah is the pivot of the child's inner world, which is made up of dreams, romantic actions, and heroic aspirations, the kerchief is at the center of the child's everyday reality, symbolizing the great love between father and mother, and cementing the family together. The legendary figure of the Messiah steps out of the child's fantasies and becomes a reality, causing the child to look for him in every beggar that he sees on the street; similarly, the kerchief, a real object with practical uses, rises to the level of legend when the child realizes its miraculous qualities, such as the fact that it never gets dirty. Thus myth is transformed into reality, and reality into myth.

The figures of both parents are painted with loving, reverential strokes. Both are censorious yet gentle, larger-than-life yet unthreatening. The father, who possesses pedagogic instincts, teaches his children the value of restraint as well as of learning. When he returns home from the fair, he first quizzes them on their studies, and only then shows them the presents that he brought from the fair. The mother serves as a model of noble discipline as she controls herself when her husband's wagon is heard, and refrains from joining her children in running to welcome him. By conducting herself in a manner opposed to her children's impulsive action, she teaches them a lesson in proper behavior, which is noted by the child who records the events, even though the mother herself never uses words to scold her children for their impetuosity: "And in a little while we heard the wheels of the wagon. . . . At once we threw our spoons down while they were half full, left our plates on the table, and ran out to meet father coming back from the fair. Mother, peace be with her, also let her apron fall and stood erect, her arms folded on her bosom, until father entered the house" (49, 50). When separated from her husband, the mother is seen as incomplete and deficient. She even becomes less of a nurturer when she serves her children only dairy meals during that time, and turns her eyes from them, looking outside the window in an attempt to conquer the distance between herself and her husband. She becomes a nurturer again when her husband returns and she immediately offers him a meal. Both the mother and her daughter are endowed with powers of telepathy which enable them to feel close to the father and identify with him, even when he is far away.

While the boy's love and admiration for his father are genuine, his attitude to him is subconciously colored by masculine rivalry, and by the immature male's inevitable sense of inadequacy, compared with the grown man. During the father's absence, the mother's feeling of emptiness is obvious to her son, who unsuccessfully tries to fill the vacuum left by his father. He sleeps in his father's bed, and fantasizes about the Messiah and his own role in hastening the Messiah's arrival. Since the mother is raised by her son to the level of a sacred symbol, that of the desolate Jerusalem, it is clear that by trying to effect the Messiah's arrival the boy is thinking about redeeming both his people and his own mother. The dream that turns into nightmare, and in which the boy is finally rescued by his own father, teaches the protagonist that he has failed both as his people's rescuer and also as his mother's redeemer. When the father returns home the boy is still haunted by his dream and filled with a sense of failure and ineptness, while the father looks to him bigger than usual: "How big my father was then! . . . now even the chandelier hanging from the ceiling in our house seemed to be lower" (50).

Arnold Band emphasizes the centrality of the kerchief which becomes, in the tale, "the matrix around which" all the narrator's fond memories of home are spun.[40] The kerchief also serves as a private symbol of the strong bond between the man and the woman. When the father presents the kerchief to the mother, there is a subdued erotic feeling in the air that the child records unwittingly: "Mother opened up the kerchief, stroked it with her fingers, and gazed at Father; he gazed back at her and they were silent" (52). Appropriately, the mother wears the kerchief at home only, and puts on a hat when she goes to the services, thus emphasizing the private, intimate meaning that the kerchief carries for her.

The story climaxes on the Sabbath of the boy's bar-mitzvah, when he finds himself alone on the street after the services, wearing his mother's kerchief. The boy meets a beggar who, again, bandages his sores in the same fashion that the Talmudic legend envisions the beggar-Messiah adjusting his bandages. Reality and dream merge in a mystical moment when the boy feels that he "sees in waking what has been shown him in dream" (57). The boy hands the kerchief to the beggar, to be used by him as a fresh bandage. In terms of the young protagonist's inner guilt, which stems from the early dream, he has now succeeded in redeeming himself and correcting the squeamishness and selfishness that he exhibited in that dream.

Now he no longer turns his eyes from the filthy old man, but gazes at him; furthermore, the boy hands the beggar the most precious thing that he has with him, the kerchief. While this is meant to be a redemptive act, the boy suddenly realizes that it is also a childish act, anchored in his tendency to confuse dream and reality. On the level of real life, the boy now realizes, he has committed an unforgivable act, giving the beggar the mother's most cherished possession, while any plain piece of cloth would do as a bandage for the beggar. The reverse side of this seemingly noble act is the boy's attempt to give away the symbol of his parents' love, and the object which is emblematic of the father's possession of his wife. Thus the act of giving away the kerchief is dialectical, stemming from two diametrically opposed motives. In terms of his grand dreams of salvation, the boy has done the right thing, and he has also redeemed the many young people in Jewish folk tales whose attempts to bring about the coming of the Messiah failed through their own follies. At the same time, he has committed a foolish act that reveals his hidden defiance of the bond between father and mother in which he does not share, and which is embodied in the kerchief.

Appropriately, the climactic moment of the story occurs on the day that marks the boy's transition from childhood to adulthood, and it is his ambivalent deed that epitomizes the boy's twofold existence as a child and as an adult. His sudden feeling of guilt is a moment of emergence from childhood fantasies, as well as from his Oedipal envy. His regret at giving away the kerchief means both that he can now distinguish between fantasy and reality, and that he no longer vies with his father for his mother. But it is the mother's approving gesture at the end of the story that helps her son rid himself of the shame and sorrow that he suddenly feels for having lost the kerchief, and for having acted out his submerged jealousy of the other man in his mother's life, his own father:

> When I entered I found mother sitting in the window as was her way. Suddenly I felt that I had not treated her properly; she had had a fine kerchief which she used to bind around her head on Sabbaths and festivals, and I had taken it and given it to a beggar to bind up his feet with. Ere I had ended asking her to forgive me she was gazing at me with love and affection (58).

The mother's immediate, instinctive sanctioning of her son's deed, when she gazes at him with love and affection, without asking for any explanation, purges the child's gesture of its selfish, Oedipal elements, and transforms it into a mature, selfless, and redemptive action.

The stages in the son's interaction with his mother in "The Kerchief" correspond to the universal course, delineated by Erich Neumann, which starts with the child's dependence on the mother, progresses into "the relation of the beloved son to the Great Mother" (displayed in the young protagonist's elevation of his mother to the mythic image of Mother Zion), and culminates in "the heroic struggle against the Great Mother."[41] Agnon's young narrator is blessed with an understanding, selfless mother who facilitates her son's attempts to grow up and free himself of her. Indeed, the son is not even fully aware that his newly found maturity has been won after a struggle. In Agnon's model family the son does not need to engage in conflict in order to emerge from the state of dependence on, and complete immersion in the mother. By contrast, in Agnon's novella *A Simple Story* (1935),[42] in which the writer abandons the legendary style and adopts the realistic mode, the relationship between the son and his mother takes the other route described by Neumann, where the Great Mother becomes the Terrible Mother and stands for the "black abysmal side of life and of the human psyche."[43]

As in "The Kerchief," the mother in *A Simple Story*, Tsirel Horovitz, is a pivotal figure in her son's life, wielding great power over him, and capable of shaping and altering his mental growth. Yet Tsirel is a catalyst of madness and is seen as the direct cause of her son's descent into insanity, both because of her own genetic heritage and of her oppressive treatment of her weak-willed son. Tsirel herself married late in life because of the blemish in her family background resulting from her own brother's insanity. The man who married the unattractive Tsirel abandoned the young woman that he loved for Tsirel's money. The domineering, unromantic Tsirel, aware of both her husband's and her son's timid, submissive natures, rules over her household, as well as over her grocery business, and makes all the important decisions in the family. When Tsirel's son, Hirshel, falls in love with Bluma, the orphaned daughter of her husband's first love, Tsirel cunningly engineers a match between her son and a rich heiress. The gentle Bluma, who resides in the Horovitz household and serves as a maid, leaves home in disgust, waiting for Hirshel to resolve his conflict with his parents. Hirshel's mother shrewdly commiserates with her son on being deserted by his girl, and convinces him that Bluma was not right for him. Tsirel avoids a confrontation with her son and succeeds in gaining his trust, persuading him that she, his mother, is his best friend. The insecure Hirshel, driven by his mother to view himself as betrayed and deserted by his beloved Bluma, marries the woman that his mother has chosen for him, and gradually sinks into depression that culminates in a breakdown.

Tsirel's responsibility for her son's loss of sanity is double. While she herself is a strong person, she carries the genes of madness in her; moreover, she does not allow her son to extricate himself from her tight grip, and thus causes him to sink into the dark unconscious, to use Erich Neumann's words, rather than emerge from it into full consciousness. Unlike the mother in "The Kerchief," Tsirel approves of her son only when he acts in accordance with her wishes, and thus prevents him from maturing into an independently minded man. If the mother in "The Kerchief" redeems her son from the primal male complex, Tsirel enhances her son's descent into the dark recesses of the "negative unconscious." The man that she has formed is not only a passive, acquiescent person, but one whose will has been broken, and whose grip on the world is tenuous.

In her relationship with Bluma, Tsirel is motivated both by her jealousy of Bluma's dead mother, and by her determination to dominate her son's life and discourage him from creating a strong bond with another woman. Furthermore, having created a life for herself and her husband in which money has taken the place of eros, and material comforts the place of strong passions, Tsirel is unwilling to allow love to enter into her son's life. When she forces her son to marry the rich Mina, Tsirel is driven not only by her crude materialism but also by feminine hostility towards even the mere phenomenon of love, adopted by a woman who has never known love.

Woven into the fabric of the language in this novella are references to early Judaic texts, prominently the Song of Songs. Hirshel and Bluma reenact the search for the beloved and the agony of love that characterize the Canticles lovers. To reinforce the spirit of this biblical paean to love, Agnon uses the phrase "upon the handles of the lock" (Song of Songs 5:5) in a climactic scene in the story. The separation of Hirshel and Bluma, effected by Tsirel, is thus transmuted from a mere breach of promise between two people to the breaking of the biblical covenant. Furthermore, in Hirshel's perception of Bluma, his beloved is "almost his twin," a phrase weighted with midrashic and Kabbalistic echoes. According to the Midrash, Cain and Abel, as well as Jacob's sons, were each born with his own female twin, who became his mate. And both according to the Midrash and the Zohar, Adam and Eve were initially created as a creature resembling Siamese twins, before God separated them into male and female. The notion of the bride as sister, evoking the Canticles verses "my sister my bride" and "my sister, my love, my dove," (5:1, 2), as well as midrashic and Kabbalistic images, suggests that the union between the man and woman in this story is divinely sanctioned. It also implies that Hirshel and Bluma's love transcends the erotic and is rooted in a spiritual, even mystical bond. The actions of the ostensibly pious Tsirel are revealed as defying not only the sanctity of the human heart, but of the very religious norms that she supposedly believes in. Within the context of the Judaic symbolism that suffuses the story, Tsirel is converted from flesh-and-blood mother into an evil force of colossal proportions that disrupts domestic, psychic, and cosmic harmony.

Like Mrs. Morel, the overbearing, stifling, and ultimately destructive mother in D. H. Lawrence's *Sons and Lovers,* Tsirel allows her son sexual gratification but begrudges him the spiritual union with a woman. Appropriately, the wife that Tsirel chooses for her son is Mina, whose name in Hebrew enfolds the noun *min,* 'sex'. Though not a spiritual person herself, Tsirel understands that in Bluma she would have a rival who has a hold on her son's very being, while in Mina her son will find merely erotic fulfillment that will not threaten the mother's power over him.

As a work written in the European tradition of social realism, *A Simple Story* positions Tsirel as the representative of the petty materialism and crass practicality of the middle class. Yet Agnon's novella, which captures Jewish society in transition, is in itself a genre in transition, since it often abandons social realism to convey the protagonist's interior monologues and associative flow of consciousness, especially when it traces his gradual sinking into mental chaos. In the psychological aspect of the story, Tsirel serves as the transmitter of madness in her son, epitomizing the Terrible Mother. She counters her son's "upward-striving consciousness," as Neumann puts it, with her successful attempts to pull him into "the regressive, devouring, dangerous unconscious" [44] which she embodies in her role as mother. Therefore, while Tsirel herself is a figure that belongs in the social novel, her role as the "negative unconscious" in her son's life warrants the novel's periodic excursions into the "stream-of-consciousness" mode that records the inner reality of the protagonist. Tsirel ties together the two aspects of the story, the social and the psychological, and emerges as a far more important factor in Agnon's novella than her secondary role initially suggests.

Agnon's two stories exemplify the two universal, diametrically opposed aspects of motherhood. In "The Kerchief," the mother is not even named, and thus her mythic quality is enhanced. She becomes larger-than-life, the mother of the family as well as "Mother Zion," embracing in her kindness her young son, and radiating her goodness over the total reality. In *A Simple Story,* the mother is an individual anchored in time and place, with a particular family history and name; yet she enfolds in her character those archetypal qualities that

result in the fear of the Mother. Significantly, the mother as a negative force in her son's life is a figure in a realistic story, written by an
objective, unbiased observer of a society in transition. The mother as
a healing, redemptive figure in Agnon's writings is at the center of a
nostalgic, idyllic, and legendary tale, written by the homesick adult
who revisits, in his mind, the admirable mother who is no longer
alive and the Edenic childhood that has vanished.

Man's sexual partner reveals a demonic side, turning anticipated pleasure
into physical and psychic torment. His progenitor, who releases him
from the darkness of the womb, may become his jailer, who drives
him to the nether land of the unconscious. These images, created by
the male mind, betray a misogynic gynephobia, embedded in the
collective male psyche. In reality, however, these reflections of femininity, coupled with socioeconomic circumstances that were disad-
vantageous to women, resulted in the oppression and victimization
of the flesh-and-blood female. Our next chapter explores some of the
instances of the woman's confrontation with male tyranny.

Notes

[1] *The Great Mother,* op. cit., 39.
[2] For instance, when the Lord saw that Leah was hated by her husband, he
"opened her womb" (Gen. 29:31), and when Hannah was barren, it was assumed that God "shut up" her womb (1 Sam. 1:5).
[3] For the different aspects of the Shekinah see Y. Tishbi, *Mishnat HaZohar,*
vol. 1 (Jerusalem: Mosad Bialik, 1949), 119–31.
[4] See Neumann, 55–63.
[5] Neumann, 65. Tishbi discusses the two faces of the Shekinah and relates
this phenomenon to archetypal, mythic configurations common to all man.
See Tishbi, 126.
[6] Neumann, 65.
[7] Neumann, 69.
[8] See Sigmund Freud, *Three Essays on the Theory of Sexuality* (1905), in *The
Standard Edition of the Complete Psychological Works,* ed. and trans. James
Strachey, vol. 7 (London: Hogarth Press, 1964), 121.
[9] Freud, *New Introductory Lectures on Psycho-Analysis* (1933), in *Works,* vol.
12, 116–17.
[10] On Freud's misogyny, see Philip Rieff, *Freud, the Mind of a Moralist* (New
York: Viking, 1959), 174–85.
[11] See Erik Erikson, op. cit., 261–94.
[12] For a discussion of the cultic as well as the social and economic importance of fruitfulness in the Middle East, see Raphael Patai, *Sex and Family in
the Bible and the Middle East* (Garden City, N.Y.: Doubleday, 1959), 71–80.

[13] George Eliot, *Middlemarch* (Cambridge, Mass.: Riverside, 1956), 3. First published in 1871–2.

[14] Yalkut Shim'omi, Sam. 1:1.

[15] *The Art of Biblical Narrative* (New York: Basic Books, 1981), 185.

[16] See Harold Fisch, "Ruth and the Structure of Covenant History," *Vetus Testamentum* 32, no. 4 (1982):425–37.

[17] For updated summaries of the scholarship on the biblical Book of Ruth, see Fisch's essay; see also E. F. Campbell's Introduction and Commentary in the Anchor Bible edition of Ruth, op. cit., and Phyllis Trible, *God and the Rhetoric of Sexuality*, op. cit., 166–99.

[18] Fisch, 436.

[19] On the cave as representative of the womb, see Neumann, 44 et passim.

[20] The translation of Ruth used in this discussion is that of E. F. Campbell's in the Anchor edition.

[21] On the dialectical pattern of death and renewal, emptiness and fullness, see D. F. Rauber, "Literary Values in the Bible: The Book of Ruth," *Journal of Biblical Literature* 89 (1970):27–37.

[22] Campbell maintains that Boaz did say these words, but that the storyteller chose to put the theme of "fullness" in Ruth's mouth when she speaks to Naomi, in order to complete the *inclusio* structure. See the Anchor Bible, 129.

[23] Trible, op. cit., emphasizes the women's destitution and deprived circumstances. According to Boaz's own testimony, however, it seems that Ruth could have found a man to rescue her from poverty, but that she waited for a legal "redeemer."

[24] On the double meaning of the language describing this episode, see Campbell, the Anchor Bible, 130–33.

[25] Trans. Nicholas de Lange. In *Eight Great Hebrew Short Novels,* ed. Lelchuk and Shaked, op. cit., 271–317. The Hebrew text consulted is the Am Oved edition, 1979.

[26] The Book of Ruth is read in the synagogue every year on the spring holiday of Shabuot.

[27] Interestingly, Oz's title takes us away from the Judaic historical experience by evoking a scene of betrayal from Christian lore. The "hill of evil counsel" is the place in Jerusalem where evil designs were formed against Jesus.

[28] Oz plays with the analogy between biblical models and modern characters in his other works, too. For instance, in his novel *A Perfect Peace* (New York: Harcourt Brace Jovanovich, 1985), each of the contemporary characters is a reflection of a biblical persona and, at the same time, a diminished and reduced copy of the ancient model.

[29] Another modern recreation of the Ruth tale worth noting here is Harold Pinter's play *The Homecoming*. Pinter, too, reverses the main premises of the biblical story through his protagonist, Ruth, a modern, sophisticated woman, and wife of an American professor of British descent, who chooses to remain in England with her husband's relatives, serving them as nurturer and whore, rather than return home to the "new world." The reality into which this modern Ruth settles is prehistoric and primitive, replete with images of blood and butchery, where naked, primal desires predominate.

[30] Kiddushin 31b.

[31] Kiddushin 31b.

[32] In Devarim Rabbah 1. Another story about the shenanigans of Dama's mother is told in Kiddushin 31a.

[33] See "The Martyrs of Mainz," in Carmi, *Hebrew Verse* (New York: Penguin, 1981), 372–73.

[34] See 2 Macc. 7:27–29. See also Chapter 5, "Female Strategy," n. 93.

[35] The story is told in Midrash on Proverbs 31. Also see the discussion of Beruria in Chapter 5, "Female Strategy."

[36] For a translation of the poem and an introduction to Bialik's poetry see Chaim Nachman Bialik, *Selected Poems,* bilingual ed., sel. and trans. Ruth Nevo (Tel Aviv: Dvir, 1981). See also Baruch Kurzweil, *Bialik and Tchernichovsky,* in Hebrew (Jerusalem: Schocken, 1971).

[37] See Nevo, 14–20.

[38] Bialik's works reveal an ambivalence towards the patriarchal figure as representative of the world of traditional piety that stands in the way of the creative individual. See Kurzweil, *Bialik and Tchernichovsky,* 3–22.

[39] In S. Y. Agnon, *Twenty-One Stories,* ed. Nahum N. Glatzer (New York: Schocken, 1970), 45–59. The story was translated by I. M. Lask. All page references are to this edition. For a detailed analysis of this story, as well as references to other major interpretations, see Band, 224–28 et passim. See also Samuel Leiter's interpretation in *Selected Stories of S. Y. Agnon* (New York: Tarbut, 1970), 20–27. Leiter mentions the possibility of a Freudian interpretation. While the reading of the story offered here is not exclusively Freudian, it does take into account an Oedipal substratum in the child-narrator's consciousness.

[40] *Nostalgia and Nightmare,* 226.

[41] *The Great Mother,* 148.

[42] In Hebrew, *Sippur Pashut.* The Hebrew text consulted is the Schocken edition, 1971.

[43] *The Great Mother,* 178.

[44] *The Great Mother,* 149.

Woman and Oppression

And the spirit of jealousy came upon him and he be jealous of his wife, and she be defiled; or if he be jealous of his wife, and she be not defiled. Then shall he bring his wife to the priest. . . . And he shall cause the woman to drink the bitter water that causes the curse, and the water that causes the curse shall enter into her, and become bitter. . . . Then it shall come to pass, that, if she be defiled, and have done trespass against her husband, that the water that causes the curse shall enter into her and become bitter, and her belly shall swell, and her thigh shall fall away, and the woman shall be a curse among her people.

    Num. 5:11–28

From that time she {the moon as a female figure} has had no light of her own, but derives her light from the sun. At first they were on an equality, but afterwards she diminished herself; for a woman enjoys no honor save in conjunction with her husband.

    Zohar I, 20a

$\mathcal{T}$he patriarchal structure provided the woman with protection and shelter. She was declared the sexual mate of one man only, not to be touched by the other males. At the same time, the woman became the chattel of that male, part of his worldly possessions, and she lost her freedom to choose and decide for herself. In biblical times, women of childbearing age were constantly confined in the home, tending to the children and domestic matters. The socio-economic realities were such that a person's worth was measured by his or her labor input. Consequently, female children were less desirable than male children, since they were not able to offer the same manpower to the family as the male children. The responsibility for supporting the family was man's, but this created a male-dominated unit in which the woman was economically completely dependent on her father and later, on her husband. A woman's earnings belonged to her husband, and she did not share in her father's estate. If the Bible cannot be blamed for conspiring to subjugate women, its male-dominated laws inevitably perpetuated the image of women as subordinate to the male and inferior to him.

Two types of feminine oppression come to the fore both in ancient works and, in subtler ways, in more modern texts. As a minor and a dependent within the law, the woman found herself, in ancient times, within a legal system that was male-centered and designed to protect men's rights and interests. The woman also existed in a certain social and cultural ambience, not defined by the law, in which her femininity—her ability to arouse desire in man, and her reproductive powers—was regarded with a mixture of awe and jealousy. This resulted in a situation where the woman's sexuality was both guarded and exploited, and where she was often seen as a being tyrannized by her own anatomy, who had to pay the price not only for her own excesses but for those she may have aroused in the male.

Women and the Patriarchal System

A large portion of biblical legislation touches upon women's lives and roles in the family, society, and cultic practices. As we turn to the narratives, however, there are very few examples in which fully individualized women, rather than a collective legal entity, are actually seen to come in contact with the law. In those few cases where a law that affects women is at the center of a dramatic tale, the female characters in question do not fare badly and are described as taking an active role in either the implementation of the law or its modification.

An episode that describes women's contribution to the understanding of the law is that of the daughters of Zelofhad whose petition for an amendment in the law was accepted by Moses under God's orders. Significantly, instead of just stating the amendment that gives certain privileges to women, the Bible tells the origins of that legal addition, and how women had a role in initiating that particular law. The Bible narrates that by special legislation, daughters were permitted to inherit where there were no male heirs. When the children of Israel were divided into tribes and families for the purpose of distributing the land, the daughters of Zelofhad approached Moses: "And they stood before Moses, and before Elazar the priest, and before the princes and all the congregation, by the door of the Tent of Meeting, saying, Our father died in the wilderness . . . and had no sons. Why should the name of our father be done away from his family, because he has no sons? Give us a possession among the brethren of our father" (Num. 27:1–5).

The daughters ask for the land not for their own sake, but in order to perpetuate their father's name. Yet the daughters' initiative triggered the special legislation that allows women to inherit from their father where male descendants are lacking. The only constriction that accompanied this amendment was the requirement that the daughters marry within their own tribe, so that the land will not pass to another tribe.

The biblical narrator is not oblivious to the dramatic potential inherent in the story. This episode follows a detailed listing of the Israelite tribes and subtribes; the social structure is patrilineal and women are not mentioned. Yet out of the faceless, anonymous multitude of women in the background, the names of five women are listed. Soon after, these five women suddenly separate themselves from the rest and become individuals; the name of each of the five daughters is again spelled out. It is obvious that the daughters need to muster all the courage that they have, since they approach not just the head of their own tribe or family, but Moses himself. The text therefore lists all the awesome male authority figures whom the sisters have to confront: Moses, the High Priest, and the heads of the tribes. The sisters challenge the law and give voice to other women who may find themselves in the same predicament in the future. The women's speech is wisely and diplomatically structured. They start by telling their background, emphasizing that their father was a worthy man and did not take part in the rebellion against Moses; they ask a rhetorical question, "Why should the name of our father be done away?" and they then proceed to make a demand: "Give to us a possession among the brethren of our father." Zelofhad's daughters make sure that their claim stay within the patriarchal legal system; they ask for a piece of land for their late father's sake. They are also careful not to seem rebellious against the basic tenets of the patriarchal ideology. Therefore, they do not question the logic behind the law that bans daughters from sharing in their father's inheritance. Instead, they focus on their particular predicament, emphasizing that they want land "among the brethren of our father." The sisters understand implicitly that if they appear to wish to change the status quo and question the patriarchal worldview and social system, they would fail. Their careful and shrewd speech is calculated not to antagonize the patriarchal authorities, yet at the same time to insist on the justice and logic of their demand. Moses is so overwhelmed by the power of their rhetoric that he immediately consults God. Significantly, God, too, seems to be impressed not only with the women's argument but with their carefully worded speech: "The daughters of Zelofhad speak right." This is one of the few biblical occasions when the woman's voice is raised and is being noted.

The Midrash felt the slightly argumentative tone in the women's address and broadened it into a questioning of the patriarchal system. In the midrashic recreation of this story, the women imply that in the present social structure there is solidarity among men against women, and a tacit agreement to protect men's rights; while God's outlook, so they believe, is egalitarian and nondiscriminatory: "They said: The compassion of men extends to men more than to women, but not so is the compassion of God; His compassion extends equally to men and women and all."[1]

Surprisingly, the Midrash sages, who were often intolerant of any indication of women's independent spirit and challenge to patriarchal authority, are quite sympathetic to Zelofhad's daughters. They see in the women's request for an allocation of territory in a land that has not yet been conquered an indication of the women's strong feeling that the divine promise will soon become a reality. The sages thus juxtapose the women's implied faith in the Israelites' eventual possession of the Land of Israel with the periodic surge of doubt and lack of faith that characterized the generation of the desert: "The daughters of Zelofhad said to Moses: 'Give unto us a possession among the brethren of our father.' Rabbi Nathan said: The faith of the women was, therefore, stronger than that of the men. For the men had said: 'Let us make a captain, and let us return to Egypt.'"[2] It seems that both in the biblical text, and in the midrashic version of this episode, the daughters of Zelofhad are commended and rewarded for their spunk, their attempt to whip the biblical law into a somewhat more egalitarian record, and, simultaneously, their implied faith in the Mosaic legal system and its historical promise.

Another example of a woman who moves within the patriarchal legal system and shapes it to her advantage is Ruth the Moabitess. The Book of Ruth describes how the childless and destitute Ruth, shrewdly and subtly, and with her mother-in-law's help, alerts a man to his legal obligations. She cunningly brings to Boaz's attention the levirate law that requires a man to marry the childless widow of his brother. Furthermore, Ruth succeeds in making Boaz understand the spirit of the law, rather than cling to its narrow meaning. She makes him realize tht the law itself does not always cover all the cases confronted in real life. With Ruth's subtle help, Boaz broadens his conception of the levirate custom to include in the obligation not only the widow's brother-in-law, but even a more distant male relative.

The institution of levirate marriage works in Ruth's favor. It saves her from destitution and enhances her cultic and social assimilation into the society of ancient Israel. Yet the same law, still adhered to in the nineteenth-century shtetl, is seen as an irrational, myopic, and stringent dictum, left over from primitive times, that ruins a woman's life and her chances for happiness. The poem that illustrates the evil of this custom is Y. L. Gordon's *"Shomeret Yabam"* ("Keeper of Levirate").[3]

To understand the background of this poem we have to remember that the Bible offers a way out for the brother who does not wish to perform his levirate duty and marry his childless sister-in-law. In a specific religious ceremony, the man is released from his obligation towards the widow. If this biblical edict was initially intended to alleviate the financial burden that marrying another woman meant for many men, it has also offered more freedom to women in postbiblical times. In reality, the levirate custom became obsolete and, in cases where it applied, the man and woman concerned underwent the religious ceremony that freed them both from any obligation to each other.[4]

The poet Gordon, who was ardently committed to "enlighten" his fellow Jews and make them realize the backwardness and outdated character of Judaic law, creates a dramatic situation in which a woman is seen as victim of Jewish law as well as of its standard bearers, the contemporary rabbis. The female protagonist of this poem is a young woman by the name of Jonah. She is first described as she is sitting at the deathbed of her beloved young husband, who suffers from a terminal disease. Jonah has been married for three years, yet God has not blessed her with a child. Ironically, Jonah's mother-in-law has just recently borne another child, so that the young woman will have to wait until her newly born brother-in-law reaches legal age and is able to release her from the levirate obligation. Her parents are aware of their daughter's difficult situation and, after much deliberation, decide to approach the dying young husband and ask him to divorce his wife. If Jonah is a divorced woman, there will be no legal tie between her and her brother-in-law and she will be able to remarry while still young and pretty.

The dying man is finally approached by his own mother, and he agrees to divorce his wife. The rabbi who is summoned to perform the hasty ceremony demands an exorbitant fee, however. The family, already impoverished as a result of the medical costs incurred through the young man's illness, begs the rabbi to reduce the fee, but the man stubbornly refuses. While the negotiations go on, the young man dies, and the childless widow will now have to wait for many years until her infant brother-in-law reaches the age of thirteen and is able to release her.

The young woman is thus victim not only of an antiquated law that puts her at the mercy of a man, but of a corrupt patriarchal system in which the legal authority, always a man, is ruthlessly insensitive to the predicament of women, and sees in their legal plight a way to pad his purse. Gordon's poetic barbs are especially poisonous in his depiction of the rabbi; he uses bitter sarcasm to portray the "holy" man whose hypocritical sense of the sacredness and importance of his position will not let him reduce the fee for a simple legal procedure that will rescue the young woman from disaster. The unyielding rabbi is a simple charlatan, a criminal in whose hands the fate of the young woman is placed. Beyond that, Gordon questions the validity and wisdom of adhering to a religious-legal code that oppresses women and wreaks havoc in their lives.

The young widow is seen as a pathetic figure, and while her predicament is real, her individuality does not come through. She is tritely described as beautiful, gentle, modest, and innocent. But it is obvious that the poet is not interested in his heroine's personality, in those qualities that would make her unique and different from other women; she is simply a case history that illustrates a prevalent situation. The poet ends with a tongue-in-cheek lament for the rabbi who, through the death of the young man, lost a chance to perform a divorce and make some money.

Religious inflexibility and masculine despotism combine to destroy the life of another Gordon heroine in the poem *"Ashaka DeRispak."*[5] The title of the poem is taken from the Talmudic story that portrays how a board that fell off a carriage caused the destruction of the city of Bethar. The Talmudic epigram that says that Bethar was plundered because of a board is used here for its metaphorical message that a tragedy can be caused by a minor, unimportant thing.

The poem opens as the family of a poor wagon driver is sitting at the Seder table, conducting the ceremony to the minutest details, and waiting for the mother of the house to serve the long-awaited meal. As the woman busies herself in the kitchen, she suddenly observes a grain of wheat in the soup; this means that the meal is not fit to be served on Passover, since a leavened ingredient has found its way to the soup. For the woman this means a catastrophe of the first order; her kitchen has not been properly "koshered" for Passover, and the lavish meal that she slaved over should be immediately removed from the premises. The unhappy woman tells her husband what happened and prepares to go to the rabbi and ask for his advice. Her uncouth, boorish husband, who is hungry and tired after days of hard work and insufficient food, forbids her to ask the rabbi's advice and commands her to serve the meal to her famished family. The pious woman reluctantly feeds her family, but does not taste a thing herself. When, on the next day, she finds another grain in her pot, she hurries to the rabbi, without her husband's knowledge. She relates to him the problem and also adds that her husband threatened to beat her if she consulted the rabbi. Gordon now slows down the story and gives rhetorical vent to his anger. "Do you think," so Gordon asks his reader, "that the rabbi provides the family with kosher food for the rest of the holiday?" The answer is, of course, no. Instead, the rabbi strictly forbids the woman to serve any of her food to her family, and orders that the impious husband be arrested for violating the Passover law. The rabbi is completely insensitive to the plight of the impoverished woman, who now has nothing to feed her young children for the rest of the holiday.

When the woman's husband returns from jail, he beats her up, then throws her out of his house and later divorces her. To describe the abuse that Sarah, the poem's protagonist, suffers at the hands of her husband, who is named Elipelet, Gordon comically paraphrases the biblical verse that tells how God remembered the ancient Sarah and rescued her from barrenness: "And Elipelet visited Sarah as he had said / And Elipelet did to Sarah as he had spoken." Elipelet's making good on his threat to beat up his wife as soon as he comes out of jail is a parody of "And the Lord visited Sarah as he had said / and the Lord did to Sarah as he had spoken" (Gen. 21:1), which introduces the story of the matriarch Sarah's giving birth to her son. Interestingly, by evoking the biblical phrase in which a woman is treated kindly and lovingly by God, Gordon avoids condemning the Bible itself. Rather, he implies that, if biblical law was good for its time, in its presently fossilized state it is only destructive and oppressive. The object of his attack is therefore not the biblical record itself, but the irrational tradition that perpetuated these ancient laws and insisted on applying them to contemporary situations.

Gordon's most vehement attack against the oppression of women by Jewish law and its zealous keepers is presented in his poem *"Qotso Shel Yod"* ("The Point of a Yod"),[6] which opens with a jeremiad on the fate of the Jewish woman, whose life is "eternal slavery," devoid of pleasure and joy. The poem's heroine is the beautiful Bat-Shu'a, the stereotypical "daughter of Israel," who has been blessed with every possible virtue. The poet is excessively effusive in his description of his heroine's perfect physical and moral nature and her many talents. When her time comes to be married, her rich father finds for her a Talmudic scholar, and the marriage is arranged without asking for the girl's opinion. The young bridegroom is described sarcastically; he may be knowledgeable in the faded leaves of the Talmud, but he lacks social graces, is completely ignorant in worldly matters, and is physically unattractive to boot. Bat-Shu'a does not say a word as the wedding preparations are under way, but there are rumors that she cries at night. The young couple is generously supported by the wife's father while the husband continues in his studies and the young woman starts a family. After three years, however, Bat-Shu'a's father loses his fortune, and the young people are left to fend for themselves.

The husband decides to go abroad with the hope of returning to his wife and children after he succeeds in making a fortune. Bat-Shu'a is left to support her young children by herself and waits to hear from her husband. As time passes and she gets no word from him, she is regarded by her townspeople as an *'agunah*, a woman whose husband's whereabouts are unknown. She cannot be released from her marriage bond since she is still legally married. After a while, a report arrives in town that the ship which the husband had boarded sank in the ocean with no survivor left. The rabbis, however, refuse to grant Bat-Shu'a the legal status of a widow, claiming that they have no solid proof that her husband is indeed dead. It is also learned that the young husband left a document in which he divorces his wife in case he disappears and the woman is left an *'agunah*. Thus the woman has a double claim to being released from the limbo state in which she finds herself. Bat-Shu'a is now anxious to be declared a divorced woman since she has, in the meantime, fallen in love with an "enlightened," liberal-minded man who wants to marry her.

The deed of divorce is brought before the local rabbi for approval and all seems to go well until the sanctimonious rabbi finds a fault in the document. The husband's name is spelled without a *yod*. The name Hillel in Hebrew can be spelled both with the letter *yod* or without it; yet the rabbi stubbornly maintains that the only acceptable way is with a *yod*. He declares the deed of divorce invalid, in spite of the fact that the two other scholarly authorities, the rabbi's subordinates, see no fault in the spelling of the husband's name.

Bat-Shu'a's fate is now cruelly sealed. She refuses to be supported by the man who loves her, not only for fear of the scandal that this might arouse, but also because her piety forbids her from maintaining any kind of relationship with another man, as long as she is considered married in the eyes of the law. The cynical community has in the meantime gossiped about Bat-Shu'a and her admirer, implying that the woman compromised herself, although the two have behaved chastely. For the sake of her children and her good name, Bat-Shu'a is now forced to sever all ties with her suitor. The last glimpse that we have of her is that of a miserable peddler, old and withered before her time, offering her meager merchandise at the train station, with her poorly clothed children at her side.

The numerous tales focusing on the predicament of the *'agunah,* the deserted woman who is in a limbo situation in the eyes of Jewish law, point to the prevalence of this unfortunate phenomenon in the East European pious communities. But Gordon's perspective was one-sided and tendentious. He aimed at exposing the absurdity of clinging to a custom that had originated in a primitive socioeconomic culture but was no longer viable in a modern reality. He also wished to deprecate the rabbinic authorities, whose pedantic adherence to the letter of the law and intellectual obtuseness to the needs of their people in changing times, rendered them incompetent to lead their flock into the modern, secular world. The literature of the turn of the twentieth century offers other aspects of the encounter between the woman and the rabbinic authorities. In S. Y. Agnon's novella, "And the Crooked Shall Be Made Straight," the domestic situation is similar to the one in Gordon's poem. The protagonist leaves home for the purpose of collecting alms and after a while stops sending letters to his wife. In the meantime, a dead beggar is found in a distant village and on his body the letter of recommendation that was given to the protagonist by his rabbi before he left town. Taking this document as evidence that the protagonist is dead, the town's rabbi declares the woman a widow, free to remarry. The rabbi behaves in a reasonable and humane way; the husband has long stopped writing letters to his beloved wife, and now the rabbi's letter has been found on a beggar's body in one of the towns that the husband planned to visit. The rabbi does not ask for more proofs that the corpse is indeed that of his townsman, in order not to prolong the misery of the protagonist's wife. As the reader knows, however, the corpse is not that of the protagonist; the latter sold the rabbi's letter to another beggar, who soon after died. The rabbi's lenient, rational decision leads to tragic results when our protagonist returns home only to find that his wife has married another man and is now the mother of a small infant. Agnon's story seems to be a response to Gordon's poem, and offers an example where the rabbi's supposedly liberal, benevolent decision turned out to be a hasty, ill-advised act. The converse side of Gordon's tragedy, as described by Agnon, is not a happy situation, either, but another kind of tragedy, though motivated, perhaps, by entirely different attitudes. Agnon's story sheds a new light on Gordon's tale in that it directs us to see the rabbi's stubborn rigidity in a new light. These two works—one presenting a vindictive, hostile patriarchy, the other a lenient, humane one, yet both ending in disaster—comment more on the ironies of life and of the narrow, circumscribed existence of both men and women in the East European reality, than on the roles of the rabbis in causing the respective tragedies.

The works of a woman, the short story writer Dvorah Baron (1887–1956), provide many examples of women coming in contact with pedantic, God-fearing male authorities and with various manifestations of a domineering patriarchy, in the Lithuanian shtetls at the turn of our century. In the tales that Baron spins she conjures up vividly and powerfully the bleak, poverty-stricken and persecution-ridden reality of Lithuanian Jewry. Baron's work is significant for the character sketches that she offers of men and women in dire straits. Though she is careful not to stereotype, generally speaking, many of Baron's male characters are hardened people, whose tough life and the meager living that they eke out in sorrow and hard work make them embittered, withdrawn, and unable to show affection. Most of Baron's character portraits are those of the shtetl women who contend courageously and proudly with poverty, lack of love, barrenness, and various other disasters.

The speaker in Baron's stories is the girl Hannah, the rabbi's daughter and undoubtedly the writer's alter ego, who tells of the cases that came before her father. Mainly these were cases related to death, loss of business, or divorce. The heroine of the story "Family,"[7] which narrates one such case, is a young woman who escapes an unhappy home situation by marrying a hardworking, innocent young man. The first years of the couple's life together are idyllic, but as time passes and the woman does not conceive, the man's family begins making unpleasant remarks to the woman, and the community as a whole starts taunting the man for not producing heirs. Though the young people never fight, they understand that when the customary ten years of marriage are over without their having produced off-spring, they will have to be divorced. For the fragile young woman who has no family of her own and who regards her strong husband as a rock that protects her against the sorrows of life, the divorce would be a catastrophe.

Hannah the narrator now intrudes into the scene and describes her father, the saintly, sickly rabbi, as he prepares himself for the divorce ceremony over which he is soon to preside. As a rule, so Hannah tells us, her father fasted on the day of a divorce, and spent the night before studying the case and reading the law pertaining to it. The rabbi also explained to his children that the noun for divorce in Hebrew, *kritut,* meant 'excision', and that it signified the attitude of Jewish tradition to divorce as a violent tearing off of one soul from another. When the hour came, the rabbi's chamber was filled with family members and other idle witnesses. Suddenly, perhaps because one of the women fainted, or because another began to cry, the hand of the old scribe trembled and one of the letters in the deed of divorce came out disjointed, like an "amputated leg," and the ink dripping from it as from a "dark wound" in the script (35). The rabbi then decided to invalidate the document and postpone the ceremony to another time.

The rabbi appears to be unduly particular; after all, the man and woman both have given their consent to the divorce in front of witnesses. He seems to reveal the same kind of pedantic inflexibility that the rabbi in Gordon's poem does. This is another case where the small "point" of a letter makes the deed of divorce invalid. And yet, the ending of this tale is different. The young couple, still lawfully married, go home together, and after nine months the wife gives birth to a healthy, strong son. The same kind of rabbinic rigidity that caused a tragedy in Gordon's poem, results in a happy ending in Baron's tale and rescues an innocent woman from a life of sorrow and misery. The heroine's name, Dinah, is significant in this context. It foreshadows the woman's encounter with Jewish law since it enfolds in itself the noun *din* which means 'law' in Hebrew. In this case, the rigid and uncompromising law is revealed as benevolent, since it is because of the rabbi's adherence to the letter of the law, the *din,* that Dinah the woman gets another chance and is saved.

Yet not all of Baron's tales end happily; in fact, most of her female protagonists appear to be doomed women, whose emotional and economic dependence on men is always exploited either by callous, uncaring males, or by a tyrannical system which views women as slaves and instruments of reproduction. If a woman has the misfortune of being stricken with paralysis (as in the story "The Thorny Path"),[8] or being barren, then it seems that the whole community, both men and women, turns against her, and questions her right to live within the family. In spite of the humane, saintly rabbi who figures in some of Baron's stories as the narrator's beloved father, Baron seems to condemn a system in which men could divorce their wives very easily and effortlessly. In the story "Excision"[9] Baron discusses two kinds of divorces that the narrator witnessed in her father's court. One type of divorce was a result of the husband's sudden falling out of love with his wife. No matter how many years the couple had lived together, how devoted the wife was, and how many children she had borne her husband, he could suddenly, on a whim, decide that he no longer loved his wife, and that would be ground enough for the rabbis to grant him the divorce. Within the Judaic legal system, the woman had nothing to say in the matter, and even the saintly rabbi was unable to help the doomed wife. The other reason for divorce was the wife's barrenness, and in this case, too, the husband was granted a divorce easily; he usually remarried immediately, and his first wife was destined to a life of poverty and destitution.

Between the biblical examples of women benefiting from the patriarchal law (Ruth), or bringing about a change in the law that protects their interests (Zelofhad's daughters), and the nineteenth-century tales in which women are often victimized by the very same legal system (such as Gordon's poems), lies a large body of Hebraic letters that illustrates the oppression of women, on the one hand, and the protection of women within the Mosaic code, on the other. In terms of social premises, too, a dual attitude towards the place and role of the woman is reflected. Though it was relatively easy for a man to divorce his wife, the Talmud asserts that "when a man divorces his first wife, even the very altar sheds tears over him."[10] The wife's positive influence on her husband is reflected in the midrashic story that tells how a man had to divorce his pious wife because she had no children. The man married a bad woman, and she made him bad. The woman married a bad man, and she made him good.[11]

In another context the Talmud declares that "when a man's first wife dies, it is as if the Temple were destroyed in his day."[12] Yet the constrictions set on a woman's existence, and the spatial and mental limitations imposed on her are evidenced in the following homily: "'All glorious is the king's daughter within.' Rabbi Jose says: When a woman keeps chastely within the house, she is fit to marry a High Priest and rear sons who shall be High Priests."[13] A woman's place is within the four walls of the patriarchal household, and her only fulfillment is through her husband or her children; she can thus experience life only vicariously and secondhand, through the achievements of the males in her life.

Post-Talmudic literature holds fast to the tenets of patriarchy. The Kabbalistic conception of the Shekinah as the feminine principle in the deity introduced a renewed element of respect towards women and a certain egalitarian attitude towards gender, with masculinity and femininity both seen as cosmic forces of equal magnitude. Yet when it comes to real-life situations, the Kabbalistic work the Zohar states unequivocally that "a woman may not do anything without the consent of her husband,"[14] and "a woman enjoys no honor save in conjunction with her husband."[15]

The Hasidic stories were narrated and written for and by men; therefore, the woman's voice is rarely heard in them. The Hasidic masters, the Rebbes, are portrayed as saintly figures who were generally loving and kind towards men and women alike. In the Rebbes' homilies and sermons, mutual respect between husband and wife and harmony in the household are seen as necessary for a sane and pure existence and for obtaining mental, and sometimes even cosmic, redemption. In theory, the oppression of women was tantamount to the creation of domestic, psychological, and cosmic disharmony and chaos. The Hasidic thought had a built-in egalitarian quality, since it started as a populist movement that opposed the elitist structure of Jewish society in Eastern Europe. Yet in reality women were victimized by a system that encouraged male bonding, where only the men congregated in order to form a spiritual environment of religious fervor and mystical closeness to God. In the East European communities the custom of leaving the family and staying at the Rebbe's court for long periods of time, even years, was quite prevalent. The wives were left to take care of the business and rear the children. The agony that this custom caused the women and the havoc it wreaked on their lives are described in the literature outside the Hasidic world, for instance, in Sholem Asch's novel *The Tehilim Jew.*

In spite of the democratic spirit that characterized the Hasidic movement at its inception, the Hasidic masters portrayed in the tales that originated in the movement itself are seen as awesome authority figures and strict patriarchs. Martin Buber tells the story of Rabbi Mendel of Rymanov who ruled that the daughters of Israel should not wear gay-colored, lavishly trimmed dresses, and who severely persecuted a young woman who dared go out in the street dressed in the latest city fashion.[16] Other stories, on the other hand, reflect the Rebbe's compassion, especially towards poor, hard-pressed women. In one such tale involving the Rabbi Yitzhak of Vorki, a widow sued some merchants who refused to pay her the debts that they had owed her late husband. To discredit the woman, the merchants told the Rebbe that she had borne a child out of wedlock after her husband's death. Instead of censuring the woman for immorality, the Rebbe expressed sympathy for her, explaining that her destitution had caused her to lose her sense of self-esteem.[17]

The Sephardic Jewish community had its own brand of strict, oppressive patriarchy that maintained its old-fashioned ways even after the male-dominated East European Jewish family began to erode rapidly under the onslaught of Jewish Enlightenment and outside influences. The novelist Yehuda Burla, himself of Sephardic origins, portrays the customs, mores, and family values of the Jewish community in Jerusalem in the early years of the twentieth century. The various Jewish communities that originated in Arab countries and came to settle down in the Land of Israel, or those families that had lived in the Land for many generations, led a far more insulated existence than their contemporaries in the European Jewish ghetto. They conducted their lives with a mixture of genuine orthodox piety and religious superstition that they shared with their Middle Eastern neighbors.

The story of the female protagonist in Burla's novel *His Hated Wife* (1920)[18] evokes the memory of the prototypical "hated wife," the biblical Leah, who won Jacob through trickery, bore him six sons and one daughter, yet was never able to gain his love. In the biblical story, Leah's status as the "hated wife" is doubly enforced; first, when God himself realizes it, and then when Leah admits that she "was hated." Leah's predicament as the unloved wife in Jacob's polygynous family is amply illustrated. She is seen as the victim of both her father and her husband. Her voice is not heard in the episode describing the tricking of Jacob, yet she grows quite vociferous when her life as the rejected wife becomes unbearable and as she starts shifting her dreams and affection from her husband to her sons. Interestingly, though it was Jacob who was duped, his anguish is not elaborated on; after all, seven years later he also wins his beloved Rachel. Burla's novel, however, is written almost exclusively from the point of view of the man who reluctantly marries a woman that he finds unattractive and then suffers all his life from emotional starvation and longings for a passionate love relationship.

Ironically, Burla names his female protagonist after the biblical woman who was ardently loved by her husband, Rachel, and he also sets the first meeting of the young couple at Rachel's Tomb in Beth-Lehem. Like Jacob the patriarch, the young Daud marries a woman who is not his first choice, yielding to the pleading and threats of his domineering mother. He finds the timid young woman unattractive because she is short and dark-skinned while he is tall and fair. As the years pass and the family grows, Daud's passive resentment towards his wife turns into violent hostility as he periodically beats her up, throws her out of his house, or falls into long depressions, refusing to talk to her for days at a time. Like Jacob, Burla's protagonist discriminates between his sons; he loves the firstborn, who looks like himself, and dislikes his second son, who looks more like his wife. Daud is afraid to divorce his wife because, in his superstitious mind, he ties his financial success, which coincided with his marriage, with his wife's good fortune, and regards the woman as an amulet that can ward off financial disaster. During the years, Daud often threatens to take a second wife, a practice that was accepted, yet slightly frowned upon, in the Sephardic community.

While the man's point of view dominates the novel, Burla does not refrain from describing Daud's darker side. If the reader is made to sympathize with the love-starved man, he is also made aware of Daud's grave faults; he is mean-spirited, stingy, and even ruthless. Daud has his lavish meals by himself, and rarely invites his wife and children to join him. They usually have the leftovers in the kitchen.

The wife's point of view is revealed only indirectly, when Burla offers us a glimpse into the letters that she writes to her mother in Hebron. The analogy with the biblical Leah is also apparent here; in Leah's case we also learn of her suffering indirectly, through the different names that she gives to her sons, all depicting her plight and her diminishing hopes of winning her husband's love. In the case of Burla's heroine, the letters reveal the tragedy of a woman who loves her husband hopelessly and passionately, and whose love seems to grow even as his attitude turns into open hostility. Burla's Rachel is seen as a pathetic victim, a figure not strong enough to gain the reader's interest, since the novel's mainspring is the man's anguish and his frustrated existence. Burla's preference for the husband's point of view speaks much of the social attitudes of the era that he describes. Morally, the wife is superior to her husband and would therefore be more deserving of the reader's sympathy and attention. Yet socially, within the structure that subordinates women and pays no attention to their feelings, Rachel's point of view cannot become of pivotal interest. Thus by choosing the male's perspective, Burla comments on the mores of a patriarchy for which love is the male's domain and his indisputable right, very much as it was in ancient biblical times.

Male Tyranny and Women's Sexuality

The area where male authority and patriarchal domination manifested themselves most clearly and oppressively was feminine sexuality. In ancient Israel polygyny was a normal practice and the male's extramarital sexual activities were accepted. A woman's sexuality, however, was regarded as the exclusive property of her husband, just as her virginity was jealously guarded by her father and brothers before she was married. A woman's main contribution to the family was her sexuality, her ability to provide pleasure to her husband and manpower to the family. The penalty for adultery was death for both the woman and her lover; they both were considered to be robbing the husband of that which was exclusively his.

The laws dealing with sexual transgression recognize not only man's rights but also the complex web of emotions that his relationship with his intimate female partner might arouse in him. The Bible acknowledges sexual jealousy as a legitimate male experience. In the example cited in the opening to the present chapter, a husband who suspects his wife of infidelity, but has no proof of it, may require her to submit to a humiliating ordeal. If she is found to be innocent, the husband will have to pay no penalty for his false accusation; the emotional scar that this incident might leave on the woman is not considered. Similarly, rape is not seen in terms of the emotional damage it may cause to a woman, especially the young girl, and the perpetrator is not regarded as a vicious criminal. He must simply marry the girl, and make the appropriate marriage gift to her father.

In matters of the heart, too, only the male's point of view is considered. Isaac loved Rebecca, Jacob was fiercely in love with Rachel, and Elkanah loved his barren wife Hannah. But we are not told of the women's response, although a great part of the narratives about these men shows the women in various states of mental agony. The woman's right, or ability, to love a man of her choice was not a matter of concern to the biblical narrator; only a man's amorous feelings were of importance. The Apocryphal work The Wisdom of Sirach, composed around 180 B.C.E., sums up the patriarchal conception of the differences between the sexes with regard to erotic choices by claiming that a woman can "receive" any man; yet for the male, one girl "surpasses" another.[19] In other words, a woman has no special sensitivity when it comes to choosing a sexual partner, since all men are alike to her; yet man's erotic discrimination is extremely developed, so that he prefers one girl over the other. This epigram seems very simplistic and imperceptive as a psychological observation, yet it is possible that the speaker meant it as a social comment that revealed cultural attitudes. It is not that women are lacking in sexual sensitivity, but that, in reality, whether they possess this quality or not is immaterial, because society allows only the man to act upon his fastidious taste in choosing his female sexual partner.

Woman's sexuality was thus regarded not so much as part of her feminine being but, rather, as an exclusive form of male experience. If the patriarch had indisputable rights over his wife's erotic life and her heart, his attitude towards his daughter's sexuality was even more complex. Within the context of ancient cultural attitudes, the daughter epitomized the family's honor, and her sexual transgression constituted a stigma for the whole family. The daughter was, therefore, protected in the home by both her father and her brothers, since her virginity and purity symbolized the family's power that manifested itself in its ability to protect its women. The Wisdom of Sirach describes the daughter as the cause of sleeplessness to her father. When she is young, the father is concerned that she will "pass her prime," and when she is married, he is afraid that she will be hated by her husband. When she is a girl, the father is afraid that she will be "profaned," and when she is married, he worries that she will not be able to have children. And the strong-willed daughter, who is not closely watched by her father, may become the "talk of the town," and fill her father's enemies with "malignant joy."[20]

The daughter is a source of concern for her father, mainly in matters that have to do with her sexuality and with the threat that it poses to the family's name. Interestingly, love and affection are not recognized among the feelings that a father may have for his daughter.

*   *

The story that best exemplifies the daughter's predicament and her precarious and paradoxical status in the family is that of Dinah, Jacob's daughter, narrated in Genesis, chapter 34. This story has come to be known as the tale of the rape of Dinah. The truth, however, is that the main focus of the story is not the girl who has been violated, but rather the tense and complicated relationship between Jacob and some of his sons. It is not a story about a woman, but about men, with the woman as the element triggering certain events but taking no active part in the actual plot that develops.

Prior to the present tale Dinah is mentioned only as Jacob's daughter by Leah. Although her parentage is known to us, the narrator repeats it at the opening of the present chapter. Dinah is mentioned not as Jacob's daughter but, surprisingly, as Leah's daughter by Jacob. The narrator's intention is, undoubtedly, to bring to the fore the special circumstances of Jacob's household. Dinah is the daughter of the unloved wife who won Jacob by trickery. The tension in Jacob's family where, ironically, the unwanted woman is fruitful, while the beloved wife Rachel is barren, is made clear in previous episodes. The fact that Dinah is Leah's daughter certainly plays a part in the ensuing events. The story opens with the woman: Dinah "went out to see the daughters of the land." While the narrator does not stop to describe the particular predicament of the only daughter in a tribe that attempted to separate itself from the neighboring communities, Dinah's going out to look for women friends implies her sense of loneliness and isolation. The biblical narrator does not judge Dinah for the act of "going out" and explains her motivation as quite innocent. From our modern perspective, the mere fact that a woman should be raped on her first venture out of the confines of her immediate family tells about women's circumscribed existence in ancient times, and their status as easy prey. However, the verb *yz'*, to 'go out', is replete with sexual associations in the Hebrew language; both the Hebrew and the Aramaic nouns for prostitute are coined from the root to 'go out', *yz'* (*yaz'anit* and *nafqa'*). It is hard to say whether the connotations of sexual promiscuity linked with this verb had already existed in biblical language or came into being later, partly as a result of our story. There is no indication in the biblical material that our storyteller, or for that matter any of the protagonists, condemns the girl. It is significant, however, to know that in its Akkadian and Aramaic equivalents this verb can connote coquettish or promiscuous conduct.[21]

In a sequence of three verbs, the narrator describes Dinah's ordeal; Shekhem the Hivvite "takes" her, "lies" with her, and "forces" (or "tortures") her. He then falls in love with the young girl and decides to marry her. Jacob's reaction is that of the stern patriarch, not the loving father. Jacob's initial response is a cultic evaluation: his daughter has been "defiled." For Jacob, Dinah now has a new status within the religious frame of thinking; she is in a state of defilement and impurity. But Jacob has no reaction to his daughter's feminine and human predicament; he does not think about her suffering and personal humiliation, but reacts as head of a religious community that has specific cultic terms for the particular state in which Dinah now finds herself. Jacob further acts as the diplomatic and responsible head of the tribe, but not as the concerned father, when he decides to wait for his sons, who are in the field, before he reacts. We know Jacob from other episodes as a highly passionate man; he bursts out crying the first time he sees Rachel, and he is inconsolable when Joseph is lost. Therefore, his apparent lack of emotion and his sober, calculated reaction, while politically wise, seem to reveal a certain coldness and lack of fatherly affection for his daughter. Is it because Dinah is Leah's daughter, or simply because she is a girl? It is hard to say. The reaction of Dinah's male siblings, however, is markedly different and stands in obvious opposition to the father's attitude.

The brothers' initial reaction is emotional and human: they are sad, in other words, they feel sorry for their sister. This is followed by anger at the offense against the moral values of the Abrahamic family, "because he had done a disgraceful thing in Israel," as well as against basic human norms that ought to be universally accepted: "Which thing ought not to be done" (v. 7).

The following scene describes the marriage negotiations between Jacob and his sons and the Hivvites; here, too, Jacob has a very passive role, and it is the brothers who do the talking. The Hivvites' position may seem rather human and their offer generous, especially if we consider the Israelite tribe's position as nomadic foreigners who are at the mercy of the masters of the land. Shekhem offers to pay as much bride price as the sons of Jacob would demand; yet it is made clear to us that Jacob's sons only pretend to be negotiating and that no monetary compensation would mollify them. The brothers regard the act of rape as an atrocity that requires severe punishment, and the Hivvites' failure to apologize, coupled with an attempt to bribe the brothers, only intensifies the latter's sense of injustice. From our modern perspective we can sympathize with the brothers' reaction to the molestation of their sister in a way that, perhaps, biblical man could not. The girl's father, for instance, gives no indication that he, too, thinks that the penalty for rape should be something more severe than mere monetary payment.

Furthermore, the Hivvites' offer seems fair and human only because the biblical narrator cunningly withholds a very important detail that he discloses only later; while the men are negotiating, the woman is still held hostage in the Hivvites' home. The cards are in the Hivvites' hands; if the brothers did not agree to a settlement, the girl would still remain in the Hivvites' home. The Hivvites thus emerge as less generous than they first appear to be; they negotiate from a position of strength, giving the brothers no real option but to agree to their request.

The brothers refuse to speak about a monetary settlement and, instead, introduce a religious and cultic aspect to the discussions: anyone who marries their sister must be circumcised. We know that this is only a trick to make the Hivvites vulnerable and unable to defend themselves. At the same time, the brothers sincerely indicate that if the Hivvites refuse to be circumcised, the family will be pleased with just getting the girl back. Unlike the Hivvites, the brothers offer a real alternative to the party that they negotiate with; either the Hivvites subject themselves to circumcision, or they should release the girl, "then we will take the girl, and we will be gone" (v. 17). At this point, the brothers are very far from appearing bloodthirsty and anxious for revenge; after all, there is a chance that the Hivvites would not agree to the exorbitant demand of circumcision and would prefer to release the girl. The brothers are eager to get their sister back, either in a peaceful manner or through violence, but they refuse to strike any deal in which they will enrich their coffers at their sister's expense.

Thus, when the brothers finally resort to violence, we understand that this was the only option open to them. Dinah is still within the walls of the city of Shekhem, and the only way to get her out is by force. If the excessive killing might seem unnecessary, we must remember that the only way to get to the imprisoned Dinah, and to insure her safe return, is by clearing the route that leads to the place where she is held. Dinah's two full brothers, Simon and Levi, force their way into Shekhem's house, killing all the males, and then take their sister and leave. The other brothers, however, both Dinah's full- and half-siblings, stay on to plunder the city and loot it. At this point, the underlying family tension that has always existed in Jacob's household erupts. Jacob's wrath is directed only at Simon and Levi, the two sons who did not take part in the looting. After a long silence Jacob finally speaks up; but he has nothing to say about his daughter's ordeal, nor does he find it necessary to talk to the girl herself. Instead, Jacob exhorts his sons for acting recklessly and endangering the entire clan. Jacob thus betrays his dislike for the sons of his unloved wife, as well as his lack of paternal affection towards the daughter born to him by this wife. Later, when Jacob is on his deathbed he also censures Simon and Levi severely for the violence and cruelty that they supposedly committed: "Cursed be their anger so fierce / and their wrath so relentless" (Gen. 49:5–7). Ironically, while Jacob singles out Simon and Levi to condemn them, in the story itself they stand out as more sincere and devoted to their sister, and less greedy, than the other brothers.

The biblical narrator, however, allows the brothers to have the last words, thus subtly implying that his sympathy lies with the fierce brothers. After listening to their father's rebuke, the brothers answer with a rhetorical question: "Should he deal with our sister as with a harlot?" Dinah is now no longer "Jacob's daughter" but "our sister" whose honor will be loyally guarded by her male siblings.[22]

While the brothers' reaction to their sister's ordeal might seem excessive to some, or admirable to others, the woman's silence is extremely significant. The biblical narrator does not give expression to the girl's point of view. Did she feel humiliated and violated? Did she thank her brothers for rescuing her? How did she react to her father's silence and aloofness when she was finally returned home? We are not told, and thus, what should have been a woman's story became a tale about the power struggle in a polygynous family that had four different sets of male half-siblings. Furthermore, although the brothers appear to genuinely care for their sister, their attitude to her is somewhat impersonal and very possessive. They do not refer to Dinah by her name, but only as "our sister," implying that their concern for her is also motivated by the fact that whatever happens to their sister reflects on them. In a sense, if the daughter is molested, the whole tribe is seen as raped, and by courageously rescuing their sister, the brothers are making a political statement to the neighboring tribes, signaling to them that they will not tolerate any form of threat to their honor. The brief episode of the rape of Dinah, inserted within the larger story of the early Israelites' struggle to strike roots in the Land of Canaan, is a correlative of the geopolitical tension as well. For Jacob's sons, who attempt to transform their status from that of foreign nomads to lawful residents and landowners, the violation of their sister by the son of the lords of the land is a political warning. The age-old close identification of woman with land and earth is meaningful in this context. It converts the story of the woman to a parable about men's fight for a land, and the real woman is once again submerged and forgotten.

Dinah's silence, her father's coldness, and the narrator's reticence about the woman's feelings might suggest that one of the links in the story has been intentionally suppressed. As we know, the only available males in the Hebrew tribe were Dinah's own brothers; the question of whom she could marry is not addressed in the biblical text. Is it possible that she was looking for a man? One might also conjecture that Dinah preferred to stay in Shekhem's home when he asked her to marry him because she knew that her chances as a deflowered girl were slim. Did she, then, cooperate with her violator once she was "defiled" and realized the gravity of her social situation? If so, perhaps the father's enigmatic silence indicates his anger and disapproval of his daughter's actions. Furthermore, the language that describes the rescue of Dinah implies that the brothers had to use a certain degree of force in order to take their sister out of Shekhem's home, when, in fact, they had already killed all the males and there was no need to use force in order to set the woman free. The text describes the act of releasing Dinah from captivity with the verb 'to take', the same verb that it employs when Shekhem "takes" Dinah by force. Did Dinah resist her brothers' attempts to release her since she was reluctant to come back to the family that would view her as a "defiled" woman? She most probably knew her father's state of mind and figured his reaction to her. If she were not yet aware that Shekhem had been killed, she may have felt that staying in the home of the man who professed to love her was preferable to returning to a strict, unloving, forbidding father.

As in many biblical tales, the terse, economical language puzzles the reader and teases him into asking more questions. But more than in other cases, it is clear that the many narrative lacunae in the Dinah tale are not only a matter of style but that they point to a deliberate attempt on the part of the narrator to shift the focus of the story away from a delicate problem that is best kept untouched. Whatever the reason for the narrator's decision to highlight some aspects of his story and leave other aspects in the dark, he has successfully and powerfully portrayed the sexual predicament of the woman in a male-centered environment. If she is curious and daring, she runs the risk of being molested. If she stays within the four walls of the patriarchal tent, she surrenders her freedom to choose for herself. Her virginity is no more than a pawn in the power struggle that takes place within her own family and that which occurs between her tribe and the other communities.

If the biblical narrator saw Dinah mainly as a victim, the Midrash sages viewed her with very different eyes. Their treatment of Dinah is, perhaps, the earliest example of men accusing the molested woman of being responsible for her own victimization. The Midrash suggests that the phrase used to describe Dinah's venturing out, "And Dinah the daughter of Leah . . . went out," deliberately evokes Leah's earlier "going out" to invite Jacob to her bed (Gen. 30:16). For the Midrash it is clear that just as Leah "went out" in order to ask a man to sleep with her, so Dinah, her daughter, "went out" with the intention of luring a man sexually. Moreover, unlike Jacob, the Midrash condones the actions of Simon and Levi, but blames the young woman for causing the savagery because she behaved immorally. The Midrash also calls Dinah a "gadabout," and tells us that she deliberately exposed her arm. Furthermore, the sages' sensitive reading of the biblical text focuses on the verb 'to take' which is used both to indicate Shekhem's forceful seizing of Dinah, and the brothers' rescuing her. They unequivocally state that the repetition of the verb indicates that Dinah refused to leave her tormentor's home: "Rabbi Judah said: 'They dragged her out and departed.' Rabbi Hunia observed: 'When a woman is intimate with an uncircumcised person, she finds it hard to tear herself away'."[23] Dinah is thus accused of seducing Shekhem, of enjoying the sexual relations with him, and of refusing to return to her family. In the eyes of the Midrash, then, Dinah is completely to blame for this unfortunate episode. Unlike the Bible, the Midrash explains Dinah's motives and actions clearly and unequivocally, and leaves no doubt in the reader's mind that the young woman was promiscuous, that she was looking for a sexual adventure, and that she is to be held responsible for the bloodshed, for turning her brothers into bloodthirsty savages, and for the rift in Jacob's household.

The paradigmatic nature of the tale of Dinah and, particularly, of the male attitudes to the "fallen" woman revealed in the ancient documents is borne out by later works which manifest similar values. Shakespeare's Leonato, father of the falsely accused Hero, is concerned only with his own grief when he learns of his daughter's supposed indiscretions. Like Jacob, he shows no compassion for the suffering daughter, and without looking into the circumstances, he hastens to label her "fallen," lamenting that ". . . the white sea / Hath drops too few to wash her clean again" (*Much Ado About Nothing,* Act 4, scene 1). In the same episode, the young woman is treated as a damaged piece of merchandise, a "rotten orange," by her intended husband. In general, the young woman is regarded merely as a commodity in a business transaction by both her father and fiance. Hero's voice is only faintly heard, while the men who surround her are allowed to give vent to their rage and humiliation, using the occasion for their own histrionics.

The paradox of the daughter's pivotal role in her brothers' and father's destinies, on the one hand, and the complete suppression of her voice, on the other, is also central in William Faulkner's *The Sound and the Fury.* The promiscuous Candace, a latter-day version of the "defiled daughter," becomes the focus of a variety of male anxieties and hostilities: she is the cause of her brother Quentin's suicide and her father's untimely death, as well as the victim of her evil brother Jason and the only glimmer of hope in the bleak existence of her idiot brother Benjy. Furthermore, as in the biblical context, the daughter's wrecked honor is subtly but inextricably tied to larger questions regarding the future survival of the family and the ownership of land, as well as to cultural and regional transformations. The rape of the woman as an "objective correlative" for the clash of cultures is also at the heart of Tennessee Williams' *A Streetcar Named Desire*, where the frail Blanche is the "raped" South, deprived of its former glory and taken over by strangers.

Furthermore, underlying the ancient Hebraic mind that produced the tale of Dinah is the merging of the concepts of sin and guilt. Jacob the father, for whom Dinah is unequivocally in a state of defilement, does not concern himself with the question of his daughter's moral guilt. Yet the Midrash sages probably felt the subtle paradox in Dinah's state as sinful in religious terms and innocent in moral terms. The rabbis therefore interpreted the story in such a way that Dinah's cultic "impurity" became not only a matter of an arbitrary sectarian definition, but it coincided with the woman's personal guilt. In the Midrash, therefore, Dinah is both sinful and guilty. Nevertheless, this paradox inevitably surfaces in the works of modern writers who are still steeped in the biblical spirit yet at the same time are attuned to secular definitions of morality and guilt. Critics have long been puzzled by Hawthorne's seeming inconsistency regarding his heroine Hester's guilt; to Hawthorne, the bearer of the "scarlet letter" is sinful and pure at the same time. As the violator of the Puritan religious code and biblical law, Hester is the sinful adulteress. Yet in psychological terms as well as in broader secular and humanistic terms, Hester has not committed any violation. A similar ambivalence pervades Tolstoy's treatment of his heroine Anna Karenina. Although he sees in his female protagonist more of a victim than victimizer, Tolstoy, who opens his novel with the New Testament verse on divine vengeance, finds it necessary to ultimately "punish" Anna for her sins, while at the same time maintaining her psychological and moral purity.

If Dinah's voice is suppressed in the early sources, it is fully heard in the poem "The Dinah Affair" (or "The Dinah Portion," 1936) by Saul Tchernichovsky.[24] The poem starts with a prose section that imitates the style and cadence of the biblical text. The opening lines fill the narrative vacuum that exists in the Bible regarding Dinah's life after she was rescued from Shekhem. Dinah's first words are that she wants to die. She later finds out that she is pregnant, and she prays for the innocent child to live. When she bears a daughter she remarks on the bitter irony of bearing a child to a hated man. She is so disgusted with her violator that, during her difficult labor, when she thinks that she is about to die, she begs to be buried in Egypt and not in

Canaan, so that her ashes will not mingle with his. When she thinks that she is on her deathbed, she calls eleven of her brothers (excluding the youngest, Benjamin) and delivers a blessing to each of them, very much in the manner that Jacob does before he dies, and in imitation of his language patterns and imagery. Her father is, significantly, missing from this family gathering. At this point Dinah becomes the forceful speaker, and the brothers the passive, respectful listeners. This reversal of the biblical situation—with the family depatriarchalized and centering around the vocal woman—is accompanied by the reversal of Jacob's blessings. While she uses the language formula of the biblical text, Dinah mostly twists and parodies Jacob's blessings (Gen. 49). She subtly rebukes all the brothers, except for Simon and Levi, for not responding quickly and decisively on her behalf and for cowardly seeking a compromise. But she praises Simon and Levi for their fierce anger and courageous action, mocking and overturning her father's harsh words. Jacob said, "instruments of cruelty are their swords," while Dinah says, "Instruments of nobility are their swords." Thus while Jacob singles out Simon and Levi for condemnation, Dinah singles them out for praise.

As the poem evolves, Dinah survives the agonizing childbirth and raises her daughter with tenderness, protecting her fiercely because, she says, a woman is like a "wild flower" that anyone "can pick." The poet Tchernichovsky, who was also a physician, records the state of mind of the molested woman with almost a clinical precision that, nevertheless, does not dilute the biblical-poetic language. Dinah experiences many of the symptoms connected with the aftermath of rape; she comes to resent her own femininity, and she pities her daughter for being a woman. She refuses to get married because the memories of the rape, of the forced kisses and physical contact with "the pig," have handicapped her sexually and mentally. Tchernichovsky thus corrects the narrative imbalance of the early sources, which did not find it necessary to consider the feelings of the violated woman. He also offers a new perspective to the Dinah affair, by making the reader aware of the crippling effects of rape on a woman, and by letting Dinah express her gratitude to the brothers who cared enough to risk their lives and save her, Simon and Levi. If Dinah is almost nonexistent in the biblical story, except as an object to be acted upon, it is Jacob who is absent in Tchernichovsky's poem. Dinah addresses her other brothers with a mixture of condescension and affection; she chastises them for dragging their feet and not acting swiftly and decisively, but she is not very angry at them, either. In contrast, her failure to discourse with Jacob or even mention him indicates the bitterness and anger that she feels towards the father who did not behave in a fatherly fashion.

Tchernichovsky's Dinah shuns any physical contact with a man because the memory of the rape has made the thought of an erotic experience nauseating and sickening. Thus, although she recovers physically, she will forever carry the emotional scars of being violently invaded at a young age. The other side of this experience would be the point of view of the man who falls in love with the "defiled" woman. This perspective is offered by S. Y. Agnon in his powerful tale "The Doctor's Divorce."[25] The biblical tale of Dinah is an underlying structure in this story, reinforced by the name of the female protagonist, which is Dinah. The story itself, though, is set in Vienna, in the years prior to World War II, and revolves around a physician and his wife who is a nurse.

Three circles of consciousness, which represent three different narrative points of view, manifest themselves in the story. The first circle, that of the physician who is actually going through the ordeal described in the story, is the narrowest and most limited, since the protagonist is so embroiled in his experience that he is unable to look at the events objectively. The second circle is that of the same man, who now tells the story from a distance of time and place. The first-person narrator of the tale is the physician who records a traumatic episode in his life that happened quite a few years ago. The man is obviously no longer practicing in the Viennese hospital that serves as a background to the story, and it is doubtful that he is still in Vienna. The tale is narrated after the War, since the teller has information about the torture–death of the head physician of this hospital at the hands of a Nazi. The chronological and geographical distance of the narrator from the subject of his story enlarges his perspective; the broader point of view enables him to look at the events as they occur and then to remove himself from the situation and comment on the events from an outside vantage point. The third circle of consciousness is that of the writer himself who listens to the doctor's confession and then transforms it into a story. Agnon's voice is not heard directly since the writer himself never intrudes openly into the scene. But the tight narrative structure, the sets of grotesque images interlaced in the story, and the implications of the heroine's name, especially in view of the anonymity of all other characters, suggest the presence of a third point of view, that of the writer who controls the tale and has a much broader perspective than his own protagonist.

In terms of the history of this tale, it is significant that it started as an episode in Agnon's novel *A Guest for the Night* and only later became an independent story.[26] In the novel, the identity of the physician as well as his name and family background are given. Furthermore, while the teller of the episode in the novel is the same physician who speaks to us in the independent story, the novel sets a dramatic scene, in which the doctor confesses, and the writer, the latter's childhood friend, listens. Agnon's persona is absent from the independent story, and therefore the dialogue that is possible in the novel between the listener-writer and the teller has also been eliminated. The story itself fails to give much information about the physician, and, with the listener and the element of dialogue removed, the story concentrates solely on the single-minded, obsessive preoccupation of the physician with his wife's past.

The heroine's name becomes significant precisely because all the other characters, including the protagonist himself, remain unnamed. The story opens with a description of the beautiful, tender nurse who is loved by patients and colleagues alike. She is first mentioned not by name but by her profession; the patients keep calling for her: "Nurse, nurse come to me" (135). The noun for nurse in Hebrew is "sister," and thus, when the nurse's private name is finally disclosed, "sister Dinah" of the story evokes the biblical "sister Dinah." The narrator confesses that he was drawn to the beautiful nurse the very first time that he saw her; he also describes the color of her eyes several times as being a mixture of both blue and black. The system of opposites that dominates the whole story is thus foreshadowed in the colors of Dinah's eyes, which signify innocence and experience, openness and secretiveness at the same time. Already the very first lines of the story contrast the strict discipline of cleanliness and order, instituted in the hospital by the old professor, with the chaos and irrationality of the Nazi regime when this old man dies of a blood infection, after having been tortured by a sadistic soldier.

Prewar Vienna is described as a curious mixture of civilized gentility, on the one hand, and decadence and disease, on the other. Images of beauty, good taste, and decorum suddenly give way to grotesque, heinous scenes that seem to come from a subterranean existence. The motif of duality or of a bi-focal vision is reinforced on the doctor's first date with Dinah when he suddenly sees her as "a new person," and her charm "doubles" with this "metamorphosis" (137). Finally, the theme of the duality of opposites finds its expression in the doctor's attitude to his beloved Dinah after he learns that she had a sexual affair with another man in the past. When Dinah tells her fiance that she was "once involved with another man," the doctor's reaction is ominous: "A chill ran through me and I went weak inside. I sat without saying a word. After a few moments I told her, 'Such a thing would have never occurred to me'" (141). While our protagonist claims that "I treated her just as before, as though she had in no way fallen in my esteem," his protestations imply the opposite. From this moment on, the doctor becomes increasingly obsessed with Dinah's past. He torments her with questions, expresses his disappointment that her former lover was just a low-ranking clerk, and constantly returns to the subject of Dinah's blemished past.

The doctor now vacillates between two states of mind and two visions of Dinah's affair and character. As a rational, liberal-minded man, he genuinely tries to dismiss Dinah's previous sexual experience as unimportant, and Dinah as an innocent victim of a crafty, more experienced man who took advantage of her youth and gullibility. Nevertheless, the doctor seems to be governed by feelings and attitudes that are beyond his control, even as he knows that they are wrong and irrational. Although he does not say it in so many words, the feeling that Dinah is now "defiled" cannot be shaken off from his mind. Dinah's name and the biblical character that it evokes become significant. The doctor shuttles between the biblical rendering of the episode in which Dinah is the victim of a brutish man, and the midrashic reading of the story, in which Dinah is described as a prostitute who seduced the man. Moreover, the doctor alternates between a precivilized, primitive attitude that considers a woman who had sexual relations before her marriage as tainted and blemished, and a modern, enlightened attitude to a premarital experience. His treatment of his wife is domineering and patriarchal. On their wedding night the doctor tells Dinah, "You don't have to wait, your lord has already come" (145). The doctor's possessiveness toward his wife implies that, in spite of his secular education and scientific training, the male in him is still the primitive head of the family who regarded his wife as chattel. For the protagonist, Dinah is now a damaged piece of merchandise that he "bought" in an unthinking moment.

The doctor gradually descends into a manic state of mind, when he can no longer control his tormented imagination. But the doctor-narrator recognizes the duality not only in his conception of Dinah but in the modern male culture: "We are enlightened individuals, modern people, we seek freedom for ourselves and for all humanity, and in point of fact we are worse than the most diehard reactionaries" (146–7). He confesses his hypocrisy: "for I was pretending to be decent while my thoughts were contemptible" (147).

Dinah's married life starts with a disastrous wedding night during which her husband suspects that the courtesy roses which have been placed in their hotel room are a gift from her former lover. Her husband keeps hearing footsteps from the next room that he attributes to the clerk. The wedding ceremony itself forebodes disaster. It is a grotesque affair in which the witnesses are "miserable creatures who an hour ago were called for a funeral and now were summoned for my wedding" (142). The bridegroom imagines that one of the heinous witnesses looks at his wife in a lewd manner, and finds out that he is a clerk who was recently fired. In his obsession, the protagonist keeps seeing his wife's former lover everywhere; when he kisses her, he hears "the echo of another kiss that someone else had given her" (146). The lowly clerk is constantly on the doctor's mind until, at last, the doctor actually comes in touch with him when the latter enters the hospital and becomes the doctor's patient.

Images of disease, infection, and foulness dominate the story. Yet the afflicted person is the one who is supposed to be the healer, the doctor himself, while the person who is regarded as contaminated, Dinah, is actually healthy and sane. The obsessed protagonist knows that he is mentally disordered and, unconsciously, he tries to demoralize his strong wife and shake her mental stability. When she falls sick, he says, "I healed her with medicines and battered her heart with words" (148). In Agnon's story the modern Dinah is almost as reticent as her ancient namesake. Whereas the biblical Dinah is declared "defiled" by her father, however, Agnon makes it clear that it is not his heroine, Dinah, who is "defiled"; rather, it is the man whose mind is polluted and who needs help. Agnon's Dinah withstands her trial with fortitude and dignity, and never loses her sanity. Jacob's description of his daughter as unclean is both subjective and cultic. In our story, which is secular in its orientation, the cultic aspect is nonexistent, of course. We have the doctor's subjective point of view, which regards the woman as contaminated, and the writer's point of view, which is nonjudgmental and enlightened.

Moreover, though the writer does not let us into Dinah's innermost thoughts, we understand from her behavior that she sees herself as the potential healer of her husband's mind, trying different tactics to help him overcome his irrational prejudices and jealousy. When at last she understands the depth of her husband's agony and feels that he is beyond cure, as far as his attitude to her is concerned, she suggests a divorce.

The theme of disease takes a new turn when Dinah's former lover becomes the doctor's patient. The protagonist treats him with special care, with a compulsive, insane dedication, and refuses to let him leave the hospital even when the patient is cured. He makes sure that the clerk has the best food, and simply forces the latter to eat and drink until he becomes almost disfigured by obesity. The doctor confesses that the patient disgusts him physically, and yet at the same time he continues to feed him and see to his needs. This forced attention and excessive care is a form of revenge that the doctor takes on his patient; he tries to kill him with kindness. At the same time, it is clear that as the patient begins to get better, the physician sinks more and more into madness.

The nature of the doctor's obsession, its primitive roots and its link to the biblical story are made clear in a strange dream in which the doctor's monomania becomes clear and focused. In the dream, his wife's lover appears to him, and his face seems sickly but, surprisingly, also likable. The lover turns to the doctor and says: "What do you want from me? Is the fact that she raped me any reason for you to have it in for me?" (155).[27] This new interpretation of Dinah's affair sounds very much like the midrashic recreation of the Dinah story in which the woman is condemned for seducing the man. The doctor, in his poisoned state of mind, goes even a step further; he blames Dinah not only for seducing the clerk, but for actually raping him. The midrashic tendency to blame the woman takes here a grotesque twist and points to the depth of the doctor's obsession. When the doctor tells his wife about the dream, she understands that she will never be able to cure him, and at the same time she pities him; she embraces him in love and pity and realizes that the only cure for him would be removing herself from his life. And it seems that Dinah was right. The first-person narrator of the story is no longer the manic protagonist whose mind is contaminated by his primitive prejudices. He seems to be cured of his sick obsession and is even able to criticize his past behavior and explain its origins as the heritage of precivilized times. Yet the man is now sane and rational only because Dinah is already a memory and is no longer with him. He will never be completely rid of this possessive, unhealthy, and basically primitive conception of woman's sexuality. Beyond him stands the writer of the tale, who knows his hero's limitations and sees them as a collective male problem, deeply seated in the male consciousness and not easily eradicable.

The doctor's treatment of Dinah combines the prejudice of Jacob the patriarch, who sees his daughter as "defiled," the fierce jealousy of the brothers, and the biased, one-sided, judgmental attitude of the Midrash sages. While Agnon adheres in his story to the biblical principle of telling the tale from the male point of view, his story contributes a modern perspective to the Dinah chain of tales. By giving a biblical substructure to his story, Agnon attempts to trace the roots of man's irrational jealousy towards the woman's sexuality and expose it as unhealthy, primitive, and wrong.

The story of the rape of Dinah, and especially the male attitude to the event, seems to have fertilized the imagination of modern writers precisely because of the enigmatic and unexplained reaction of the girl's father, as well as the twist given to the story by the Midrash rabbis. A similar incident, repeating almost identically the different reactions of the father and brother to the daughter's molestation, and set against more civilized times, is recorded in II Samuel 13, in the tale of the rape of David's daughter, Tamar, by her half-brother Amnon. The rape of the daughter becomes here the pivot of a political power struggle and of a son's attempt to dethrone his father that results in civil war. Again, the woman's tale recedes into the background and serves only as the initial link in a chain of male intrigue and conspiracy.

The story's interest, however, lies also in the fact that it traces the violator's changing feelings towards his female victim with a psychological insight not always provided in the biblical story. The story first introduces Tamar as the beautiful sister of David's son. Tamar may be named Absalom's sister rather than David's daughter, just as Dinah is the sister of Simon and Levi, rather than the daughter of her indifferent father. Some commentators suggest, however, that Tamar indeed was not David's daughter but the daughter of Absalom's mother from a previous marriage. The latter possibility seems reasonable in view of the fact that Tamar later suggests that Amnon marry her. Amnon's obsession with his half-sister (if Tamar is David's biological daughter) or with his step-sister (if she is only Absalom's sister), is initially depicted as manic and diseased. He desires her so much that he becomes sick. Later he feigns sickness in order to lure his sister to his bedroom.

When Amnon tries to seduce Tamar, she refuses, and describes the act as a violation of the Israelite moral values, using the same words that Dinah's brothers did when condemning Shekhem's act: "For no such thing ought to be done in Israel" (v. 12). When an appeal to Amnon's sense of morality fails, the woman points out the social stigma that this act will create for both of them: "And I, where should I carry my shame? And as for thee, thou shalt be as one of the base men in Israel" (v. 13). Tamar now realizes that Amnon is in an irrational state of mind and tries another tactic, in an attempt to gain time and, perhaps, avert the disaster. She suggests that Amnon ask David for her hand, and expresses her conviction that David will not withold his consent. If Tamar is not Amnon's biological sister, then this argument makes sense. However, if she is, then Tamar's tactic, suggesting an incestuous marriage, proves her despair. She probably realizes that Amnon is so mentally disoriented at this point, that he might accept such an improbable solution.

The scene where the woman pleads with her attacker, and uses both rational and irrational arguments in order to stave him off, is absent in the Genesis tale of Dinah. In the present case, the biblical narrator removes any blame from the woman, the innocent victim, who still has the presence of mind and strength to reason with the crazed man and try to save herself. Yet Tamar, though using the right tactics from a modern, psychological point of view, fails, and she is brutally raped by her brother. Amnon's mood in the aftermath of the attack is clearly recorded by the narrator: "Then Amnon hated her exceedingly; so that the hatred with which he hated her was greater than the love with which he had loved her. And Amnon said to her, Arise, be gone" (v. 15). Now that he is rid of his obsession, Amnon blames the woman who, unwittingly, aroused his desire and clouded his rational judgment. In Amnon's mind, Tamar turns from the object of his desire to the cause of it; when his desire is spent, his "love" changes into hatred. Shakespeare's memorable verses about lust in Sonnet 129 aptly describe Amnon's shifting moods: "Enjoyed no sooner but despised straight / Past reason hunted; and no sooner had, past reason hated . . . ."

It is clear that the biblical narrator is in full sympathy with the woman and understands her predicament in a male-centered society; he describes her as virtuous and intelligent. Tamar's words after the rape might help the reader understand Dinah's state of mind, too. While we must assume that Tamar hates Amnon for what he has done to her, she pleads with him to let her stay in his home. If this is surprising to the modern reader, within the patriarchal culture in which a woman like Tamar is now "tainted," the woman prefers to stay with her hated violator than go back to a life of social isolation. Thus, if the Genesis storyteller implies that Dinah was not anxious to leave Shekhem's house, the attitude of a sensible woman like Tamar helps us understand the reason behind Dinah's reluctance to return home. Unlike the female protagonist in the Genesis story, the victimized woman in the Samuel story emerges as an individual with a distinct personality who has a strong and intelligent voice. But even such a woman fares badly in a closed-minded and rigid society: Tamar "remained desolate in her brother Absalom's house" (v. 20).

The woman's father, David, is as silent as was Jacob the patriarch, but his reasons are different. Unlike Jacob, he does not label his daughter as unclean; he is also described as very angry, though we do not know whether he feels any compassion for his suffering daughter. David's silence and lack of active reaction is due to the erosion of his own moral stature at this particular moment. The rape of Tamar follows the Bat-Sheba episode in which David's own morality has been put into question. Within the narrative framework of the David saga, the story of the rape of Tamar is not an independent episode but serves as a link in the growing chain of tales that trace the deterioration and demoralization of the house of David in the aftermath of the Bat-Sheba episode. The rape of Tamar is followed by the murder of Amnon at the hands of Tamar's loyal brother, Absalom. As a result, Absalom has to flee the court, and though he returns later at David's request, he harbors plans to rebel against his father and usurp the throne. As in the case of Simon and Levi, we never know whether the act of revenge is motivated solely by feelings of righteousness and anger, or whether it is also intended as a political gesture. In Absalom's case, it seems more likely that Absalom seizes his sister's rape and the killing of Amnon as opportunities to assert his political power, display his defiance of his father, and expose the growing political and moral impotence of the king.

The story of the rape of Tamar displays more compassion and respect towards the female victim than its Genesis counterpart. It also allows the woman to speak and thus reveal her personality. It seems a more enlightened story, less confined to cultic dogmas, and more interested in psychological processes than the Genesis tale. It is similar to the Genesis story in that the function of the brother, rather than the father, as keeper of the daughter's virginity and purity is again confirmed. Yet the fate of the violated woman in the days of King David was as bleak as in the days of the nomadic tribes. The female protagonist quickly recedes to the background, as her story gives way to the momentous, historical events that follow, and in which only men take part.

The cultural postulate that the daughter's femininity is the father's property which he can use as a bargaining chip or payment of a debt or compensation for favors is behind the David-Michal story in 1 Sam. 18. The unfortunate King Saul, the first monarch of ancient Israel, decides to entrap David, his armor-bearer and musician, who is increasingly gaining in popularity among the people. Saul offers David his daughter Merav on the condition that David fight the Philistines. Saul's inner motives are made very clear to the reader: he hopes that the young man will be killed on the battlefield. But publicly, of course, the gesture of giving the daughter as an award to the brave warrior is a form of incentive that seems to be a prevalent custom, and does not arouse any suspicion. The fact that the girl's opinion is not solicited is also within accepted social premises.

While Saul does not ask for his daughter's consent, the Bible surprisingly tells us that in the midst of the negotiations, Merav was given to someone else. One might conjecture that the girl refused to have David; but this is very unlikely. Merav is not seen as choosing another man; rather, she "was given" to another man. It seems that the withdrawal of Merav is part of the king's machinations and has nothing to do with the girl's wishes. The very next verse introduces a new character, Saul's other daughter, Michal, and a new fact: Michal is in love with David. Robert Alter, in his insightful reading of the story, correctly points out that this is the only instance in the Bible where we are explicitly told that a woman loves a man.[28] This outstanding piece of information colors the whole relationship between David and Michal and foreshadows future events. While the Bible states twice that Michal loves David, it ominously omits David's response; when David finally marries Michal, he will not be motivated by amorous feelings, but by political considerations. Apparently, Michal is so much in love with David that her passion becomes public knowledge, and the word finally reaches her father. From this point on, the tale of the tumultuous history of David and Michal is told in fragments that are interlaced in the long narrative dedicated to the rise of David and the establishment of his dynasty. The story is not that of the woman, but that of the man, David, and the woman appears only periodically on occasions that are presented as landmarks in the progress of the hero from a lowly armor-bearer to a glorious monarch.

Michal seems to be a doomed woman from the very first moment that she appears on the scene. For her father, she is an instrument through which he plans to get rid of David. First, Saul demands a very unusual bride-price, one hundred foreskins of Philistines, in the hope that David will get killed while trying to perform this feat. When David survives, Saul sees in his daughter a spy who would help him entrap David in the future. But Michal's greatest vulnerability lies in her love for the ambitious David, for whom she is no more than the reward due to him for his heroic deeds, and a symbol of his rapid climb in the king's court. Michal starts as a rather independent woman who, contrary to cultural attitudes and norms, is not ashamed to make public her love for a man. She also succeeds in marrying that man, although we do not know what would have happened if her love for David had not coincided with her father's conspiracy to destroy him.

Michal's initial actions as David's wife display her great love for him as well as her assertive and independent spirit. She defies her father and helps David escape when Saul's men come for him. In the ensuing events, Michal emerges as crafty and quick-witted. First, she puts a dummy in the bed to mislead Saul's messengers into believing that David lies sick in bed, thus allowing David enough time to reach safety. Secondly, when the ruse is revealed and her father asks for an explanation, Michal quickly answers that she was forced to help David because he threatened her life. Michal's allegiance is now clear and unequivocal, and yet the narrator's silence regarding David's feelings towards the woman does not bode well for the future.

The biblical text now abandons Michal and follows David's career as a fugitive from the law, on the run from the wrath of a paranoid king whose world now centers on destroying the charismatic young warrior. The reader is left to wonder about the fate of the smart, enterprising, and very loving woman, Michal, who was left behind. The next time that Michal is mentioned, she is only referred to passingly, and does not appear in the scene directly. In chapter 25, the story takes a pause from the narration of the military and social adventures of David the outlaw, to tell us about the man's marital doings; in this connection, there is a brief statement to the effect that Saul gave his daughter Michal to another man. While we do not get a direct glimpse of Michal, her compliance, or her silence as this transaction goes on, points to the metamorphosis that this young woman has probably experienced. Earlier, she dared to defy her father and blatantly lie to him, yet now she does not even put up a fight. She may be disillusioned with David, who did not send for her and has married two other women, or she may have lost her spunk during the long waiting at the home of her obsessed father. David's reaction to Michal's marriage is, typically, not mentioned, and it was probably nonexistent.

When Michal next appears on the scene, she is the typical woman in a patriarchal society: she is being acted upon. The occasion is David's rise to the throne after the death of king Saul. Saul's loyalists are now ready to make peace with David who, in turn, demands Michal back. His claim is couched in a legal, not emotional language; he wants his wife back not because he loves and misses her, but because she is legally his, and he paid the bride-price demanded by her father: "Deliver me my wife Michal, whom I betrothed to me for a hundred foreskins of Philistines" (II Sam. 3:14). At this sensitive point in David's political life, the return of Michal to his home will mark the final surrender of the former royal family, and would serve as a symbol of the consolidation of power in David's hands. Michal's husband cries bitterly as he accompanies the woman to David's place, yet Michal does not say a word and is probably much less heart-broken than her present husband. Again, one might surmise that Michal understands David's motives and does not delude herself as to his feelings towards her, yet perhaps she still hopes that the long lost love would be rekindled.

Later, when David dances before the Ark as it is brought into "the city of David," Michal criticizes him for making a spectacle of him-self and behaving in an unregal manner (II Sam. 6:20). She is now identified as "Michal the daughter of Saul," which implies her isola-tion in the court of her father's successor. Some commentators see in Michal's words an expression of nostalgia for the older regime that was less populist and more regal. Yet we know that Michal was happy to betray her father and help David in any way that she could. Michal's words are those of a woman scorned, and they display the last stage in her career: from David's lover, she has turned into "Saul's daughter."

The Michal narrative ends with the statement that "Michal, the daughter of Saul had no children to the day of her death" (v. 23). This piece of information follows the angry exchange between Michal and David in which the former criticizes the king for not behaving regally and the latter crudely reminds her that God has taken the kingdom from her father and given it to him. The biblical narrator does not explain the connection between the two events, but the proximity between the last episode in which David and Michal are seen together and the fact that the woman had no children is mean-ingful. We can read the statement about Michal's barrenness as an ex-planation of what has transpired before; Michal's bitterness towards David is due to the fact that, though he forced her return from her second husband, David did not receive her as a wife but as a symbol of his political triumph. Thus her acid words mark the eruption of the pent-up anger that the humiliated Michal has long felt towards her neglectful husband. On the other hand, Michal's barrenness can be seen as a consequence of the last episode; after the hostile ex-change David withdraws his sexual favors from the woman he never really loved.

The four episodes in which Michal appears, while spread out and interspersed into the main narrative, which is about David, still form an independent literary unit. The first and last episodes echo and re-verse each other, thus giving the Michal story an envelope structure. Both when she makes her first appearance, and when she makes her final exit, Michal acts and speaks out, while in the middle episodes she is silent and is being acted upon. Yet the parallelism between the first and the last episode draws our attention to the woman's transfor-mation from a spirited and independent young woman, motivated by love and hope, to a bitter and neglected wife, shrunken in stature and depleted in spirit. In her first appearances, Michal is verbal and expressive about, and for the sake of, her love. In her last scene, she is also outspoken; yet her cutting sarcasm and acrimonious tirade reveal a tortured woman who no longer shares in her husband's triumphs and joys.

The David and Michal story seems to be an ironic reversal of a romantic tale, precisely because it starts with all the right ingredients. We have the dashing, brave soldier, beloved by men and women alike, and the king's daughter. Michal's looks are not mentioned, and this omission might be meaningful in understanding the nature of the relationship between David and her. The story consists of daring adventures and last-minute escapes, and yet the spirit of romance never materializes. It is partly due to the nature of biblical narrative, which stays away from both the heroic and the romantic. Yet in the David saga the Bible comes very close to creating a larger-than-life hero in the epic tradition with more than a dash of romance. Michal initially seems to be the right female counterpart of the romantic hero, yet her career ends in disillusionment and pain. If she presents herself in the role of the heroine of a romance of adventure, David denies her the opportunity to play this role in his life. We know that, while persecuted by Saul, David still managed to meet with Saul's son, Jonathan. It is very likely that Michal expected David to come back for her, and we know that she was daring enough to risk her life in an adventure that would unite her with her lover. But this did not happen. It seems that David's lack of love for Michal, and the latter's excessive, unconditional love for David, reiterated in the text, caused Michal's tragedy.

After Michal's barrenness is noted, she disappears from the biblical arena, traveling into her bleak future childless and loveless, alienated from her husband and his court. The cruelty of Michal's fate and David's part in contributing to the woman's tragedy were felt by the Midrash sages, who tried to mitigate the harshness of the woman's destiny. They interpreted the biblical verse that said that Michal had no children to the day that she died as implying that on the day she died she did have a child, in other words, that she bore a child and died during the delivery.[29] The Midrash prefers to overlook the link that the Bible suggests between the tense and unloving relationship of David and Michal and the latter's childlessness. David is thus exonerated of treating the woman ungratefully and heartlessly, and Michal is redeemed of her biblical role as the deserted and humiliated wife.

The attempts of the Midrash to soften the dreariness of Michal's life do not take away from her role as the sexual pawn of the two patriarchal figures in her life, her father and her husband. Saul uses his daughter's sexuality as a prize that he bestows on the person he favors, and that he withdraws when that person falls out of his good graces. Similarly, David punishes Michal's womanhood when he no longer cohabits with her, thus degrading her as a wife and denying her the only other feminine fulfillment known in ancient times, motherhood.

A romantic and idealized version of the Michal saga is offered in the poem "The Love of David and Michal" by Y. L. Gordon.[30] Gordon remolds the biblical text into a romantic story that glorifies the eternal bond between the two lovers, David and Michal. He explains the estrangement between the two as a painful sacrifice that David has to make in order to devote himself completely to the burdensome task of monarch and conquerer who puts his national mission ahead of his personal life. Gordon also sees in David's polygynous practice a necessary evil which does not imply betrayal of his beloved first wife, Michal, but rather, indicates the man's dedication to establishing a dynasty and securing a stable monarchy for his people when he dies.

It seems, however, that both the Midrash version and Gordon's fictionalized treatment of the Michal story, in their efforts to relieve the somberness of the ancient tale, further highlight the frustrating and even disastrous fate of a biblical woman who dared to deviate from the feminine mold by unabashedly making known her sexual desire for a man and then committing herself fully and unequivocally to the choice of her heart.

One of the most disturbing tales in Hebraic letters about man's use of female sexual vulnerability as a form of punishment, or as an attempt to put the independent woman in her "right" place, comes to us in an enigmatic legend about the charismatic Beruria.[31] Like her husband, the venerable scholar Rabbi Meir, Beruria was counted among the Tana'im, the rabbis who produced the Mishna. In her several appearances in Talmudic literature, Beruria's scholarship, intelligence, and right judgment are exhibited. She is a unique case in Talmudic literature in that she is regarded as the intellectual equal of her male contemporaries and as a respected rabbinic authority. The legend tells us that Beruria used to challenge and ridicule the rabbis' famous saying that "women are light-minded." She cited her own profound knowledge of the law as an example which refuted the rabbis' denigrating comment on women's intellectual capacities. To teach Beruria a lesson, her husband asked one of his students to seduce her. Beruria submitted to her husband's student but later, overcome by shame and guilt, she committed suicide.

While this tale's origins are shrouded in mystery, its message is clear: even a knowledgeable and extraordinary woman like Beruria was tyrannized by her feminine body. If Beruria's mind offered her the intellectual freedom to teach and challenge the male authorities, she was still a prisoner of her anatomy, following the dictates of her biological nature over which she had no control. But Rabbi Meir's position is extremely puzzling. In other encounters with his wife he seems to listen to her and show deference to her judgment. Nevertheless, the relationship between this unusual couple must have been often put to the test in a society where only men were expected to devote themselves to studying the Torah. Indeed, the classic story about a woman and learning, that of Rabbi Akiba's wife, puts on a pedestal the woman who gladly accepted poverty and destitution in order to allow her husband the freedom to study. The woman defied her father by marrying an ignorant shepherd, and later allowed her young husband to stay away for twenty-four years so that he could devote himself completely to his studies.[32] Against this cultural background, it appears that there must have been some kind of intellectual rivalry between Rabbi Meir and his wife that finally culminated in an outrageous scheme devised by the husband in order to put his hubristic wife in her place.

*   *

A number of modern works give testimony to a variety of tangled male emotions and premises regarding female sexuality, that result in the victimization of women. Yet often the heroine's femininity, whether exploited or protected, or rejected, becomes the focus of an amalgam of cultural myths as well as sociohistorical undercurrents. While the woman continues in her role as the literary other, in conformity with her secondary position in society, her sexual odyssey paradoxically serves as a potent symbol of changing mores and often portends social catastrophes.

In the short stories of I. D. Berkowitz (1885–1967), the woman protagonist enfolds in her sexual predicament the social and economic upheavals of a tumultuous era in Jewish life. Berkowitz depicts the decline of the Jewish family and erosion of patriarchal power in the Russian Jewish communities that resided in the small villages or the countryside, at the turn of the twentieth century. Some of his stories, especially those set in the country, reverberate with Chekovian echoes of the disintegration of traditional social values, the boredom and degeneracy of country life, and the false allure of the city and modern culture.[33]

In the story "Mariashka,"[34] which is set in the countryside, the heroine who gives her name to the story is a young girl who serves as a maid in a rich household where the boorish and coarse head of the family treats his wife with derision and contempt. Mariashka does not speak much but she daydreams quite a bit, and is immersed in the beauty and mystery of her awakening womanhood and in romantic dreams of love and sexual fulfillment. Mariashka functions as the magnetic center that attracts various male reactions, which, although different in some ways, share in common the relinquishing of patriarchal responsibility and its replacement with an exploitative, dehumanizing treatment of the young girl.

The men who surround Mariashka seem to encompass almost the whole spectrum of Jewish society at the time. The father of the family, Mariashka's employer, sees both in his maid and in his own wife stupid, undeserving, less than human creatures. When he calls his wife *behema* or 'animal', he includes Mariashka and that part of the female race that is there to serve his physical needs. He is an uncouth man, contemptuous of both traditional piety and learning and modern culture and education. He therefore treats with derision Mariashka's God-fearing and strictly observant father, as well as his children's tutor, a student whom he hired to give his sons a secular education.

Another patriarchal figure is Mariashka's own father, who, with her mother, comes to visit his daughter at the home of her employers. The father is a pitiful creature, sickly and destitute, who seems constantly to apologize for the space that he occupies in this world. In his total lack of self-esteem and his fawning, apologetic posture in the world, Mariashka's father serves as a negative force in his daughter's life, at a stage where she gropes for identity and seeks personal happiness. Both paternal figures represent the corruption of the patriarchal institution. One uses his wealth and power as a means of abusing and maltreating the women who may need his support and help. The other transmits to his daughter a sense of worthlessness and insignificance. None of these two older men is able to direct, protect, or sustain the bewildered adolescent girl.

The eldest son of Mariashka's employer, as coarse and unfeeling as his father, harasses the girl sexually and taunts her as she tries to fend him off. This is another form of encounter with the male world that Mariashka experiences, in which the young girl is regarded as a sex object to be enjoyed momentarily and then discarded. The bestial nature of the young man's treatment of Mariashka is evident in the fact that he does not try to court the girl or seduce her with compliments and promises; he simply jumps at her in the barn at night like an animal, and leaves the young girl upset and mortified.

The most unscrupulous conduct is exhibited by the man of whom Mariashka expects the most, the attractive and educated young tutor, who represents for the girl the realization of her romantic dreams. The idealistic and enlightened young man impresses the sensitive Mariashka with his lectures about the value of education, the nobility of menial labor, and the equality of man. This man, too, however, aims only at bedding the gullible young girl, and while he speaks words of love to her when they are alone at night, he hardly acknowledges her during the day when other people are around. The tutor, Levinson, represents the greatest form of male betrayal because he has succeeded in gaining the girl's trust and admiration. In a moment of truth, Levinson reproaches himself for raising the girl's expectations and instilling in her ideals that she will never be able to realize. In this interior monologue Levinson wonders about the polarity between the pretty and sensitive Mariashka and her worn and miserable father. Levinson thus provides for the reader, in a moment of truth, an objective assessment of Mariashka's nature as a sensitive, bright woman, full of potential that circumstances will never allow her to fulfill.

Mariashka's mother provides the reader with a vision into the future, since she represents a more mature, worn-out, and haggard version of the young and blooming Mariashka. The tall and still imposing mother, whose weary face reveals vestiges of beauty and spirit, seems resigned to her fate as the wife of a powerless, downtrodden, and cowardly man. If her husband has disappointed her, she wishes for Mariashka a different kind of marriage and destiny. And yet the mother is so weighted down by her distressed circumstances that she is unable to recognize Mariashka's needs for romance and love. Confined within the narrow boundaries of her existence, the mother describes a young man, who works "like a horse" and easily carries "heavy loads of flour," whom she would like Mariashka to meet. This young man, homely looking but very strong and a good provider, is the opposite of Mariashka's frail and emasculated father. The mother's limited and low expectations serve as a reminder for Mariashka of her true situation in the world. The scene in which the talkative mother delivers a long sermon that is meant to bring her daughter to her senses, and the silent Mariashka listens with tears in her eyes, brings home to the young girl the harsh reality of her own existence, and the folly of her dreams. At the end of the story the young girl is seen gazing at the river, contemplating suicide.

In "Mariashka" patriarchy is seen as both corrupt, in its boorish denigration of women, and impotent, in its inability to protect the woman. In Berkowitz's story "Neched" ("Grandchild"), patriarchy no longer exists, yet it has still left behind its irrational rigidity and constrictive dogma.[35] In this story, the young girl Ḥaya (the name also means 'animal', in Hebrew), who works as a maid in a wealthy household, unexpectedly returns one evening to her widowed mother's dilapidated home, to give birth to an illegitimate child. The mother first thinks that Ḥaya is merely sick, and she wonders what ails her "virginal," "pure," and "innocent" daughter. Yet at the moment that she realizes the truth, the mother turns viciously against the young woman, now in the grips of labor pains, and calls her "promiscuous" and a "murderess." Berkowitz does not elaborate on the circumstances preceding Ḥaya's arrival at her mother's poverty-stricken home, yet it is clear that the girl has been a source of material support to the family, providing them with food and money. The mother's surprise at her daughter's condition thus seems unwarranted, and her righteous disappointment with her hypocritical. As an older and more experienced person, the mother should have asked about the origins of her daughter's relative prosperity before the disaster occurred.

For Mendel, Ḥaya's brother who is studying to be a scribe, the young woman's situation is a source of agony and terrible shame. He, too, condemns the girl, calls her a prostitute and blames her for defiling the family's name, tainting their dead father's memory, and violating the sacred principles of their religion. The young Mendel stands for patriarchal piety and its heartless treatment of the exploited daughter. Behind him hovers the figure of their dead father whose sanctity the daughter has violated. Yet the father's memory is twofold, appearing as powerful and ineffectual at the same time. Mendel evokes his father as a pious and learned man, respected by his fellow Jews and known for his fine voice as he read the Torah in the synagogue. On the other hand, Mendel also remembers how the same father, frail and humble, stubbornly and foolishly argued with their mother over two rubles that he wanted for himself and that she needed to pay their debt at the grocery store.

Ḥaya is seen by her family as violating the patriarchal-religious values, exemplified in her brother and her father. At the same time, patriarchy and matriarchy both have failed the girl by ignoring her predicament, exploiting her, and then condemning her in an hour of need. Unlike Mariashka, Ḥaya is not an individual but a type; Berkowitz has created here a stereotypical situation, using the sexually exploited girl as a didactic vehicle to expose the ignorance and inhumanity of the pious community. Ḥaya's name, 'animal', is significant, as is the fact that she "lows like a cow." She has been reduced to the state of nature both by the circumstances of her family and by her vulnerable and, in this case, treacherous femininity.

The story *"Ha-Michtav"* ("The Letter")[36] presents a similar situation in a tragicomic manner, treating the emasculated yet censorious father with humor. The male protagonist asks a young boy to help him write a letter to his daughter in America. He wishes to tell his married daughter about the trouble at home: her unmarried sister has just had a baby. At the same time he cannot bring himself to utter the shameful news, and he is also concerned that the young boy will understand his secret. It seems that Berkowitz has little sympathy for the paternal figure whose ability to protect his daughter has eroded, yet whose principles remain as strict as ever. Since the young female victim is not seen in the foreground, Berkowitz can allow himself to use the comic mode in his description of the father's verbal manipulations and euphemistic tactics as he unsuccessfully attempts to hide the truth from the curious young stranger.

The story changes gears at the end and turns pathetic when the enraged father can no longer control himself; he drags his sleeping daughter out of her bed, puts the baby in her arms and throws her out of the house. As in the other stories on the same subject, the young girl who has been victimized by poverty, ignorance, and an unscrupulous man is not treated with pity, either by her victimizer, or by her father, who is concerned with his own sense of shame and humiliation.

The male's conception of female sexuality as a mystery to be dreaded and rejected, an attitude that results in another form of feminine suffering, is at the center of Agnon's story "The Tale of the Scribe."[37] Its male protagonist, Raphael the scribe, is seen at one point as studying the Kabbalist Book of Splendor, the Zohar. The scribe might be studying the mystical correspondences between the heavenly male and female and their earthly counterparts. This Kabbalistic idea suggests that the sexual union of man and woman imitates and reflects the sexual relationship within the deity, and is therefore sacred. Yet it seems that the pious scribe must have been reading another Kabbalistic passage, one in which human sexuality is seen to conflict with man's spiritual life. Perhaps he was reading those lines which tell us that Moses had sexual relations with the Shekinah and therefore withdrew from his earthly wife.

In the character of Raphael the scribe Agnon offers a study in self-denial, obsessive preoccupation with the cleanliness of the body, and physical self-abnegation that cripple the saintly man and prevent him from leading a normal life with his spouse. The scribe's dedication to the sanctity and purity of both his mind and body, and, consequently, his inability to consummate his marriage are rooted in mental disorder as well as in a distorted interpretation of the Judaic idea of holiness. While Raphael the scribe does not make a decision to abstain from his beloved wife Miriam, in reality, it seems that the couple is so overwhelmed by the husband's sense of purity in both the personal and cosmic sense, that they are never able to express their desire for each other in physical terms. The scribe's occupation of copying Torah scrolls, phylacteries, and mezuzot demands his subjection to a regimen of ritual purification which he follows religiously and excessively. The scribe moves within the narrow periphery that consists of his home, the house of prayer, and the bathhouse. He is so immersed in his holy work that he rarely notices his virtuous wife who shyly and unsuccessfully tries to draw his attention to herself.

The embroidery that covers the eastern wall in the scribe's home and that was made by his wife in her youth epitomizes the two poles between which Miriam shuttles. It depicts a garden full of fruit trees, which represents Miriam's earthy nature and her yearnings to be fruitful herself. But it also contains the picture of two lions holding an inscription of the verse from the Psalms: "The earth is the Lord's and the fullness thereof," as well as the words "I have set the Lord always before me" in each corner of the embroidery; this exemplifies the spirit of sanctity and the fear of God that prevails in Miriam's household.

Miriam is seen as a healthy woman who possesses sexual desires, a feminine impulse to be attractive, and maternal feelings. She is characterized by the paraphernalia that she surrounds herself with: a mirror and an amulet that chases evil spirits at the time of birth. Yet when she makes herself up in front of the mirror, and dresses like a bride to please her husband, the mirror reflects the embroidery with its forbidding inscription; Miriam and her husband turn away from each other and retire separately to their respective corners.

From a retrospective scene that Raphael the scribe evokes after his wife's death, we understand that the relationship between Miriam and her husband was initiated by the young Miriam and was rooted in Miriam's passionate nature. When the young Raphael was dancing with the Torah scroll in his arms on the Festival of Rejoicing in the Torah, the girl Miriam suddenly leaped forward, "sank her red lips into the white mantle of the Torah scroll in Raphael's arm, and kept on kissing the scroll and caressing it with her hands. Just then the flag fell out of her hand, and the burning candle dropped on Raphael's clothing" (23, 24). The images of fire and flame, the redness of Miriam's lips, and her ecstatic kisses indicate Miriam's craving for physical contact, and her ardent emotions. They also suggest that Miriam's bashful and restrained conduct in her husband's house meant a suppression of her warm and passionate nature.

Agnon does not try to delve into his heroine's heart and depict the collision of two equally demanding forces, one rooted in her own nature, and the other instilled in her by her admired husband. Instead, Agnon prefers to chart the mental course taken by Raphael the scribe after his wife's untimely death. But the reader cannot but wonder about Miriam's inner feelings as she begins to see her rejected femininity as part of the defiled and unclean universe from which her saintly husband strives to free himself. Miriam's sudden death may be a form of rebellion against the oppressive purity and sterile existence imposed on her by her righteous husband. Ironically, after Miriam's death the house is no longer clean; "a mouse plays with a discarded quill, and the cat lies dejected on the abandoned oven" (19). Raphael now learns that his wife was a source of purity, not a threat to it.

Before her sudden, untimely death, Miriam asks her husband to write a Torah scroll for the two of them, as a way to ensure a form of posterity for themselves, since they are childless. After his wife's death, the scribe continues in this holy task, and before its completion, he goes to immerse himself in the river since the bathhouse is closed. Raphael catches a bad cold, and when he returns home he becomes delirious.

The ending of the story fuses symbolically the Torah cover, Miriam's wedding gown, and the shroud with which the scribe will soon be covered. As the scribe is now dancing ecstatically with the Torah, he begins to hallucinate and sees his wife dancing opposite him, dressed in her wedding gown. The dance is a ritual in honor of the Torah, as well as in honor of the scribe's earthly wife. It forcefully blends the various elements in the scribe's existence: his beloved Torah, his marriage, and his approaching death. When he drops in exhaustion, Raphael is seen with his wife's wedding dress "spread out over him and over his scroll" (25). Only now is he finally able to reconcile his dedication to otherworldly ideals, epitomized in the sacred Torah, with his this-worldly being, represented by his wife. In a moment of clarity and illumination that the scribe experiences before his death, his wife's wedding gown, symbol of love and its consummation, finally rises in importance and becomes equal to the Torah. The earthly woman and her physical being are ultimately vindicated, and the scribe's rejection of his spouse and her sexuality as antithetical to purity and cleanliness is seen as wrong and destructive.

In some of his stories written in the realistic vein, Agnon delineates the decline of the Jewish family at a historical juncture where the external forces of secularism, modernity, and religious skepticism were finally able to penetrate Jewish reality and assert their supremacy over the old values of piety and devoutness. "The Tale of the Scribe," though imbued with the fantastic and the macabre, offers another aspect of the decline of the family. The inner forces of old-fashioned Orthodoxy have deteriorated into a fanatic religiosity that was degenerative and self-destructive; thus the family began to crumble from within. While Agnon does not focus on the victimization of the woman within this cultural framework, he does present the woman as a potentially healing force in her wholesome physicality and this-worldly existence. Miriam's death marks the end of the world of traditional piety in which both men and women found themselves caught in a tangled web of constrictive values and irreconcilable forces.

For Agnon, the rejected and unfulfilled sexuality of the Jewish woman signifies the degeneracy of the old world, and thus becomes a cultural symbol. In David Fogel's novella "Facing the Sea" [38] (1932), the heroine's sexual surrender becomes a moment of historical significance. It is meant to prefigure the death of Western civilization and its rational heritage, and the rise of barbaric, untamed, and primitive forces.

Fogel's novella recalls Thomas Mann's *Death in Venice* with its suggestive visions of weariness and spiritual boredom, of the disintegration of reality, and the decay of civilization. The story itself is constructed as a series of imagistic scenes of overripe fruit about to rot, uncontrollable passions, and sexual decadence. It is imbued with a cosmopolitan flavor, and at its center are Barth and Gina, two alienated, uprooted Jews of German-Austrian origins whose identity is European rather than exclusively Jewish.

The story takes place at a resort in the French Riviera where the multilingual, multinational crowd that is gathered to enjoy the summer season encompasses the variety of European cultures and social classes. The oppressive heat and the too-bright sun, depicted as "sick," suggest not only the beginning of the season's end, but also the coming to a close of Enlightenment and civilization. In spite of the spirit of gaiety and leisure, macabre images of death, disease, and a sense of an ending dominate the scene. The young girl Marcelle, one of the vacationers, spits blood, Barth comes down with a mysterious fever, and the man called "the translator" has a false right hand. The ocean that heaves ceaselessly with "muffled breath" (242), the odor of fish and brine, and the sweltering weather affect people with languor, apathy, and lack of will. The cluster of images that impart the sense of inertness and decay suggest a glorious civilization that has already reached its climax of beauty and glamor and is about to decompose.

Barth and Gina seem to be a breed apart from the rest of the crowd. They are handsome and tall, aristocratic-looking, and very genteel. Their polar opposites, and also literary doubles, are Marcelle and Cici. While Barth and Gina are described as overcivilized, languid, and lacking in strong passions or wills, Marcelle and Cici are animalistic in their hunger for life and their search for physical, sensual gratification. Barth and Gina love each other in a desperate manner, as if holding on to something that will soon be violently taken away from them. Both experience a sudden, unexpected, and unwanted moment of passion with partners who are their social and cultural inferiors. Both feel that their sexual ecstasy means a betrayal of their refinement and culture and capitulation to their beastly nature. When Barth goes to bed with Marcelle the latter sinks her teeth into his neck, his shoulders and chest, like a wild animal; and Gina remembers her sexual experience with Cici as a "beastly" event.

Yet is is Gina's sexual episode with the Italian Cici, in a scene in which the boundaries between rape and volitional surrender are purposely blurred, that takes on a symbolical significance of universal magnitude. Cici is described as sturdy and virile, "squat and square," with muscular arms, round and thick like iron bars. Gina resembles a ripe, velvety fruit which is about to burst or to rot. The antithesis between the patrician Gina, daughter of an Austrian professor, and the plebeian Cici, an Italian construction worker of dubious background and past, is reminiscent of that between Blanche and Stanley in Tennessee Williams' *A Streetcar Named Desire*. But Gina is a healthier and saner early version of the neurotic Blanche, and Cici, as the European precursor of the crude Stanley, is less secure and more admiring of the woman than his later American incarnation. Nevertheless, Cici the laborer, who pursues Gina ardently and insistently, represents the emerging European middle-class which is about to replace the frail, sensitive aristocracy, just as Stanley stands for the "new blood" that would dispossess the old, decadent Southern gentility.

Another literary counterpart of the Gina-Cici pair is Strindberg's aristocratic Miss Julie, who is weak and decadent, and her father's plebeian valet, the robust and virile Jean. In Miss Julie's surrender to the coarse and vulgar Jean, and in her eventual suicide, something refined and noble is seen to be annihilated by a primitive, yet vital and healthy force. Strindberg's attitude to the social climber Jean was not entirely negative. He saw in him the Darwinian "fittest" who was bound to survive, and in the destruction of Miss Julie he saw the inevitable, and not necessarily negative, evolutionary march of history.

In contrast to Strindberg's "naturalist" play, Fogel's literary style, which is reminiscent of the Symbolist technique that characterizes his poetry, produces a reality dotted with images and signals that transcend the narrowly realistic realm. For Fogel, Gina's surrender to Cici is more than a social comment on the supremacy of the robust survivor over the decadent, and inevitably destructible, older guard, since the polarity between the two is not only socioeconomic. The animallike Cici serves as a catalyst forcing Gina into an encounter with the subterranean, irrational nature that she tries to suppress. Gina facing the sea is Europe on the brink of a major catastrophe in which hysterical, barbaric, and primeval forces will surface and take control, overpowering and erasing the long tradition of rational humanism. In this context Cici as a social type is irrelevant; his role is that of the transmitter of irrationality. It is the duality between Gina's refined veneer, which is nevertheless too weak and fragile, and her seething, uncontrollable, and unhealthy passions that is the focus of the novella. Unlike Strindberg, Fogel mourns his heroine's sexual lapse, and in her lack of vigor, coupled with her surrender to the brutish and uncivilized, he sees an ominous sign for European civilization as a whole. Fogel, who disappeared in a Nazi concentration camp, sounds almost prophetic in his employment of Gina's moment of sexual weakness as a metaphorical foreboding of the decline of the West.

The subjugation and humiliation of the woman through sex thus becomes a literary motif that ties together the various works studied in this section, which belong to different historical phases of Hebrew letters. At the same time, we have seen an underlying idea that has also traveled through the ages: feminine sexuality, belittled, maligned, and relegated to the lower stratum of the human experience, actually emerges as a potent cultural sign that illuminates social mores and premises, mirrors the male power play and struggle for domination, interprets man's psychological handicaps that are symptomatic of a whole era, and foreshadows, or even allegorizes, the decline of the West.

For Jacob and his sons, the daughter's abused body meant the desecration of the whole tribe. For Saul, the daughter's femininity is a bait that he throws in his enemy's direction, and the prize that he will bestow on the man that he favors. For Agnon's doctor, positioned on the opposite end of the cultural and historical spectrum, the wife's tainted past is no less traumatic than is Dinah's rape to her father and brothers. If it is not the doctor's religious sensitivity that is threatened, it is his shaky psychic strength that is put to the test. For Agnon's protagonist, who originates in the poverty and destitution of the East European shtetl, the position of a physician in a Viennese hospital is the peak of his social ascent. The union with a sexually "damaged" woman is regarded by him as regression on the human and social ladder. The paranoia created in the doctor by the knowledge of his wife's earlier sexual experience encapsulates the insecurity of the emerging European lower classes in their misguided search for respectability; thus the "enlightened" doctor is seen as an inhabitant of a much darker age. For Fogel, the deterioration of his heroine's vibrant sexuality into the nether land of the savage and the chaotic signals the death of a refined, sensitive era, and the imminent arrival of a cataclysmic, nightmarish event. In sum, while the feminine figures that we have studied are seen as tyrannized by their biological existence, their sexuality is used by the male narrators as a forceful image that captures social and historical processes.

The paradoxical status of female sexuality as filtered through the male vision into literature finds its counterpoint in the woman's use of her sexual weakness and strength as a weapon to overcome her powerlessness. Our next step is to examine the variety of tactics adopted by women in their struggle to hold their own in a male-centered universe.

Notes

1 Sifre Numbers, Pinehas.

2 Ibid.

3 In *The Collected Poems of Y. L. Gordon* (Vilna: Raam, 1898), 43–51.

4 On the law of *yibbum* and its historical evolution, see Rachel Biale, *Women and Jewish Law: An Exploration of Women's Issues in Halakhic Sources* (New York: Schocken, 1984), 114–20.

5 Gordon, *The Collected Poems*, 50–58.

6 Ibid., 5–43.

7 In Dvorah Baron, *The Thorny Path*, translated by Joseph Shachter (Jerusalem: Israel University Press, 1969), 1–37.

8 Ibid., 208–52.

9 "Kritut" ("Excision"), in *Parashiot*, Dvorah Baron's collected stories in Hebrew (Jerusalem: Mosad Bialik, 1951).

10 Gittin 90b.

11 Genesis Rabbah 17, 7.

12 Sanhedrin 22a.

13 Tanhuma, Wayishlah, 36.

14 The Zohar 1, 22a.

15 The Zohar 1, 20a.

16 See Martin Buber, *Tales of the Hasidim: The Later Masters* (New York: Schocken, 1948), 127.

[17] Ibid., 293.

[18] Yehudah Burla, *'Ishto haSenu'ah* (Tel Aviv: Massada, 1920).

[19] The Wisdom of Sirach, or, Ben Sira, 36:21.

[20] Ibid., 42:9,10.

[21] See Nahum M. Sarna, "The Ravishing of Dinah: A Commentary on Genesis, Chapter 34," in A. Shapiro and B. Cohen, eds., *Studies in Jewish Education* (New York: Ktav, 1984), 143–56.

[22] On the biblical narrator's balancing tactics, as he tries to maintain an evenhanded, nonjudgmental attitude to the two fierce brothers, Simon and Levi, see Meir Sternberg, "A Delicate Balance in the Rape of Dinah," in Hebrew, *Ha-Sifrut* 4, no. 2 (1973): 193–231.

[23] Genesis Rabbah 80,1.

[24] Saul Tchernichovsky, *The Collected Poems,* in Hebrew, (Jerusalem: Schocken, 1950), 571–76.

[25] In *Twenty-One Stories,* 135–61.

[26] For the history of the story and a comparison of its different versions, see Hillel Barzel, *Agnon's Love Stories,* in Hebrew, 13–51.

[27] The Hebrew is ambiguous. In the English translation by Robert Alter, with which I agree, the clerk is saying that "she [Dinah] raped me." Barzel reads the clerk's words differently. In Barzel's reading the clerk says that "you [the doctor], raped me."

[28] In *The Art of Biblical Narrative,* op. cit., 118.

[29] Genesis Rabbah 82.

[30] In *The Collected Poems,* in Hebrew (Peterburg, 1884), 15–99.

[31] This legend about Beruria is cited by the medieval commentator Rashi in his discussion of Abodah Zarah 18b where the Talmud enigmatically tells us that Rabbi Meir left for Babylon because of "that incident with Beruria."

[32] The stories about Rabbi Akiba and his wife are told in Ketubot 62b.

[33] For an introduction to Berkowitz's works and a translation of some of his stories, see Avraham Holtz, *I. D. Berkowitz: Voice of the Uprooted* (Ithaca, N.Y.: Cornell University Press, 1973).

[34] In *The Collected Works of I. D. Berkowitz,* in Hebrew (Tel Aviv: Devir, 1959), 64–72.

[35] Ibid., 59–62.

[36] Ibid., pp. 132–34.

[37] Trans. Isaac Franck, in *Twenty-One Stories,* 7–25.

[38] Trans. Daniel Silverstone, in *Eight Great Hebrew Short Novels,* ed. Alan Lelchuk and Gershon Shaked, op. cit., 219–68.

Female Strategy

And when Boaz had eaten and drunk, and his heart was merry, he went to lie down at the end of the heap of corn; and she came softly, and uncovered his feet, and laid herself down. And it came to pass at midnight, that the man was startled, and turned over; and behold, a woman lay at his feet . . . And he said, Who art thou? . . . And she answered, I am Ruth thy handmaid; spread therefore thy skirt over thy handmaid; for thou art a near kinsman.
  Ruth 3:7–9

That night I was a clockwork doll
And I turned to the right and to the left in all directions,
  From Dalia Ravikovitch, "Clockwork Doll," 1959

*W*omen have reacted to oppression in various ways, ranging from complete acceptance of patriarchal values and resignation to a subordinate place in society, to rebellion that is sometimes external but more often is internalized and results in madness and the fragmentation of the self. The instances of outright feminine challenge to male authority, or insistent questioning, albeit respectful, of some of the patriarchal laws are rather few. The ancient documents reveal a universal feminine conduct that is timid, mild, and unassuming; after all, very few women are actually heard in the Bible and Midrash. Yet a woman's reticence is not always acceptance; it may mean that the woman harbors feelings of hostility and anger that may erupt and find expression in various forms of behavior.

In the literature produced by men, reflecting the male writers' conception of the world, which constitutes the bulk of the works discussed here, one has to see in every example of feminine conduct a form of feminine response. Even a passive, acquiescent stance, or a secondary, marginal role adopted by a feminine figure, which is not consciously meant by its creator to serve as an example of feminine reaction to a constricted and oppressive existence, is in itself an indication of a strategy the woman is using in an attempt to survive in a male-dominated culture. In other words, the male narrator may not even be aware that the muted presence of his female characters, which he has faithfully copied from life, may enfold in itself a statement made by women in his society, or a tactic employed by them and carried into fiction by the unsuspicious recorder of life. Thus the passive role and the silence adopted by most unnamed female characters in the Bible and Midrash should be seen both as the males' attempts to suppress the woman's voice, and as the woman's own strategy of survival in a potentially crushing reality.

The majority of women in the ancient documents remain anonymous; even those who are named, like Dinah, are not always given an opportunity to express their voice. Yet those few female characters who step forward and into the limelight in the biblical texts are seen as tough, active, and vocal. Some of them use subtle "feminine" wiles, some blatant lies, and others resort to a variety of underhanded means to get what they want. In fact, most of the admirable biblical women, the matriarchs among them, are portrayed as conniving and manipulative, with a proclivity for deception and a quickwitted adjustment to difficult situations. Sarah conspires to get rid of her husband's mistress, Hagar, and her son; Rebecca manipulates her son into fooling his father; Rachel lies to her father about the terafim that she stole from him; and Leah seems to be a willing accomplice in the tricking of Jacob.

That women were very often seen as using underhanded, dishonest means to accomplish their wishes may not necessarily reflect the male writers' slanted view of reality or their biased conception of the female nature. It may be a true representation of realities and times when an underprivileged group had to resort to devious tactics to offset the built-in injustice in its legal and social circumstances. At the same time, treachery, falseness, or even just a circuitous manner of dealing with problems should not be seen as congenital, inherent in the feminine nature, but rather as an acquired evil, a device used by women who were very often barred from decision making, and whose opinion was rarely solicited, even in cases directly involving their own lives and fates.

Tricksters and Wise Women

The masses of anonymous women in the ancient documents come across not only as reticent and nonverbal; their seeming lack of ability to articulate and express themselves and, especially, the apparent poverty of their creative imagination are borne out by the mere fact that they did not share in the labor of creating the Judaic literary legacy. In their roles as manipulators and hoaxers, however, women are seen as great creators of fiction, as spinners of tales and producers of imagined realities. Perhaps the first case of a woman setting up a theatrical mask scene, intended to benefit her son through a case of mistaken identities, is the matriarch Rebecca.

We know Rebecca as a determined woman who takes part in her own marriage negotiations; as a young girl she "hastens" and "runs" and is seen as subtly but actively prompting Eliezer, Abraham's messenger, to make the marriage offer to her, on behalf of his master. But when we meet her as wife and mother, she is seen, like Sarah before her, in what becomes a prototypical feminine pose: overhearing the men talk, and then pulling the strings from behind the scenes. The aging and blind Isaac tells his son Esau to prepare a feast for his father, after which the son will be blessed by the patriarch. Rebecca the mother, apparently younger and more robust than her husband, probably feels that Isaac has lost his powers of discrimination together with his sight. She will do everything in her power to put her favorite son, Jacob, in his brother's place, so that the younger son will get the patriarch's blessings. She devises an elaborate scheme that calls for her not only to cook a lavish meal but also to disguise her "plain" and "tent-dwelling" son in such a way that his father will mistake him for Esau, the "cunning hunter," and the "man of the field" (Gen. 27).

In a frenzy of energetic activity, Rebecca cooks a meal, takes the best clothes of her older son and puts them on her youngest son; she then puts goats' skins on Jacob's smooth hands and neck, gives him the "savory food and the bread" which she prepared, and sends the apparently reluctant young man to his father. Rebecca thus helps in adding a link to the twisted, tortuous, and complicated history of her son Jacob, who from now on will either be outsmarted by others, or will have to devise strategies to outwit his enemies and, in a sense, his own fate. The biblical narrator neither condones nor condemns Rebecca's and Jacob's actions. He does make it clear, however, that while Rebecca was resourceful and inventive in her ability to create a make-believe situation and fool her blind husband, she was far from instrumental in the selection of Jacob as the successor of the Abrahamic mission. As Nehama Leibowitz shows in her analysis of this tale, Isaac understood the difference between his sons, and he therefore prepared a separate blessing for each of them, in accordance with their respective personalities and destinies.[1] Thus when Isaac unwittingly bestows on Jacob the blessing he designed for Esau, he promises his son material things such as abundance, fatness, and dominion; but he does not mention the Abrahamic mission, the blessing of seed and the promise of the land. Therefore, when the ruse is discovered, Isaac not only has to bless his son Esau, but he sees fit to bless his son Jacob again, this time giving him the promise of the land and charging him with upholding the Abrahamic mission (Gen. 28: 34). It turns out that though Isaac's sight is gone, his mental abilities are intact, and he knows very well which of his sons should become the third patriarch.

Subtly and indirectly, then, the biblical narrator lets us know that Rebecca's elaborate scheme was completely unnecessary, and that her energy and talents were wasted on a ruse that only complicated her and her son's lives. Rebecca is punished for interfering in what was conceived of as the patriarch's domain and his prerogative, that is, mapping out the future of his sons, for she now has to send her beloved son abroad, away from his brother's vengeful hand. It also becomes clear that though Isaac loved his wife very much, he did not share with her his opinion of his sons and his plans for them; ignorant of Isaac's state of mind, and not trusting his judgment, Rebecca decides to take matters into her own hands. Thus Rebecca the matriarch emerges as a woman discontent with her derivative status, who is confident of her wisdom and adamant about asserting her influence, and whose sense of powerlessness leads her to using wiles and trickery that, ironically, lead only to disaster. At the same time, Rebecca's unused talents and energies are unraveled before the reader, who is forced to draw conclusions about all those feminine abilities and gifts that were laid to waste in ancient times.

Another woman who takes part in a duplicitous scheme that again involves imposture and impersonation is Leah, who marries Jacob by pretending to be Rachel, her sister. Unlike in the previous case, the trick is not initiated by the woman but rather by her father, the devious Laban. But it is evident that Leah is a willing accomplice; she must know the art of dissembling if she is able to convince the lovesick Jacob, throughout the entire ceremony and wedding night, that she is indeed his beloved Rachel. As we know, the deception of Isaac and the deception of Jacob are causally connected and mirror each other; Jacob's deception at the hand of Leah constitutes "poetic justice" in correlation to the earlier episode; it stands as punishment to Jacob: from the deceiver he turns into the deceived, and the punishment fits the crime.[2]

Leah's presence, however, remains nonvocal; while the biblical narrator explains what led Rebecca to devise the scheme—her disaffection with Esau's Canaanite wives and Isaac's blindness—he does not elaborate on Leah's motives for forcing herself on an unwilling and unloving groom. The Midrash tells us that Leah was afraid that, as the older daughter, she will have to marry her older cousin, Esau. The Midrash also dramatizes the wedding night and describes how Jacob did not take the hints of the local people that he was being duped. It also enlarges Leah's part in the trick by having her answer to the name "Rachel" several times during the wedding night.[3] Yet the biblical text itself, through its spare, lean prose, allows the reader to fill in the missing gaps. Let us look at Leah's predicament from the woman's point of view. Here is the firstborn daughter in a family headed by an authoritarian paterfamilias. As a woman, she is powerless and lacks any control over her own life and destiny. At the same time, she has some rights that are protected and enforced by her society, one of which is the assurance that she will be the first one of her father's daughters to be married. Jacob's appearance in her life naturally raises hopes that are soon crushed when, like everyone else, she learns that "Jacob loved Rachel." It is apparently common knowledge that Jacob's ways are unorthodox and that he believes that the biological firstborn is not necessarily the one who should enjoy extra privileges; Jacob is also known to regard the status of the firstborn as transferable (he "bought" his own from his older brother). Both Laban and Leah are, therefore, prepared to set Jacob straight. When Laban tells Jacob, after the deception is discovered, that "it must not be so done in our country, to give the younger before the firstborn," he speaks also for his daughter Leah. In other words, Leah was fully within her rights when she tricked Jacob; the latter should have realized that the first wedding to be held in Laban's house would be that of the oldest daughter, Leah.

Both Rebecca and Leah are seen as entering into a complicated scheme that involves pretense, make-believe, and playacting. Leah, like Rebecca, is eventually punished; for, no matter how just she was in insisting on her birthright, she will never be loved by her reluctant husband, and will always suffer rejection and humiliation. In both cases the powerless woman creates an illusory world as a way of attempting to change reality and mold it to her own liking. Rebecca's action constitutes defiance of patriarchal authority and confidence that the woman knows better. In Leah's case, however, the rebellion is not against the status quo but, rather, against the unorthodox ideas of freedom of choice in matters of the heart, introduced by the newcomer Jacob, that seem to threaten the daughter in the patriarchal structure and deprive her of those few rights that she enjoys within her constrained existence. Defiance of male authority, exhibited by Rebecca, and enforcement of the patriarchal tenets, exhibited by Leah—as different and polarized as these two attitudes seem to be—both stem from the women's innate feeling of powerlessness coupled with a strong will and faith in their ability to defeat the man, if only through duplicity and dishonesty.

But women manipulate events and create new realities not only through subversive means. The story of Deborah the Judge (Judg. 4–5) manifests how a charismatic woman is instrumental in boosting the morale of her people, and in urging the discouraged chief of staff to round up his army and go out to war, thus averting the military and political disaster that was threatening the Israelites. In fact, the tale that centers around the war between the Israelites and the Canaanites in Deborah's time is significant in that, though apparently a "male" story that describes a battle and a military victory, it is actually a "female" story. It starts with Deborah the Judge serving as military advisor to the head of the Israelite army, climaxes in the suspenseful scene where another woman, Jael, kills the formidable enemy, Sisera, and ends with Deborah envisioning the Canaanite mother of Sisera, surrounded by her "wise women," anxiously awaiting the arrival of her victorious son from the battlefield. The three women display three distinctly different feminine tactics that become prototypical feminine responses to a male-dominated environment and reappear in later literature.

Deborah is first introduced to the reader as "a prophetess" and "the wife of Lappidot"; thus, if the first title implies acceptance of woman as spiritual leader and an authority figure, the second immediately reinforces patriarchy: a married woman is identified through her husband. However, some of the Midrash sages read the phrase *'eshet lappidot* as 'woman of fire,' analogous to *'eshet ḥayil,* 'woman of valor' in Proverbs—a comment on the woman's mettle rather than on her subordinate status.[4] Deborah is further described not only as prophetess, a spiritual leader, but as judge, a social and legal authority. But it is with the power of her language that she initiates events and makes things happen. The people of Israel have been oppressed at the hands of Sisera for twenty years, yet only Deborah has the courage and stamina to suggest military action. She summons Baraq and commands him, in God's name, to recruit ten thousand people and challenge Sisera, pronouncing to him the divine promise that Sisera will be delivered to his hands. Baraq stipulates that she come with him, to which Deborah retorts with "I will surely go with thee; however, thou shalt scarcely attain honor on the journey that thou goest, for the Lord will yield Sisera into the hands of a woman" (Judg. 4:9).

Deborah's answer may imply acquiescence to the patriarchal tenets of male supremacy and an attempt on the woman's part to protect the man's position, even if it means minimizing her real power. She warns Baraq that if she comes with him, his eventual victory will be attributed to her, rather than to him. If this reading is correct, then Deborah, who up until now did not seem to be aware of her unique status in the male-dominant culture, is actually seen as a woman walking a very tight rope. On the one hand, her real position within her people is very powerful: she is accepted as God's messenger as well as a legal authority. Yet on the other hand, Deborah seems to realize that her continued success depends on her ability to stay within the limits of her position as prophetess and judge. If she adds a military victory to her laurels, then she would certainly be seen as overstepping her feminine boundaries and intruding into an exclusively male domain—war and military action. Thus while she warns Baraq that including her in his soldierly activities may harm his military reputation, Deborah betrays her own fears and the awareness that, as a woman, she must remain an outsider to some spheres of life.

Another way of looking at Deborah's words to Baraq, suggested by early commentators, is to see her reference to a woman in whose hands God will yield the enemy as prophetic and alluding to Jael, who will later kill Sisera.[5] Deborah is thus not betraying her own inner conflict, but declaring, rather bluntly and fearlessly, that while the men will spend much energy and effort in the war, the actual victory will be accomplished by a woman. This interpretation not only attributes an ironic edge to Deborah's speech, but also presents Deborah as a courageous woman, somewhat vigilant, who seizes every opportunity to point out to the men that women have a role in every area of life, even in the actual war effort. If it seems that there would be a division of labor in which the woman, Deborah, will serve as the spiritual inspiration but the men will have to do the fighting, Deborah announces, in her position as prophetess, that even the actual killing of the enemy will be a feat performed by a woman. Thus Deborah not only epitomizes in her own existence an egalitarian conception of the roles of the sexes, she also reinforces it with the announcement that implies that women cannot be excluded even from the bloodshed of war, the last bastion of male domain.

Both interpretations present Deborah as a woman eager to maintain balance between the sexes, and cautious not to tip the scale in any direction. The first one shows Deborah as heedful of male sensitivities, and therefore attempting not to draw more of the limelight to herself than she already enjoys. It reveals the charismatic woman's uneasy position in a culture that promotes male supremacy, but that is not utterly sexist and allows the unique woman to find an outlet for her talents and transcend the constrictive existence of her sisters. The second interpretation reveals Deborah as somewhat militant in her attempts to promote the social role of the female. Both readings of this verse, originating from male commentators, bring to light the commentators' awareness of the delicate social position that Deborah finds herself in, and the skillful diplomacy that she exhibits in her efforts to create good will and avoid any source of potential hostility between the sexes.

Deborah's feminine strategy is thus twofold: by capably holding a venerable position in her society, she serves as an example of female reach, and by articulating her nonsexist views, she reinforces her faith that she, Deborah, should not be looked upon as a unique case, but as indicative of feminine potential that can be fully realized in every aspect of life. Deborah's tactic, which is an attempt to reconcile different social elements and unite them into a harmonious whole, is also evident in the victory ode, which she chants with Baraq. The verb *vatashar,* literally 'and (she) sang,' is in the third person feminine singular, and therefore seems to refer to a woman singer. Yet there are two syntactic subjects attached to this verb, Deborah and Baraq. While this grammatical structure is not unusual in biblical Hebrew, some of the Bible commentators note that the biblical narrator is probably trying to indicate that it is really the woman, Deborah, who composed and delivered the ode.[6] We might see in this peculiar verse another confirmation of Deborah's methods: while she alone produced the song, she lets the man, Baraq, share in the credit, so that the effect is one of unity and accord between the prophet and the soldier, the spiritual leader and the man of action, female and male.

The ode itself serves as Deborah's manifesto in which she unfolds her vision of social harmony and cohesion. Here, the prophetess becomes a poetess, and uses her creative ability to express her nation's feelings and aspirations. Just as there is no strife between the talents of the individual and his social obligations, so there is no conflict between woman and man, or female and her environment. The poet's balancing tactics are evident in her carefully structured verse using the technique of poetic parallelism as an ideological tool:

Awake awake Deborah / awake awake utter a song
Arise Baraq / and lead away your captives, thou son of Abinoam
(5:12)

Deborah's ode pays homage to femininity as a powerful theological and political factor. She sees no incongruity between the woman's role as mother and her role as social leader: "Until that I Deborah arose / that I arose a mother in Israel" (Judg. 5:7). Deborah restores the Israelite nation to the God that they have forsaken (5:8–10), and she also embraces the alien tribe of the Kenites into the host nation, by blessing not only Jael, but her whole tribe (5:24). Thus Deborah's poem reflects the prophetess' harmonious vision of the scheme of things where the individual's creativity is enhanced by his or her national commitments, the straying people finally come back to their God, the tribe of strangers is accepted by the masters of the land, and the woman becomes an integral part of her nation's life and destiny.

Deborah's ode also puts Jael's actions in the context of divine justice, thus mitigating the horrifying aspect of the Jael and Sisera scene, in which the woman kills a man who trusted her enough to fall asleep in her home. As this episode is recounted in the biblical text (Judg. 4:18–22), Jael, the wife of the head of the Kenite tribe, who has tried to maintain a neutral position in the Israelite-Canaanite conflict, makes a brave decision by defying her husband's neutrality and taking a courageous action that proves her loyalty to the Israelite nation. The murder of Sisera is seen as crucial in determining the fate of the battle, since it is only when the figurehead has been eliminated that the armies put down their weapons. Jael's killing of Sisera is thus considered by the biblical narrator as a just and wise act. Deborah reinforces this attitude by juxtaposing the cowardice of some of the Israelite neighbors with Jael's courage, and by viewing Jael's action as complying with the divine wishes. Jael thus not only takes a politically bold step, but she also fulfills God's will and operates within the divine scheme of things: "Curse Meroz, said the angel of the Lord / curse bitterly its inhabitants; / because they did not come to the help of the Lord / to the help of the Lord against the mighty men. / Blessed above women is Jael / the wife of Hever the Kenite / blessed is she more than women in the tent" (Judg. 5:23–24).

As the tale's highlight shifts from Deborah to Jael, we move from the wide vistas of Deborah's career to the narrow confines of Jael's tent; we are also introduced to another form of feminine response to oppression and to a new aspect of feminine craftiness that assume archetypal dimensions. Unlike Deborah, Jael is first seen as a home-bound, domestic person: she ventures out of her tent only to invite Sisera in, and immediately returns inside with her guest. We remember that Deborah judged the people of Israel not inside the house but rather "under the palm tree," and that she left home in order to help Baraq in his efforts to recruit people for his army.[7] If Deborah's life was not constricted either in terms of her achievements or her geographical movements, Jael, in her seemingly sheltered existence, is a more traditional woman, and therefore a more genuine representative of the feminine condition at the time. She comes out of her tent and invites the fatigued Sisera, who has escaped on foot from the battle-field, to her home; she then offers him milk, instead of the water that he requests, covers him with a blanket, and makes him feel comfortable enough to fall asleep. This seemingly harmless, domestic person, associated with nurturing (milk) and warmth (blanket), suddenly reveals a new face when she takes a tent peg and hammer, drives the peg into the man's temple and kills him. But even when she steps out of her womanly docility and turns the quietude of her home into the bloody scene of slaughter, her homespun strategy is still evident: she uses the readily available tent peg. Thus the irony of Sisera's life and destiny comes full circle; he terrorizes his neighbors with his reputation as a man of iron, "for he had nine hundred chariots of iron" (Judg. 4:3), and ends his life within the four walls of a woman's tent, defeated by a small wooden peg.

In her victory ode, Deborah again reiterates Jael's quality as a tent-dweller; yet the picture that ultimately emerges of Jael is very different from the one that the scriptural storyteller and Deborah attempt to promote, namely, that of the innocent, maternal homemaker who rises to a historic occasion that brings about a momentary mutation of her nature, and then slips back to her feminine lot. In fact, if taken out of its historical and scriptural context and reduced to its primal core, the Jael and Sisera episode is patterned along the lines of the "strange woman" episode in Proverbs (7:6–23), and contains all the elements of the archetypal male experience that results in the "fear of women."[8] Again we have the man passing by the woman's house and lured inside. In Proverbs, the woman offers the young man food and luxuries, and then sexual favors; the young man does not resist this enticement, he accepts the woman's invitation and inevitably meets his doom. In the Jael and Sisera episode, the element of food is present, but there is no allusion to a sexual bait that the woman might be using. Yet the question remains as to what tactic was employed by Jael that gained her Sisera's trust and resulted in his putting his fate in her hands.

The similarity between the scene of the "strange woman" in Proverbs and the Jael and Sisera episode is significant. While chronologically, the tale in Judges was put in final form earlier, the scene from Proverbs has the impact of a primal, archetypal experience in that it is not anchored in any specific place or time. The young man of Proverbs is "everyman," and the woman stands for "eternal womanhood." The Jael story is a concrete example of this universal experience as it fleshes out the general lines of the primary story by naming its main actors, and giving it a historical and geographical particularity. The element of sexual temptation, contained in the archetypal scene and absent in the historical tale, adds a new twist to the latter, and makes us aware of a possible earlier layer existing in the Judges story that has been suppressed or eliminated by the biblical redactor. A new reading of the story that focuses on the woman's strategy inevitably points to a submerged sexual tension that pervades the tale. Interestingly, Deborah's ode introduces an erotic strain in verse 27, which is usually translated as "at her feet, he fell he lay down: / at her feet he fell"; the Hebrew, however, is more daring, since it reads "between her feet," or, "between her legs." If we remember that the noun *regel,* 'leg,' carries sexual connotations in Hebrew, it is no wonder that an ancient midrash concluded that Sisera had intercourse with Jael.[9]

In the tale itself, Jael encourages Sisera to enter her tent by telling him not to fear; Sisera is inclined to accept her invitation since he is now dead tired, and also because the Kenites are at peace with his

people. The exhausted Sisera asks for a little water, but Jael, generously, gives him a more nourishing drink, milk; thus, presumably,
she gains his trust and lulls him into sleep. Yet this short exchange
between the man and the woman is rife with sexual tension once we
realize that, as Wolfgang Lederer tells us, in the mythological apper-
ception of early man, woman, water, and milk are tied together, and
that, in Egyptian hieroglyphics, the water jar is a symbol of femininity.[10] Thus when Sisera asks Jael for water, he implies that he wants
more than just a drink; and when Jael responds by giving him milk,
she more than hints at her readiness to satisfy him with the totality of
her femininity.

The man and the woman initially address each other in a formal
and respectful manner; she calls him "my lord," and he adds to his
request for water the word *na'* ('please,' or 'I pray thee'). And yet
after the man has had his milk, and the woman covers him with a
blanket (this latter act is mentioned twice), Sisera becomes bolder,
and commands the woman in a familiar, even masterly tone: "Stand
in the door of the tent." The sexual act, implied in the symbols of
water, milk, and blanket, is interpreted by the man as a sign of his
domination over the woman, and results in a new relationship, one in
which the woman is seen as slave and the man as master. Ironically,
the man is wrong; the sexual intimacy only gives him the illusion of
power, while, in reality, it places him at the mercy of the woman.

Jael's sexual tactic of luring the man is expunged from the story's
outer layer, but is still woven into the symbolic fabric of this small
drama. The result is a cleaned up version that is nevertheless vitalized
by a darker side which ties Jael to all those women who throughout
history were forced to use their sexuality to gain their ends. Significantly, the woman's sexual strength is always seen as a means by
which the treacherous woman overpowers the trusting man. The sexual act is never graphically depicted in the ancient documents, but the
act of killing is presented in gory details, and functions as an "objective correlative," to use T. S. Eliot's phrase, of the sexual encounter.

The Apocryphal story of Judith, who delivered her people from
the hands of the ruthless Assyrian Holofernes, is an elaborate version
of the Jael and Sisera tale. Here the protagonist is a beautiful Hebrew
woman who comes over to Holofernes' camp and bewitches him
with her wisdom and charm. The man interprets her demeanor as
signifying sexual promise, but when the right moment comes, the
woman sees to it that the man gets heavily drunk, and when he falls
asleep she beheads him, puts his head in her bag, and returns to her
people with a tangible sign of victory. Unlike in the Jael story, where
the narrator seems to be making an effort to suppress the sexual as-

pect, the narrator of Judith plays up Holofernes' desire for the beautiful woman, and delights in its frustration. What materializes is not the man's lust, but the woman's revenge. Similarly, the biblical Esther is induced by her uncle to marry the Persian king Ahasuerus, so that she can help her people in time of trouble. If the story presents Esther as the queen, it gives enough indication that perhaps the Hebrew woman was no more than a favored concubine. Again an attempt to purge the story from unseemly elements is evident. And when Esther's moment comes, she indeed uses her feminine charms to arouse sexual jealousy in the king and thus to alienate him from Haman, his close advisor and the Jews' enemy.

At the core of the Judges tale of Jael and Sisera, as well as of similar later stories, lies a well-defined feminine strategy: the use of sex as a bait to gain man's trust and then overpower him and put him under the woman's control. The biblical narrators use a known formula that stems from the male fear of women, which is the seduction of the unsuspecting man at the hands of the treacherous female. Yet as the tales are recounted and given a historical reality and individualized characters, the various female protagonists are extolled as paragons of virtue and loyalty, and the evil men are seen as being justly punished. If in the prototype of Proverbs the woman is viewed as the cosmological "other," and the man as the subject with whom the reader identifies, the formula is reversed in the historical stories. Here, the men are the "others" since they are the enemies of the Hebrews, the strangers that have to be overcome, while the women represent the Israelites' collective aspirations and they thus become lovingly ensconced in their people's consciousness.

In Deborah's ode, another female character is introduced, not by name, but in her role as Sisera's mother: "The mother of Sisera looked out at the window, / and moaned through the lattice / Why is his chariot so long in coming? / Why are the hoofbeats of his steeds so tardy? / Her wise ladies answered her, / she even returned answer to herself, / Have they not found booty? have they not divided the prey; / to every man a damsel or two . . ." (5:28–30). Sisera's mother exhibits natural maternal feelings when she worries about her son and hopes that he has emerged victorious from the battle. However, when envisioning her son's success, and the booty that he will bring home, she reveals excessive cruelty which, surprisingly, is not aimed at the enemy soldiers, but rather, at the women captives that will be taken by the Canaanite army. The various English translations use language that is much less crude, and less figurative, than the Hebrew. Deborah does not use the noun 'damsel,' but rather the synecdoche 'womb', which she repeats twice, *"rehem rahmatayim."* The prophetess thus pictures the Canaanite noble ladies reducing woman from a whole human being to a sexual organ, and delighting not only in their men's victory, a response that is understandable, but also in the way their sons and husbands will ravish and abuse the enemy women.

Sisera's mother is not presented to us directly since she acts in a scene conjured up by the prophetess. Still, while we have no way of knowing whether the historical person was that cruel, we learn much from this scene about women's treatment of their own sex; and the evidence this time is not filtered through male eyes but is given to us directly by a woman, Deborah, who, so tradition tells us, composed and delivered the ode. Perhaps unwittingly, Deborah presents here a very condemning testimony of her own sex: the lack of solidarity among women.[11] Sisera's mother and her female advisors manifest no feminine sensitivity towards the predicament of other women. They could take pleasure in the fact that the female captives will be humiliated by becoming slaves, for instance; but it seems that they enjoy imagining the women abused in their femininity, being raped by the enemy. The Canaanite women make it clear that feminine loyalty does not cross over national lines, and that fidelity to one's people is greater than any feeling of sisterhood among women. They do not realize, however, that they betray their own womanhood if they derive pleasure from viewing other women's femininity being debased. Sisera's mother's acceptance of the rules of male sovereignty, that call for establishing of mastery over another nation by raping its women, is symptomatic of feminine behavior in oppressive circumstances, and can serve as an example of Simone de Beauvoir's claim that patriarchy succeeded because women cooperated with the men, and helped in their own subjugation.[12]

That Sisera's mother represents the traditional feminine condition of confinement and incarceration which leads to narrowness of aspiration, and, therefore, to surrender to the male authority, is evidenced by her spatial limitation: "The mother of Sisera looked out at the window, / and moaned through the lattice" (5:28). The window and lattice are powerful symbols that place the woman indoors, looking outside but never really participating in life. Clearly, in the figure of the vicious old Canaanite woman, Deborah brings forth the image of this ancient tribe as extremely cruel and sexually depraved; but is Deborah not trying to tell us that feminine imprisonment and powerlessness lead to woman's denigration, even hatred, of her own sex? Surely Deborah's career, which was characterized by physical and mental mobility, was different from that of the majority of women in her time who, like Jael and the Canaanite women, were enclosed in their home and waited for men to return and give meaning to their lives.[13]

Thus the Judges story about the war between the Israelites and the Canaanites turns into a women's story that delineates for us three different feminine behaviors seen as reactions to patriarchal oppression. Deborah is active, articulate, and straightforward; she manifests no feelings of inferiority and no attempt to escape her femininity. In her constant efforts to balance and harmonize the different forces existing in her society, she reveals insight, intelligence, and recognition that life is made up of conflicting elements that need to be reconciled and synthesized. She senses the potential conflict between the sexes, but wisely puts it in the context of all the other forms of discord in life that can be worked out and solved. Yet if she is entirely secure in her unique position as a woman and a leader, she exercises caution and restraint, and shows an awareness that she does not really represent the collective feminine destiny. In her existence she serves as proof that if women are given recognition, allowed mobility, and permitted to express themselves, they can rise above the common feminine predicament. Her situation is juxtaposed with that of the two other female figures in the story, whose claustrophobic existence inevitably leads to undignified behavior.

Jael uses the age-old feminine technique of sexual temptation, and Sisera's mother reveals feminine self-hatred and compliance with the sexual abuse of women. To accommodate the didactic and moral purposes of the biblical story, Jael is put on a pedestal and her story is cleansed of its underlying sexual implications. Sisera's mother, on the other hand, is denigrated as a crude and debased human being, and the words that are attributed to her reveal a woman treacherous and hostile to her own sex. Yet the insights that are offered in this short biblical drama regarding the woman's predicament and her tactics for survival make us wonder if this is not another enclave within the biblical canon that represents the feminine point of view and that may have originated from a woman storyteller.[14]

The scene in the Canaanite palace, described in Deborah's ode, alludes to a group of female advisors to Sisera's mother and points to a custom practiced by grand ladies to surround themselves with wise women, or even to the existence of "wise women" as a separate professional group. And Deborah herself, though not labeled a "wise woman," manifests wisdom that is characterized by moderation and avoidance of discord. Both types of feminine wisdom, one indicating a professional class and the other suggesting female strategy, are present in the biblical narratives.

Proverbs presents two allegorical feminine figures, Folly and Wisdom, which personify abstract human qualities and are not depicted as individuals. Of special interest are those narratives in which a real female figure manifests the quality of wisdom, especially in her dealings with the male world. One such example is the Abigail episode (1 Sam. 25) which, on the surface, serves as a sort of "comic relief" in the saga of David's tribulations before he ascends the throne. And yet as the tale takes shape, the charismatic David recedes to a supporting role and gives way to an even more fascinating person, Abigail, the wife of the boorish Nabal.[15]

As the story unfolds we see David, now a fugitive from Saul's wrath and heading a group of outlaws, sending messengers to the wealthy and influential Nabal, asking for "protection fee," because, as he claims, his people guarded Nabal's shepherds when they camped in the Carmel. Nabal, described as "coarse and ill-behaved," angrily rejects David's demands, calling the latter a worthless hooligan.[16] In response, the impatient young David rounds up four hundred men, intent on attacking Nabal's home and property.

Each of these two men, one older, more affluent and self-confident, and the other young, ambitious, and hotheaded, clearly serves as a foil to the other. Both are too extreme and irrational in their reaction, and each one's hot-tempered conduct might lead to disaster. In fact, these two figures exemplify Northrop Frye's formula of the polarized comic pair consisting of *eirôn*, the self-deprecator, and *alazôn*, the boaster or impostor.[17] David, at the present point in his life, is less than he really is, or will become, therefore he plays the *eirôn*, and the arrogant Nabal, in his social status and wealth, has more than his character warrants, therefore he is the *alazôn*. The moderate type between these two extremes is the *alêthes*, the truthful person, a role that will be assumed by Nabal's charming wife, Abigail. If the *eirôn* and *alazôn* are two extreme types with regard to truth, another pair of comic figures consists of two extreme types with regard to pleasure or amusement: the buffoon and churl (or the clown-boor), and the *eutrapelos*, the truly witty person, representing the middle way. This formula, too, seems to apply to the three actors in this small drama, with the men assuming the roles of the two comic extremes (David is ludicrous in his impetuosity and ill-advised decision, and Nabal is comic in his crude boorishness), while the woman represents the golden mean between these two antithetical forms of comic conduct.

Nabal and Abigail exemplify a variation on the "detestable father–admirable daughter" pattern, with the forbidding patriarchal figure of the husband taking the traditional place of the father. Nabal's surname "Calebite" might affiliate him with the Caleb family, but it may also be a character or even physical description, "doglike." [18] The woman is reputable not only for her beauty but for her good sense and, therefore, one of her husband's men appeals to her, telling her of the dangerous situation that has evolved, and justifying David's demands. Abigail acts swiftly, but also thoughtfully. She journeys to David's camp, heavily supplied with food and wine. Her tactic consists of appeasement, flattery, but also of gentle exhortation. First, she condemns her husband's conduct, going so far as to call him "ignoble" or "villain," thus dissociating herself from him. She describes herself as David's "handmaid" and assures him that she believes in his divine mission to do "the battles of the Lord." At the same time, she is daring enough to point out to David the folly of shedding innocent blood, and the stigma that would be attached to his name, if such a thing were to occur. Abigail thus wisely ties her faith in David's glorious future with a warning to him not to take any imprudent, shortsighted step now that might tarnish his eventual glory.

Like Deborah, Abigail serves as a moderating force that averts the clash of two extremes, and at the same time, she is also the wise teacher, who instructs and directs the man, and whose advice is heeded. Both women seem to enjoy an amount of mobility that allows them to travel and to take action outside their home. Abigail lacks Deborah's ferocious and warlike side because of her different circumstances. Deborah must urge the man to start a war which will lead to bloodshed, while Abigail foils a potential carnage. But both are seen as peacemakers: if Deborah cannot effect peace between the Canaanites and the Israelites, she tries to reconcile the other potentially conflicting forces in her society. Abigail's realm of activity is much narrower, since she is a private person and not a leader, but the initiative that she takes when she suddenly springs out of the wife's customary anonymity puts her in the limelight, if only momentarily, and gains a place for her in the biblical canon.

Within the saga of David's tumultuous career, the Abigail episode serves as a further step in David's education, when the young man learns moderation and restraint, qualities that he will later need as a leader. [19] In this particular story, David's situation is analogous to that of the youthful Prince Hal (in Shakespeare's *Henry IV, Part 1*) who has to go through a period of training before he is ready to assume the responsibility of the throne. Comic excesses are seen by both the biblical narrator and Shakespeare as part of the young man's folly of which he has to be rid. In fact, David shuttles between one comic extreme and the other, since he is both the *eirôn,* the self-deprecator, but also the *alazôn,* the boaster, especially when he rattles his saber and vows revenge.

Yet a literary analysis makes it clear that, if taken out of its historical context, this tale is about the woman, Abigail, and not about the man, and that it carefully delineates different forms of strategy that a woman has to use in a culture where she is socioeconomically powerless yet, in reality, is allowed to intrude, interfere, and even take control and guide. Furthermore, if Abigail is seen as daring in her taking action contrary to her husband's wishes, and in implicitly warning David not to commit an irreversible error, she is also bold enough virtually to offer herself as a woman to David when she says: "And the Lord shall deal well with my lord, and thou shall remember thy handmaid" (25:31).

David recognizes the wisdom of Abigail's advice, thanks her for preventing him from shedding blood, and commends her "discretion." He is evidently also greatly impressed with her other feminine qualities because, when he hears that her insufferable husband has died, he sends for her, and she hastens to come to him and become his wife, just as she hastened before to go to David and appease him. But if she has helped in educating young David and then has managed to share in his fate by marrying him, Abigail now slips back to her feminine destiny of anonymity and marginal existence, and the biblical text, that has shifted momentarily from its main course, goes back to narrating the adventure of its central male hero, David.

Two other episodes deal with "wise women," who are not identified by name, but rather by their intellectual abilities or perhaps by their profession. The techniques these two women use in order to achieve their ends are somewhat similar to those of Deborah and Abigail, in that language is used as a powerful tool to effect a change in man's attitude. In one episode, a wise woman is hired by Joab, David's chief of staff, to make peace between David and his estranged son Absalom (II Sam. 14). It seems obvious that the custom of hiring a "wise woman" to mediate or negotiate between two sides was rather prevalent; otherwise it is hard to believe that Joab, the most "macho" of David's men, would resort to the help of a woman. One might argue that Joab uses the services of a woman in this case since it has to do with a delicate family matter and that he believes that a woman would be able to strike the right note and say the most appropriate words to settle the domestic problem. However, in a different case altogether, one that involves military decisions (II Sam. 20:16–22), Joab listens to the arguments of a wise woman and accepts her suggestions.

The method used by the "wise woman" in the first case, involving David and his son, is impersonation and storytelling. She dresses in black and pretends to be a heartbroken mother, mourning both her dead son and the son who had to escape in order to avoid revenge. As David eventually realizes, the fictional yarn that she so convincingly weaves about her own domestic problem is fabricated and serves as an analogy to David's own situation. While Joab instructs the woman what to say, the actual recounting of the story, the impromptu answers to the king's questions, the nuances of tone and voice, and the choice of words are the woman's. In other words, the "wise woman" is a combination of a spellbinding storyteller, a convincing actress, and a clever advisor.

In the second episode, Joab and his army lay siege to a city, Abel, that has provided refuge to a man who had tried to incite the people to rebel against David. The city's wall is about to cave in when a "wise woman" approaches the besieging army and asks to talk to Joab. In fact, she shows much courage when she practically orders Joab to come close to the wall so he can hear her. Surprisingly, the ruthless and hardened man of war, Joab, complies with the woman's wishes and approaches the wall, assuring the woman that he is listening. Obviously, the woman has no time for a lengthy fable, and so she quotes an apparently widespread epigram that means, essentially, that Joab should have first asked the city's residents if they were ready to hand over the fugitive, before embarking on a military action.[20] Now that the woman seems to have Joab's close attention, she continues, not losing momentum: "Thou seeketh to destroy a city and a mother in Israel." By using the known Hebrew idiom to describe a metropolitan center, "a city and a mother in Israel," the wise woman achieves several ends: she emphasizes to David's advisor the importance of the city and the wisdom of keeping it intact, and she also points out the feminine nature of the city, thus shaming the fierce soldier into further realizing the absurdity of his actions. But by alluding to the city's "femininity" the woman is also protecting herself, justifying her interference in a political and military matter, considered to be an exclusively male domain. After reaching an understanding with Joab, the wise woman still has to persuade her own people to turn the fugitive over. Again she uses her wisdom: "Then the woman went to all the people in her wisdom," though we are not told what measures she takes with her townspeople. Thus we see the wise woman engaged in "shuttle diplomacy" as she attempts to force the two sides to settle their dispute without resorting to violence. Yet though she wants to prevent slaughter and destruction, this wise woman does not display any squeamishness; before she even consults with her own people she promises Joab to throw the fugitive's head down the wall. The brutal ending of the story reminds us that many other stories involving women are not without their gory, cruel side. The women function as peacemakers and saviors, yet in the process they often take active part in the killing.

From Wisdom to Fury

The biblical "wise women" are adept at composing poetry, spinning tales, citing proverbs, playacting and impersonating. They all serve as mediators for peace and accord and never reveal a bitter or discontented edge, though they show awareness of the delicacy of their position in a male-dominant culture. Their wisdom is mainly practical and pragmatic, usually choosing the lesser of two evils. Many times they appear not to shy away from violence, thus making the accepted notions of feminine frailty, gentleness, and squeamishness seem like false myths. But they channel their low-keyed militancy into harmonizing and unifying, rather than polarizing. Some biblical female figures display jealousy and a mean-spirited bitchiness towards other women, such as Peninah, who is hostile and nasty towards her husband's other wife, Hannah (1 Sam. 1). The lack of solidarity among women is exemplified not only in the figure of the Canaanite mother of Sisera but in some of the Israelite women as well. Peninah and Hannah constitute a "community of women," to use Nina Auerbach's phrase, that is characterized by animosity and disloyalty.[21] The jealousy among women usually appears in the polygynous household, and while the biblical narrator withholds any judgment, it is obvious that the practice of keeping many wives in the same household was responsible for feminine hostility and anger.

Strikingly, however, the quality of extreme rage and almost unappeasable fury is attributed in the Bible to God and to some of the male protagonists, but not to women. The emergence of explicit feminine fury can be traced to the Midrash stories of the two charismatic women, Beruria and Yalta. In the figures of the learned Beruria, the daughter of a famous rabbi and the wife of the illustrious Rabbi Meir, and of the eccentric Yalta, the daughter of the president of the Babylonian Jewish community and the wife of an important rabbi, the thread of the biblical "wise women" is continued and, at the same time, takes a new direction.

Unlike the wisdom of the biblical women, based on pragmatism and good sense, Beruria's sagacity is mainly intellectual. She laces her speeches with erudite quotes and learned insights into the biblical text, and bases her observations on her knowledge of the written word. The biblical wise women seem to belong to an oral tradition and to possess a wisdom that stems from penetrating intuitions and life experiences. Perhaps with the exception of Deborah, who is a spiritual person and God's messenger, the other women's intelligence is firmly rooted in this-worldly experiences. And even the spiritual Deborah, though a prophetess and a poetess, ultimately emerges as action-oriented. Beruria, on the other hand, is noted for her dedication to learning and brilliant mind, and is cited by male scholars as an illustration of vast scholarship. The Midrash tells us of a rabbi who describes to his student, with a mixture of awe and deference, how Beruria has spent three years studying a certain difficult text, the Book of Genealogies, covering three hundred laws a day, until she completely mastered it.[22] When her two sons die on the Sabbath, she hides the fact from her husband until the night, when the holy day is over, so as not to disturb the sacredness of the day with grief and mourning. When the moment comes for her to tell her husband the truth, she engages him in an apparently halakic dialogue, asking whether she is obliged to return an object that was deposited with her for safekeeping. Her husband answers that, of course, she has to return that object to its original owner, since it does not legally belong to her. Beruria then shows him his dead sons and quotes Job: "The Lord gave and the Lord has taken away; blessed be the name of the Lord."[23]

Beruria thus seems stronger than her husband, trying to reconcile him to his sons' death. Like the many wise women before her, she uses a circuitous way of breaking the devastating news, telling a story and only then making her point. But the story is not simply fiction; it is couched in the language of legal deliberations, and gives proof of the woman's diplomacy as well as her learning.

It is apparent that Beruria's husband, the knowledgeable Rabbi Meir, respects his wife's erudition and listens to her. At one point, a midrash tells us, Rabbi Meir cursed some hooligans who lived in his neighborhood, and wished them dead. His wife asked him what his reasoning was for wishing such a terrible end to those people. The rabbi quotes the biblical verse that says: "The sinners will be consumed out of the earth, and the wicked will be no more." Beruria, however, argues that another way of reading the verse in Hebrew is: "Sins will be consumed out of the earth." She therefore advises her husband that instead of wishing these people dead he should rather ask for them to repent and return from their sinful ways. The midrash then tells us that Rabbi Meir took his wife's suggestion, prayed for the sinners to repent, and that his prayer was answered. Beruria, according to this midrash, takes the liberty of modifying the biblical verse so as to make it more humanistic. She is seen as having powers that are almost supernatural, when the change in the sinners' hearts, that she has wished for, comes true.

Beruria's function in these tales is that of a moderating force in her husband's life, introducing the concept of *raḥamim,* 'mercy', with which one has to deal with his fellow human beings. Yet a different string of stories reveals another side to Beruria's character, one that separates her from the biblical "wise women" and proves that the Hebrew storytellers, or the collective legend-makers with whom some of the tales about Beruria originated, have become more sophisticated in their awareness of the woman's response to an oppressive society. In a cluster of stories that narrate Beruria's various exchanges with men, including an acclaimed rabbi, a student, and even a heretic who challenged the authority of the Bible, Beruria appears to be impatient, rude, and arrogant. At one point she calls the noted Rabbi Yossi "a foolish Galilean," and she also addresses the heretic as "a fool." When she sees a young man studying in silence, instead of reading the text aloud, she kicks him and exhorts him that one has to involve all his senses in the act of learning.[24] Beruria constantly takes a polemical stand in her dialogues with men scholars; she also abuses people not only verbally but physically. It is hard to reconcile these two polar aspects of Beruria's personality, that of a calm, eventempered, and merciful human being, who keeps her stoic composure even when she loses her sons, and that of a furious, impatient individual who snaps at people and "kicks" a young student. One must conclude that at the time that the tales about Beruria were created, mostly from the second half of the second century C.E. to the fifth century C.E. (and some even later), feminine fury and discontentment were being recognized.[25] Beruria's rage may have also been due to the precariousness of Jewish existence in her times: her own father was one of the ten martyrs executed by the Romans, and, according to one midrash, her sister was forcibly placed in a whorehouse. The origins of Beruria's anger are probably manifold; they are a combination of her individual personality, the tumultuous times, and her own unique position in a culture that warned the father not teach his daughter the Torah, and that exhorted men in general not to engage in a dialogue with women.[26]

The midrashic tales revolving around Yalta are even more pervaded with rage and its physical expression. We do not know whether Yalta was as learned as Beruria, but she clearly was an educated woman belonging to an aristocratic family in the Babylonian diaspora. Yalta's moments of fury are often seen as feminine in their origin. This is a summary of one of the stories:

> 'Ulla was once visiting at the house of Rabbi Naḥman (Yalta's husband). They had a meal and 'Ulla said grace, and he handed the cup of benediction to Rabbi Naḥman. Rabbi Naḥman said to him: "Please send the cup of benediction to Yalta." 'Ulla answered: "Thus said Rabbi Yoḥanan: 'The fruit of a woman's body is blessed only from the fruit of a man's body . . .'" Meanwhile Yalta heard that 'Ulla refused to send her a cup, and she got up in a passion and went to the wine cellar and broke four hundred jars. 'Ulla tried to appease her by sending over to her another cup of benediction, but she retorted with the following proverb: "Gossip comes from pedlars and vermin from rags."[27]

Yalta is clearly enraged by the insinuation that the man is the more important part of a couple. The proverb that she quotes implies that she considers the rabbi's words to be nonsensical and foolish; but she is not above making an ad hominem argument, remarking on the visiting rabbi's ragged clothes and, possibly, his occupation. The story shows a woman fiercely protective of her feminine worth and proud of her social status and affluence, referring to the visiting rabbi's obvious poverty as indicative of the poverty of his mind.

On another occasion, Yalta becomes very impatient with her husband's inability to gain the upper hand in a learned debate with a fellow rabbi.[28] She also teases and challenges her husband on legal matters, such as the dietary laws, proving that she is well versed in the Judaic tradition.[29] The overall impression created by Yalta's presence in the tales is that of an angry, discontented woman who refuses to show any deference to men, as when she warns her husband that he will be exposed as an ignoramus, or belittles her guest's erudition, calling it nonsense and idle talk. She also does not hesitate to express her anger in harsh language and in action that is far from dignified for a woman of her position.

With Beruria kicking the student and Yalta descending to the wine cellar to break the wine jars, we clearly see a new phase in female reaction to oppressive circumstances, one in which the women can no longer contain their anger that now explodes and, surprisingly, finds its way into the Talmudic written canon. These two women are not just comic shrews, as described in Proverbs, but strong individuals whose intellectual abilities and inquisitive minds, coupled with their rebellious and antagonistic conduct, alert us to a new dimension of the feminine response that was either unrecognized or suppressed in the biblical narratives.

Feminine rage and feminine revolt find their ultimate expression in the post-Talmudic legends of Lilith. We have seen Lilith as the woman who was created prior to Eve and presented to Adam as his wife, and who was later transformed into a she-demon, becoming a paradigm of the male fear of women and his sense of the demonic side of the feminine being. But the major source of most of the legends concerning Lilith, the Alpha Betha of Ben Sira, does not dwell only on Lilith's diabolical qualities and her affiliation with other forces of evil in the world. Surprisingly, the medieval storyteller tries to explain the origins of Lilith's metamorphosis from a human into a demon, and sees in Lilith's rebellion against Adam's domination the main reason behind her escape from him. The following is a summary of this story:

> When God created His world and created Adam, He saw that Adam was alone, and He immediately created a woman from the earth, like him, for him, and named her Lilith. He brought her to Adam and they immediately began to fight. Adam said, "You shall lie below" and Lilith said, "You shall lie below for we are equal and both of us were created from earth." When Lilith saw the state of things, she uttered the Holy name and flew into the air and fled. God immediately sent three angels and told them: "Go and fetch Lilith; if she agrees to come, bring her, and if she does not, bring her by force." The three angels caught up with her in the Red Sea. She told them: "Darlings, I know myself that God created me only to afflict babies with fatal diseases." The angels would not leave her alone, until she swore by God's name that wherever she would see them or their names in an amulet, she would not possess the baby bearing it. They then left her immediately.[30]

The story clearly asserts that God's intention was to make the man and the woman equal, and that the patriarchal rules originated from the male and not from his creator. The story starts with an egalitarian conception of the sexes, and in this context Lilith's flight is viewed as the escape of an individual whose freedom is threatened, rather than as an active rebellion of an evil person. Adam seems possessive and tyrannical, while Lilith fights for her rights to be deemed equal to the man. Yet it seems that Lilith's only refuge can be the demonic; by deserting Adam she inevitably relinquishes her humanity and must assume a fiendish role and change into a monster. Lilith, then, does not choose her transformation willingly, but is rather forced into it in her frustrated attempts to establish parity with the man.

It is Lilith's anger and unwillingness to resign herself to an inferior existence that ultimately bring about her reluctant mutation into a devilish force. If in this ancient myth the woman-rebel has to descend into the nether land of cosmological evil, in later works, as we shall see, rebellion often catapults the female into the psychic underworld of madness. Lilith's monstrosity would later find its literary correlative in feminine lunacy, just as many ancient myths were to be transformed in the modern mind from cosmological into psychological truths. Indeed, as some modern feminist critics, such as Gilbert and Gubar, have observed, in other literatures, too, feminine rebellion is tied to freakishness, monstrosity, and madness.[31]

Furthermore, as Joseph Dan suggests, Lilith does not voluntarily become a baby-killer; in the story cited above, it seems that Lilith expresses resentment of the role assigned to her by Talmudic literature—where she appears only briefly—as the killer of newborn infants.[32] Lilith thus rebels against her predestined image, indeed against the assumption of evil in her nature, and perversely decides to live up to it as a way of avenging herself for all forms of injustice that she has been subject to. Preferring her fiendish existence to a life with the domineering Adam, she bribes the angels by promising them that she will never harm babies protected by them; therefore, they let her go. Lilith's rebellion thus ends in disaster; if she had wanted a dignified existence at Adam's side, she now has to resort to bribery, and she finds herself locked in the role of a killer-demon that would be forever chased away from the human community.

A later version of the Lilith story provides another answer as to why the angels did not force Lilith to come with them.[33] In this account, Lilith confesses before the angels that the "great demon" has already slept with her and, therefore, according to biblical law, she is "defiled" and cannot go back to her husband; adultery is thus added to Lilith's list of sins.

The main thrust of these two versions of the Lilith story is the underlying irony that shows how, in her fury, Lilith turns against herself. If we also remember that Lilith is doomed to kill her own baby-demons, then we have here an early version of feminine rebellion that backfires and transforms the protagonist into a reluctant, and therefore all the more raging monster. Flight, infidelity, and destruction are all tied to feminine anger and result in a new form of imprisonment, not in the patriarchal world but in the infernal realm of the devil, or, as we shall see later, in the subterranean sphere of the self's private demons.

If Joseph Dan is right in his conception of this work, which he calls "Pseudo Ben Sira," as satiric and parodic, then the inherent irony in Lilith's fate can be seen as the cruel cosmological joke that has been played on the defiant female.[34] But if the Lilith myth is a folktale with no particular parodic edge, and if we consider that Lilith's call for equality at the very beginning of the story is founded on her divinely ordained parity with man, then we can see in this tale a not unsympathetic myth of the price of female escape. Lilith now enjoys the freedom denied Eve and her daughters; for if the submissive female race will be incarcerated within the four walls of the male home, Lilith will roam the universe freely. But Lilith is stripped of her humanity and will stay marooned in the sphere of darkness and of destruction that turns on itself.

In Chapter Two we have seen Lilith as a paradigm of the male fear of the unknown in the universe and in himself, and his projection of the dark and mysterious side of life into the feminine figure. But by making Lilith the heroine of this tale and giving her a voice, the medieval narrator asks the reader to consider the female point of view. Lilith thus exemplifies the woman's strategy of channeling her rage into disloyalty, monstrosity, and ultimately, self-annihilation. The female ability to exercise self-restraint and effect moderation and sanity in her environment, reflected in the Bible, now gives way to militancy and uncontrolled wrath.

As Lilith's figure travels through the Hebraic documents, the focus is shifted from her origins as the first female rebel to her role as the embodiment of total evil and the bride of the archdemon Samael.[35] A parallel structure is created between three couples: God and the Shekinah, Adam and Eve, Samael and Lilith. But in the works of the Kabbalists, another expression to female fury is given through the figure of the exalted Shekinah. On the one hand, Shekinah and Lilith exemplify the polarity of opposites—Shekinah being the supernal mother and Lilith the satanic baby killer, Shekinah being the hallowed divine bride and Lilith the ghostly source of illicit sexual fantasies. And yet, the Kabbalists projected into the Shekinah herself a dualism that has sometimes baffled the readers; she is described as both chaste and promiscuous, motherly and bloodthirsty, a queen endowed with celestial beauty, and a woman-monster of cosmic proportions.[36]

The popular explanation for this paradoxical duality within the extolled configuration of the feminine element in the deity is summed up by Patai: "The fact that the image [of the Matronit-Shekinah] does not lack in its contradictory features betrays something of the male's ambivalence in his relationship to the woman."[37] Yet another possible source for the two faces of the Shekinah might be the Kabbalists' own observation of feminine behavior and their attempts to integrate it into their mythology. The Zohar constantly directs the reader to view the male-female relationship in reality as a reflection of the relationship of the male and female aspects of God, and vice versa. It asks us to see in the Shekinah an analogous image of the concrete woman, and in the real woman a replica of the heavenly figure. If the Shekinah is kindly, loving, and self-sacrificing and at the same time also furious, warlike, and vindictive, it is because the real woman projected both images. In a sense, the Kabbalists revealed an awareness of the other side of female timidity and subservience, that of female combativeness and insubordination, and, by reproducing it in the image of the Shekinah, they validated, if not condoned it.

Furthermore, when the Shekinah betrays God and becomes a *Sotah*, 'adulteress', she is seen as dominated by the *sitra aḥra*, the 'other side', who has won the cosmic war and now controls the Shekinah.[38] The Shekinah becomes "possessed," so to speak, by evil powers, and it is easy to substitute psychological terms for the mythological language of the Kabbalists, just as Hasidism did later.[39] The extreme fury and the antinomian traces in the Shekinah's profile, as well as her sometimes strange and inexplicable forms of conduct, are as integral a part of her image as are her kindness and goodness. Female discontent that builds up into fury and results in monstrosity is thus represented in the other face of the Shekinah.

In a medieval tale by one Abraham Yagel, the duality of feminine strategy is dramatically represented in a parable about two women and their polar opposite histories.[40] The female protagonists in this reconstructed folktale allegorize, respectively, "good fortune" and "bad fortune," and are not fully realized as individuals. Nevertheless, in the set of qualities that the writer attributes to each woman, he makes clear his conception of what the feminine conduct should be. The first woman, the one who has been blessed with good luck all her life, is passive, docile, and accepting of male authority. She is born to a very poor father but she works hard and never complains; eventually, a rich man sees her, falls in love with her, and rescues her and her father from misery. The other woman's story is diametrically opposite. She is born to a rich man who loses his fortune as soon as his daughter comes into the world. Against her father's wishes, she elopes with a man who later goes on a business trip, finds himself shipwrecked, and is sold into slavery. The woman tries suicide, and when she fails, she goes to Egypt and sells herself as a slave in order to raise the ransom money needed to free her husband. When her husband hears what his wife did, he becomes so agitated that his heart fails and he dies. The story continues in this manner, describing the woman's later travails and her unsuccessful attempts to change her bad luck. She becomes so embittered that she is sentenced to end her life in the body of a mad dog. Significantly, the woman herself is well-meaning and does nothing that is morally or ethically wrong, but she is stubborn and active, and is not resigned to her fate as a woman and a person. She relies on her own judgment and believes in her own powers, but she causes the deaths of both her husband and her father. Her fault is that she behaves in an "unwomanly" manner, defying one man, her father, and attempting to rescue another man, her husband. This type of behavior is seen as madness and therefore, symbolically, the woman is doomed to finish her life as a mad dog. The didactic aspect of the story is self-evident, and complies with the standard male view of the "proper" feminine conduct. Yet some elements in this tale go beyond its moralistic scheme. In the essential benevolence of the protagonist and in the bizarre punishment meted out to this nontraditional woman, the themes of feminine rebellion, rage (translated into a suicide attempt), madness, and dehumanization are meaningfully, and disturbingly, intertwined.[41]

The Hasidic lore, too, provides us with an example of feminine fury that dehumanizes the woman, in the figure of the contentious Schoendel, the wife of the venerable Yehudi, though she comes to us via a modern vantage point, that of Martin Buber.[42] We have seen how the shrewish Schoendel's jealousy of her mother-in-law aided the Satanic powers in their attempts to cause damage of historic and cosmic proportions.[43] But as with Lilith, we are also given an opportunity to see the woman's point of view. In two versions of the same event, Buber tells us how Schoendel once burst into her husband's study, while he was discussing the role of the Hasidic leader, and indulged in a long tirade, condemning her husband for cruelly neglecting his wife and children. She insists on having her voice heard, and becomes more and more agitated as she goes on. She blames her husband for cultivating and relishing his "dreams," while being oblivious to the needs of the people close to him. She also exposes him as an arrogant and selfish man, full of his own self-importance, who fools those who adore him into believing that he cares for them. She works herself up into hysteria and then she suddenly loses her voice.

As much as she tries, she can no longer speak and she starts crying softly. Her husband, who was used to those scenes and never answered her, unexpectedly speaks up, and in a conciliatory tone tries to defend himself, pointing out that his wife and children have a roof over their heads and enough to eat. When his wife finally leaves the room, the Yehudi is asked by his student why he departed this time from his regular silence, and chose to answer his wife. In the two versions of this story, two different answers are given. In one, the Yehudi says: "Did you observe how it throttled her that her scolding had no power over me? And so I had to let her feel that her words did strike me to the heart."[44] In the shorter version of this event the Yehudi explains to his students that he saw that his wife's soul was about to leave her body for rage because he did not let her scolding annoy him, and so he said a trifling word, that she might feel that her words did trouble her husband and draw strength from this feeling.[45]

Schoendel represents here the concerns of the home and the family that are seen as opposed to the grand vision and the historic role of her charismatic husband. She is firmly rooted in the here and now, and has neither patience nor respect for her husband's otherworldly existence. Though depicted as a cantankerous woman who talks incessantly, there is some sympathy for her when she says: "I beg of you to open your ears wide to what I have to say. I insist on being heard." Her moment of fury, when she appears almost like a madwoman in her gestures and harsh language, is a state of total abandon which gives her the freedom denied her in everyday reality. Her explosive fury so overwhelms her authoritative and aloof husband, that he finally responds to her.

In the present story Schoendel is not seen as the captive of a demonic force, but she is punished in several ways for her insubordination to her awe-inspiring, forbidding husband. The sudden inability to speak is a "measure for measure" penalty on the loquacious woman, and, in the second version of this episode, the woman's indulgence in extreme rage almost costs her her life. In the themes of the loss of speech and the fury that might result in self-annihilation, this episode heralds a new phase in female strategy and its consequences.

Dissociation of the Self

The modern literary imagination provides us with many examples of suppressed feminine fury that finally erupts in self-destruction, madness, and dehumanization. Several modern works have been selected to represent the variety of ways in which the male writers projected the female response to oppression and the cost, for a woman, of attempting to defy the patriarchal laws.

The first, "Klonimus and Naomi" (1921), is a shtetl tale written by Micah Yosef Berdichewscky (1865–1921), who started his writing career at the end of Haskalah and whose works mark the transition from Haskalah's dedication to social reform to the writer's growing awareness that the inner world of the individual deserves to be noted and explored.[46] Berdichewscky views life as the individual's struggle to free himself from an uncompromising, demanding, and inflexible society, as well as from the mysterious and arbitrary laws of fate and destiny that govern the human existence.[47] In this respect, Berdichewscky does not differentiate between his female and male protagonists.

To reinforce his conception of the human behavior as a juncture of inherited traits and environmental influences, Berdichewscky starts his short story by giving us the family background of the female protagonist, Naomi. He describes her maternal grandfather as a good-looking man, with a talent for drawing and an eye for beauty. Though being a sensual man driven by strong physical desires, who married four times, Nathan was also an avid reader and was especially interested in the writings of the Jewish mystics. The incongruity between this man's spirits and abilities and the paucity of opportunities results in the diminishing of his charisma; he reconciles himself to a life of petty concerns and narrow visions. His daughter Malkah, who is an unusual beauty, shows even more willingness than her father to resign herself to life's narrow confines, because, as a woman, she is doubly limited. Cleverly, Berdichewscky does not let us into this woman's heart and therefore, whenever her conduct indicates unquestioning readiness to submit her will to stronger forces, be it her stepmother's wishes or the vicissitudes of her own fate, the reader feels a certain hypocritical note in the woman's voice or action, and sees in her conduct a betrayal of her inherited charisma, for which she will be punished.

In deference to the wishes of her stepmother, a woman subservient to men and despotic towards her stepdaughter, Malkah marries a man whose "pockmarked face" and mediocre qualities stand in opposition to the uniqueness of his wife and her father. This man, tormented by jealousy over his wife's beauty and his own relative inadequacy, is driven to insanity and later dies. In Yagel's didactic medieval parable of the "good woman" and "bad woman," the passive and submissive woman is rewarded for her docility by becoming blessed with "good fortune," that results in a succession of auspicious events. By contrast, Malkah's acquiescence to marrying a man who falls

short of her stature creates almost cosmic discord and aesthetic disharmony and results in a string of sufferings that would extend to the
next generation as well.

Malkah remarries after a while and brings to her new husband's
home her daughter Naomi, who inherited her mother's "amazing"
beauty. Naomi, who loves nature and scenic beauty and is endowed
with a good singing voice and a feeling for rhythm and dance, falls in
love with her stepbrother Klonimus, a handsome young man who is
immersed in Judaic scholarship. The whole community notices that
these two young people are made for each other, especially when he
sits at his desk and studies, and she leans over him; also Malkah,
Naomi's mother, prays to God that the two will become a couple.
Nevertheless, when Malkah's husband tells her that a very rich match
has been proposed for his son, Malkah does not raise any objection.
Again, as when she marries an unwanted and unsuitable man, Malkah
accepts the dictates of patriarchy even if they stand opposed to
her own self-interest. Yet Malkah's selflessness, a thread that runs
through the whole story, is always a factor in triggering a tragic chain
of events; as a result of Malkah's consent to her stepson's marriage,
her daughter Naomi, lovesick and feeling betrayed, loses her mind.

Naomi's madness first expresses itself in her running away from the
house and wandering aimlessly in the woods, a twisted attempt at
freedom. When she is brought home and locked in a room, she
breaks everything that she can lay her hands on. She is now regarded
as the seat of "many fierce evil spirits," but her association with the
demonic gives her enormous physical powers. She not only loses her
beauty, but also her human image. She is sent to a sanatorium, returns home and then sent to a physician who puts her "in chains" and
beats her. She now calms down and goes home, yet she has become
completely dehumanized, and leads the life of an animal. Naomi refuses to eat cooked food, she has lost her speech, crawls on all fours,
and emits animal sounds. She does not recognize any of her relatives,
and is frequently subject to strange, disturbing hallucinations.

When spring comes, Klonimus, who has been immersed in his
own thoughts and not paying attention to Naomi's misery, suddenly
feels restless. A short time before his wedding he reveals to his closest
friend that he has lost his faith. The friend is shocked, the whole
town is scandalized, and Klonimus' father beats him up, in the hope
of chasing the unwanted thoughts from his son's heart. Klonimus
now starts a course that runs parallel to that of Naomi's. Like her, he
is being beaten into submission; like her, he tries to escape into the
open spaces, and then withdraws into himself. In analogy to Naomi's
loss of speech, Klonimus, who used to like debates and learned dis-

cussions, stops talking. Whereas Naomi's derangement first finds its expression in explosive violence, in which she runs amok and smashes things, Klonimus is never violent and, after having been beaten by his father, reveals traits of a manic-depressive.

When Klonimus begins his descent into depression, Naomi starts to show signs of partial recovery. She returns to cooked meals, then tries to sit up and even walk, and finally regains her speech. Although she never returns to her former self, she has come back to normalcy; "her soul is healthy now," says Berdichewscky, "but she has lost her soaring spirits." Klonimus' prospective in-laws break their daughter's engagement to him and, after a while, Klonimus marries Naomi in a ceremony that looks more like a funeral. They lead a life of perfect strangers, each enclosed in his own mental cocoon. Their parents' high hopes have been shattered; the brilliant Klonimus now becomes tutor for the children of the poor, and the lovely Naomi, who used to sing and dance, now fusses a bit in the kitchen and then stares aimlessly at the blank wall.

Gershon Shaked sees in Klonimus' insanity an eruption of the suppressed spirits of Naomi's grandfather. The late Nathan is a kind of *dibbuk* that possesses the young man's soul and tries to accomplish, through Klonimus, what the living man never could.[48] In his good looks, inquisitive mind, and mystical inclinations, Klonimus is indeed a replica of the old man, with whom the story starts. But Klonimus has no biological relationship to Nathan, and he was never in his company. The source of Klonimus' insanity is, undoubtedly, Naomi herself. Significantly, when the young man becomes possessed by the "evil spirits," Naomi rids herself of her own inner demons. The analogy between Naomi's route into madness and that of Klonimus inevitably makes us see the relationship between the two. The woman serves as a transmitter of madness; she emits the spirit of insanity and infects the man who is the cause of her mental agony.

In the case of Naomi, it seems that her madness is both congenital, since her father was a lunatic, and environmental, the result of her frustrated love. However, even the madness of Naomi's father is inextricably tied to a woman, his own beautiful wife. Although passive, compliant, and silent, Malkah caused her husband's mental disintegration by the sheer force of her impressive and overwhelming presence. Naomi, through her violence and raving behavior, radiates the spirit of insanity that finally contaminates Klonimus. Though in Berdichewscky's story both men and women are subject to the loss of reason, it seems that the women are the source from which the "evil spirits" flow out and possess the men.

Berdichewscky traces in this tale three forms of feminine *modus* operandi that are not necessarily premeditated, but nevertheless do not always stem from the women's inner being, but are often acquired and adopted as tactics for survival. One is that of Malkah's stepmother, who eagerly arranges for her stunningly pretty daughter an obviously inappropriate match that starts the tale's rapid course to catastrophe. By claiming ignorance of the stepmother's motives, the narrator alerts us to them. The stepmother represents typical female jealousy of a younger and prettier woman, resulting in lack of solidarity and betrayal. The second form of feminine method, displayed by Malkah, is characterized by complete submission, to the point of self-effacement and self-abnegation. The third, Naomi's, is an attempt to suppress the feelings of resentment and defiance that eventually erupt in violence and self-destruction. All three female responses, though seemingly different, bring about disastrous results. Berdichewscky's view of life in this story, as in some of his other works, is tragic almost in the Greek sense. A note of doom and predestination hovers over his protagonists, who will never be able to escape their fate. As Shaked has shown, beauty, wisdom, and an inquisitive mind are viewed as defiance of the "gods," and are punishable with the loss of sanity. The wish for true love is equally seen as a person's attempt to overreach his human boundaries; only those who compromise and reduce themselves to a vacuous, trivial existence, like Nathan and his daughter Malkah, survive. These two pay not only with the diminishing of their own stature; somehow their unspent energies and charisma find their way into the next generation, in this case the hapless Naomi, and wreak havoc in her life.

Naomi is an untraditional young woman in terms of the nineteenth-century East European shtetl. She dares to make her own erotic choice and will not compromise. Her artistic gifts and love of the open spaces set her apart from the traditional mold.[49] Significantly, when she comes back to sanity, defeated and resigned to her lot, she busies herself with the traditional feminine occupations which contradict her previous nature: she spends her time in the kitchen, and then sits in a chair and does needlework.

It is needless to remark that Berdichewscky is not a modern feminist writer, intent on exposing the narrow life imposed on women. As a writer of his generation that witnessed the Jew's emergence from the ghetto mold, he gave voice to the freedom cry of both men and women. But he also felt that the women were subjected to a double jeopardy, tyrannized by the rigid forces of tradition as well as by the patriarchal structure. Beyond that, both men and women were subject to the universal, arbitrary laws of predestination. Yet in the present story at least, Berdichewscky sees the women as more capable of violent eruptions and passionate furies; the men are better able to compromise with life. Even the insanity of Naomi is different from that of her father's and Klonimus' in that it is turbulent and ferocious, while the men's insanity is the sinking into gloom and depression.

Both Naomi and Klonimus have been defeated in their search for freedom which, for the woman, means choosing her own mate and, for the man, delving into the mystery of life with a fresh mind, not bound by preconceived notions. Berdichewscky differentiates between men and women in the intensity of their madness; he also divides the realms of human aspirations along gender lines. The woman is concerned with matters of the heart; the man, with matters of the spirit. Thus Shaked is right in seeing the legacy of the elderly Nathan split between Klonimus and Naomi. The man inherits Nathan's metaphysical yearnings and his wish to solve the most profound questions of existence, while the woman inherits her ancestor's beauty and sensuality, his strong erotic passions and the need to fulfill them.

Self-destruction and regression to the animal level mark Naomi's attempts at rebellion. At the same time, madness gives Naomi the freedom that she has craved. In her madness Naomi articulates her wish to have Klonimus, a wish that she could not express in any other way within her puritanical society. Naomi's madness also triggers Klonimus' restlessness, which results in his iconoclastic words to his pious friend. Thus Naomi achieves in her dehumanized state what she could not accomplish as a gloriously pretty woman: she brings about the cancellation of Klonimus' wedding. Naomi's derangement can consequently be seen as the result of the feminine habit of suppressing anger, and, at the same time, as a partially conscious strategy that, in a perverse manner, allows the woman to have her own way.

Naomi's emergence from madness is seen as both a compromise and an ironic victory. Paradoxically, Naomi gets what she wanted, because she is now married to Klonimus; yet she had to pay a steep price with the shrinking of her own and Klonimus' former brilliant selves. The ending of the story sounds like a parodic reversal of a fairy tale; Klonimus and Naomi live "happily ever after" in an existence that is more like death-in-life.

S. Y. Agnon's "In the Prime of Her Life" (1923),[50] is told in the first person by a young girl, Tirtza Mintz, whose mother died "in the prime of her life." A lively and curious girl, Tirtza falls in love with her middle-aged schoolmaster, Akaviah Mazal, when she learns that he was her mother's true love. Many years before, Akaviah had been discouraged from proposing to Tirtza's mother, Leah, by the latter's parents, who saw in the impoverished scholar an unsuitable match for their frail daughter. Leah complied with her parents' wishes, married Mintz, the man that they chose for her, bore him a daughter, and then died of a heart ailment.

Baruch Kurzweil saw in this story a study of the "generational strife" that plagued the shtetl Jews at the turn of our century, as they found themselves at a historical and cultural crossroad.[51] The old, traditional Jewish values, together with bourgeois morality, are rejected by Tirtza, who dares to choose her own lover and marry a secular man on the margins of the Jewish society which, in the small towns, was still largely pious. Obviously, Tirtza repeats her mother's history with a difference, realizing Leah's hidden desires for Akaviah, and defying the rigid values of her middle-class Jewish environment for whom Akaviah is undesirable because of his lack of financial as well as social status (his ancestors had converted to Christianity). Tirtza assumes the role of her mother's "double," permitting herself what her mother denied herself, and thus becoming, ostensibly, a less frustrated, more fulfilled replica of the former generation.

The theme of the double—reality and its mirror image—consequently becomes one of the major themes, as well as literary techniques, of the story. On the face of it, by becoming her mother's double, Tirtza rectifies the injustice done both to Leah and to Mazal, and therefore creates harmony where there was once lack of harmony, union, where there was separation, and consummated love, where there once was physical and emotional denial. Yet the reader soon begins to realize that the theme of the double involves falsehood, the negation of the real self, and worse, the splitting of the self into different, even conflicting entities. Ultimately, the double becomes a creator of anarchy and an emblem of souls at war with themselves as well as of a society unsure of itself.[52]

The motif of the double is enhanced by the many references to mirrors and to shadows in the story, especially in the description of Leah's last days, when her strength leaves her like "a shadow," or when there is a deceptive illusion of recovery, just before her death, and shadows that run over her body glimmer in the mirror. It seems that Leah dealt with losing her love and marrying another man by creating a double which is a shadow of her old self. She gives her shadow to the man that she is married to, but her real self is submerged under the facade of resignation and acceptance.

A pair of twins frequently mentioned in the story, the brothers Gottlieb, enhance the theme of the twin images of life. Gottlieb's infant cries when he sees the two men together, realizing that the man he thought was his father was not. The child thus protests against the phenomenon of the double, revealing in his cry that he would accept only one of the twins as the genuine person, not both of them (187).

Just as Tirtza's life is an attempt to emulate someone's else's existence, so the Hebrew that she uses is an imitation of an imitation. Arnold Band remarks that the language in this tale is "a variant of the normal Agnonic style of the period."[53] The reason for this is that the style of the story is that of Tirtza the *maskilah* or 'enlightened girl', who copies the language of the Haskalah writers.[54] The biblical cadence and locutions represent the style of the literature that Tirtza has been reading, and probably the form of Hebrew that she has learned. Thus Tirtza imitates the language of the *maskilim,* the writers of the Enlightenment, who themselves imitated biblical vocabulary and syntax.

The theme of imitation and doubleness, the genuine original and its pale reflection, extends to the emotional lives of the individual characters as well as to the social questions that the story touches. Thus the validity of reality itself is questioned: are Tirtza's feelings genuine, or is she just forcing herself to feel what her mother felt? Are Mazal and Tirtza's father rivals, or are they the two sides of the same man? Conversely, could Mintz replace Mazal and make Leah happy, or would Leah be happy only with her original lover, Mazal? Did Tirtza find in Mazal a husband and lover, or just another paternal figure, in the image of her own father?

The social questions are a variation of the personal questions. They apply to the validity of the old Jewish mold; is it a vital, enduring existence, or just an illusion, a dream that will soon fade away? Akaviah Mazal has found in his archeological research that this town is built over an old cemetery; thus his findings question the very being of this world, which still in many ways adheres to the old pious traditions: is the old Jewish world alive or is it founded on graves, on dead, obsolete ideas, and disintegrating before our very eyes? Similarly, Tirtza's Haskalah Hebrew raises questions with regard to modern Hebrew; is it going to be just a pale, artificial reflection of the biblical language, or will it possess an independent vitality, enriched by biblical Hebrew but not overshadowed by it? And, in a broader sense, is the modern, secular Jewish culture, that the Enlightenment is trying to bring about and promote, going to strike roots and become a valid existence, or will it be just a diminished reflection of the old world of tradition; will it be able to offer vital and viable ideas in the place of the old, rejected ones?

One of the main functions of the theme of the double is to illuminate and signalize the female strategy in a story where Agnon has departed from his usual custom of filtering reality through the male eyes, and allowed a woman to tell her own story. Leah's strategy is withdrawing into her private sphere of heart sickness that allows her to lie in bed, divorce herself from everyday life, and avoid sexual contact with her husband.[55] The sick Leah is a shadow of the real one, a subterfuge for the lively and pretty young woman who once knew the intensity of romantic love. But the mask that hides the old self is very sick, and once it departs from this world it marks the death of the original woman too.[56] We know that the young Leah was troubled by poor health and that her parents wanted for her a rich man who could afford the heavy medical expenses and give her an easy life. Their hope was that, with the proper care that only money could buy, their daughter would overcome her heart ailment. Ironically, when she marries and settles into a comfortable existence, her disease intensifies, until she dies. In terms of the double motif, Leah refuses to get rid of her sick self; on the contrary, she nurtures and nourishes this self, hiding and suppressing the old self that was not allowed to express itself, and that, in her mind, belonged to another man, Akaviah.

The descriptions of the sick Leah point to the fact that the woman welcomes disease and death as the only alternatives to a life of heartbroken misery. Leah dies of a "broken" heart in a medical as well as metaphorical sense. She refuses to stay at the health spas and returns home because she experiences strong longings; but, of course, she does not find the real object of her longings when she comes home. She prepares herself for death long before the doctors have given up any hope, by wearing white, the color of shrouds. Her name, Leah, means 'weary' in Hebrew, and it also recalls the biblical Leah. The ancient woman led a loveless life and was one of two wives, while the modern Leah is loved by two men, yet is even more miserable than her biblical counterpart.

The language of the Song of Songs permeates the first few pages of the story, with an ironic twist. Leah and her husband sit in a position similar, yet different, from that of the Canticles lovers: her husband's left hand rests under his head and his right hand is in hers. This is a variation on: "His left hand is under my head, and his right hand embraces me" (Song of Songs 8 : 3). The erotic flavor of the Canticles verse exposes the bond between Leah and her husband as pale and passionless. Though Leah is indeed "lovesick," no reproduction of the spirit of Canticles is possible, since Leah feels only gratitude and affection towards her husband, not burning desire.

After Leah's death the phenomenon of the double begins to pervade her daughter's existence. When Tirtza meets Akaviah Mazal for the first time, not yet aware of his past role in her mother's life, she sees in him a reflection of her mother. And, without realizing the connection between her father and Mazal, she views the two men as mirror images of each other.

Tirtza's attitude towards her mother is a mixture of love and vague resentment over being abandoned by her. She begins to feel a mysterious link to her, and the identification with the dead woman becomes increasingly close. But when her father, immersed in his grief, neglects her, Tirtza betrays some jealousy towards the dead woman, which increases when she learns of her mother's secret past and her love for Mazal. She also begins to feel sorry for Mazal, arguing that he is like a man whose lawful wife has been taken away from him.

The discovery of her mother's love for Mazal shakes Tirtza's sense of identity. She feels betrayed by the people closest to her, and at the same time she also pities them. Tirtza sees in both her father and Mazal victims but also victimizers. The previous generation submitted to powers of conventional wisdom and social mores, but at the same time they betrayed both themselves and the person they loved. Tirtza pities her father for marrying an unloving woman, but she is also furious at him for entering into this loveless relationship, and standing in the way of true love. She sympathizes with Mazal who lost his love, yet she is angry with him for not fighting for it. She refuses to accept the old generation's subjection to laws that demanded the negation of the self.

Tirtza is resolved to adopt a strategy for survival that will be the polar opposite of her mother's. If her mother surrendered to her parents' wishes and married the man they wanted for her, Tirtza will not listen to her father, and marry the man of her choice. Tirtza represents the transition from a tradition-oriented society to an inner-oriented society, where the private desires and preferences of the individual take precedence over social conventions and proprieties. Tirtza's name, that enfolds in Hebrew the verb 'will', also points to the young woman's strong will and her determination to act upon her private wishes and exercise her own volition. Ironically, for Tirtza to correct the damage that was done in her mother's generation and to act in opposition to her mother's passive submission, she has to repeat her mother's life, fall in love with the man her mother loved, and marry him.

Tirtza does not realize that asserting her own will would paradoxically entail the surrender of her own will. For Tirtza is not genuinely in love with Mazal, although for a time she thinks she is. Her infatuation with Mazal is part of her fascination with, and resentment of the past. By trying to depart from past attitudes and forms of behavior, Tirtza now has to relive the past. Unlike her mother, she marries the man who is deemed unsuitable in her father's eyes; but very much like her mother, she does not marry the man she loves. Her love for Mazal soon fades, and Tirtza's married life with Mazal resembles her own mother's life with Mintz, Tirtza's father. Like her mother, Tirtza is now planning her own death, praying to God to give her an infant girl who would tend to Mazal's needs after her own untimely death. Tirtza is now emulating the strategy of her mother Leah, who chose to die, leaving Tirtza behind as a comfort, and perhaps a token of appreciation, to the man that she married but towards whom she felt no passion.

Very early in the story, before Tirtza becomes aware of the heart-breaks of the past, she witnesses a conversation between her father and Mazal, which she only partly understands. Soon after Leah's death, Tirtza and her father visit Mazal and ask him to write the inscription on Leah's tombstone. Tirtza's father tells Mazal that he rummaged through his dead wife's drawers in order to find Mazal's old poems, that she had in her possession, since he, Tirtza's father, wished to publish them. However, Mazal's writings were love verses, composed for his beloved Leah, and meant to be read by her only. By regarding Mazal's compositions as poems that are worthy of being published, Leah's husband purposely ignores their private meaning as an expression of Mazal's love for Leah, pretending that their value was in their universal aspect. Mazal insists, however, that he made no copies of his poems, implying that the genuine original cannot be copied. His words should have been a warning to the young Tirtza, making her realize that she could not copy the love between her own mother and Mazal by recreating a similar bond between herself and Mazal. Love cannot be reproduced, Mazal, in essence, seems to be saying, and indeed, he does not love Tirtza in the same way that he loved her mother.

In the relationship between Mazal and Tirtza, the woman is the aggressive pursuer, and the man, the passive object of pursuit. As with most of Agnon's couples, it is the woman who is the active partner in the courtship and the love relationship, while the man is subdued, submitting to the woman's wishes rather than actively expressing his own. Aware that Mazal likes to take walks in the woods, Tirtza meets him there and alarms him by pretending to have been bitten by a dog. The ruse that Tirtza uses to draw Mazal's attention to her feminine presence may seem naive to the modern reader. Neither the girl-narrator's puritanical and prudish upbringing nor Agnon's own euphemistic and restrained style, would allow for a graphic portrayal of erotic situations. But Agnon makes up for the absence of explicit language by evoking archetypal symbols of sexual temptation. Baruch

Kurzweil remarked on the primal meanings of the dog as a symbol and carrier of sexual temptation, as well as of the forest which, in its noncivilized condition, stands for wild, unbridled instincts and desires, uninhibited by the laws and customs of organized society.[57] By claiming to have been bitten by a dog, Tirtza forces Mazal into physical contact with her, and into betraying some feelings towards her (191).

In terms of the times, Tirtza is daring and forward in her pursuit of Akaviah. Yet when her more "modern" methods of luring the man do not work, she resorts to her mother's strategy: she becomes very sick. Again we see the irony where the freer, more "liberated" Tirtza, intent on correcting her mother's mistakes, has to emulate her mother. Tirtza arranges another walk in the forest with Mazal, where the man tries to dissuade her from further courting him, pointing out, correctly, that she is just infatuated with him and that her amorous feelings for him will pass. Tirtza goes home and becomes sick, apparently because she caught a cold walking in the damp forest in the chilly spring weather with only a light summer dress on. In her feverish condition, Tirtza begins to hallucinate and then, in imitation of her mother's ailment, she sighs from her "heart."[58] She also tells her astonished father that she has become engaged to Mazal. As his daughter's illness intensifies, Tirtza's father, too, decides not to repeat the mistakes of the past. He apparently talks to Mazal, and when Tirtza finally wakes up from her fever, she sees both Akaviah and her father standing at her bedside and beaming at her.

Tirtza instills in Mazal feelings of guilt when she becomes ill, because he allowed her to take a long walk with him in the damp weather. In a deeper way, this guilt mingles with Mazal's feelings that he was responsible for Leah's death, because he had complied with her parents' wishes and given her up without a fight. Tirtza's deteriorating health also awakens in her father memories of another woman whose denied love caused her death, and, in his devotion to his daughter, he agrees to her union with Mazal, and even helps bring it about. It seems that each of the persons involved in the past drama of unfulfilled love now tries to correct the damage that was done many years ago, yet fails as miserably as he did the first time: Tirtza is no happier with Mazal than her mother was without him.

But Tirtza's falling into ill health is only part of the strategy that she uses in order to fight the rigid, stifling forces of tradition. In her feverish condition, Tirtza slips into another identity, that of her mother's. The close feelings of identification that Tirtza had always had towards the dead woman, together with Tirtza's deliberate attempts to repeat and improve her mother's life story by giving it a

happy ending, ultimately result in a complete split within Tirtza's
psyche: the self that was once Tirtza is now silenced and suppressed,
and a new self emerges, that of Leah. In her delirium, she speaks as if
she is the woman who was once almost married to Mazal (210).
Later, when she is still lying sick in bed, Tirtza feels her mother's
voice talking through her, as if the dead Leah is now a *dibbuk* that
possesses her daughter's body, lives through her, and even gives the
young woman her own weak heart: Tirtza now feels that her heart
beats feebly and that her own voice sounds like her mother's voice at
the time of the latter's illness (211).

In her delirium Tirtza becomes Leah, but when she recovers, the
two selves, that of Leah and that of Tirtza, coexist within her. The
two men in her life merge into one person, as they both look at her
with love and compassion and their faces become indistinguishable
from each other. Tirtza realizes that they both love her in the same
way, and that Mazal's feelings for her are paternal; vis-à-vis Tirtza
both men are fathers, and vis-à-vis Leah, both are lovers. Thus Tirtza
can win Mazal as a lover only if she stops being Tirtza and becomes
Leah. At the end of the novel Tirtza becomes aware of the irony of her
situation when she reminds herself of the Gottlieb infant who cried
when he realized that the man he was playing with, and whom he
thought to be his father, turned out to be someone else (his father's
identical twin). In his innocence, the child conveys the message that
his love is given only to the original, his own father, and not to the
impostor, no matter how much like the original he actually looks
(216). Tirtza now understands that Mazal's passionate love was given
to her mother, Leah, and that she herself is only an impostor, in spite
of all her attempts to relive Leah's situation and recreate the dead
woman's image.

Tirtza's struggle for independence, for asserting her own individuality and shaking off social conventions, ends unhappily. As in Berdichewscky's world, the deterministic laws that govern human life are
more powerful than the individual's fierce wish for freedom. Tirtza
is doomed to live someone else's life rather than her own. With all
her "progressive" ideas and schooling, she is no different from her
mother, resorting to the same subterfuges and paying with her health
and the loss of her identity. The sick self, which was both real and
invented, was an excuse for Leah not to fight against the social order
of things; for Tirtza, the sick self is devised as an instrument of ma-
nipulation, yet in the end she has only manipulated herself into an
unhappy, unfulfilled life.

The Mazal home becomes a focal point in the mind of another Agnon protagonist as he slowly sinks into madness that results from unfulfilled love. In *A Simple Story*[59] Hirshel Horovitz is a man who succumbed to his parents' wishes and gave up the woman he loved for the rich heiress that his parents chose for him. Since Bluma, his beloved, works in the household of Mazal and Tirtza, the obsessed Hirshel finds himself walking involuntarily towards that home, which is in the older part of town, outside the main concentration of the Jewish community. Akaviah Mazal and his wife represent for Hirshel the successful rebellion against the petty social mores that govern the middle-class Jewish community, and that have destroyed Hirshel's life and his sanity. Of course, we know that the Mazal household is not particularly happy and that there is no fulfillment of passionate love there. To Hirshel, however, as to the community as a whole, the Mazals are people who have dared go against the stream and who have separated themselves from their bourgeois environment. We thus get a chance to see Mazal and Tirtza through the lenses of the outside observers. If Tirtza's efforts to correct the past have resulted in unhappiness for herself, for the outside world she still stands for the individual's ability to fight against the social conventions.

Agnon's *A Simple Story* is also significant to us in that the person who loses his healthy self is not the woman, but the man. After the separation from his beloved Bluma and the forced marriage to an unloved woman, Hirshel's mental health begins to deteriorate until he goes mad and has to be incarcerated. Bluma, on the other hand, makes the best of her unhappy situation, finds a job and resumes her life. As in Berdichewscky's story, the woman is the cause of the man's madness, yet unlike in the latter, the woman herself does not lose her mental lucidity before she infects the man with insanity. In analogy with Berdichewscky's views, the compromise that follows the eruption of madness in Agnon's world results in the diminishing of the old personality. Though Hirshel is never described by Agnon as particularly charismatic, after he is cured and returns home he is even more lackluster than he was before. He compromises by pretending to love his wife and be content with his home situation. He thus lets hypocrisy rule his life, whereas before he at least attempted to be truthful to himself and to his feelings.[60] Agnon's language at the end of this novella, describing the former lovesick and passionate youth as a well-fed, well-dressed petit bourgeois, surrounded by material wealth and coarsely pleased with his fertile wife as well as with his other worldly possessions, is saturated with irony.

The difference between the splitting of the self that occurs to the woman protagonist of "In the Prime of Her Life" and the complete descent into madness that happens to the male protagonist of *A Simple Story* is that the woman manipulates herself into her condition, while the man succumbs to the loss of sanity. The same differentiation between the male fury and the feminine fury occurs, with some variations, in Berdichewscky's story. Naomi chooses madness as a form of protest, and she catapults herself out of it when she sees the possibility of getting the man that she wanted. Tirtza, too, while never clinically insane, voluntarily ruptures her psyche into two selves and lives the life of her double, instead of her own. For Hirshel, the eruption of insanity is more of a surrender to inner forces of derangement that gradually take over. In other words, while for the man the mental disintegration is a passive capitulation to the forces of psychic chaos, for the woman the mad fury and the psychic fragmentation are simultaneously both caused by forces beyond her control and self-induced—a means of manipulating a reality that is otherwise not controllable and gaining the freedom not afforded within a constrictive universe. The mad double or the gravely sick double are forms of female duplicity, a tactic to circumvent and fool the ferocious powers of fate and social authority. But freedom and self-destruction, the two extremes of the double-edged sword of feminine strategy, become at the end one and the same. Berdichewscky's mad Naomi gains the freedom that she craves at the expense of her sanity and brilliant personality; Agnon's Leah is released from an untenable situation through the shadow that becomes her sick double, but as her double's health deteriorates and it departs from the land of the living, it takes Leah with it. Tirtza wills her mother's self into overtaking her own life, but she pays with the loss of her former individuality, and with the constant knowledge that the man who acts as if he loves her, does not really feel passion for her, the young Tirtza, but for the Leah that she has become.[61]

*   *

Several female protagonists in modern Hebrew literature retreat to a suicidal state of depression or hysteria as the only form of rebellion available to women. Mariashka, the protagonist of Berkowitz's short story by the same name, is seen at the end of the tale reduced to a near-catatonic state of apathy and loss of interest in life, gazing blankly at the river, intuitively sensing that the deep waters are her only escape from an unbearable existence.[62] Another Berkowitz woman, Shifra the seamstress, the protagonist of "Cucumbers,"[63] resorts to a hysterical outburst, after which she storms out of her parents' home, intent on throwing herself into the river and drowning.

Shifra had left her provincial hometown a few years before with the hope of finding a more cultured and satisfying life in the big city. Although she has found work as a seamstress, her hopes of sewing for herself a new reality of refinement and self-fulfillment have not been realized. Defeated, she returns to her poor parents and their run-down, dilapidated home. The shabby existence of meagerness and destitution, resulting in pettiness of mind and coarse habits, contrasts sharply with Shifra's newly acquired sensitivities and tastes. She becomes imbued with feelings of "no exit," and escapes from the dreary reality into a world of fantasy, her mind fueled by the romantic novels that she borrows from the local library and reads voraciously.

Shifra is not much different from many of the Hebrew protagonists in the early part of our century who find themselves at a cultural as well as existential dead end. Berkowitz's powerful story "Severed" deals with a young physician who returns to his provincial hometown and is torn between the old world of empty piety combined with devastating poverty, and the new secular world that is, perhaps, more refined and cultured but at the same time vacuous and pretentious, having abandoned the old traditions but not found any substantial alternatives.[64] Shifra is in a similar situation, yet as a woman, her predicament is worse. The young man could more easily survive in the big city and acquire a profession than the young woman; Winnik, the male protagonist of "Severed," succeeds in obtaining a medical degree in spite of his poor origins, while Shifra's liberation still hinges on her competence in the traditional female occupation, sewing. In fact, Shifra's culture is skin-deep; it consists of a few hygienic habits that she has acquired in the big city and of her addiction to the cheap romantic novels that she borrows in the library, but she is basically ignorant.

When a matchmaker arrives at Shifra's home, offering Shifra a young tailor, the already nervous and tense girl explodes. She screams and yells, sneering at her parents' poverty and ignorance, and then runs out of the house. Shifra plans to commit suicide, yet she is too frightened to throw herself into the chilly river. She calms down and spends the night outdoors, returning home in the morning with broken spirits and hopeless melancholy. Shifra's brief minute of rebellion, which erupted in a hysteric fit, leaves her drained and exhausted, but it also helps deflate her dreams of glory and passionate love. Unlike the heroines we have previously discussed, Shifra is not strong, imaginative, and resourceful enough to resort to the more elaborate strategies that they have contrived and that resulted in self-destruction. Shifra is too timid to kill herself and therefore has now become more subdued, probably ready to compromise and settle into a life of vulgar, petty existence. Because Shifra is not described as glowingly as Berdichewscky's or Agnon's heroines, the self that she gives up and the one she would probably settle for are not so different. In a sense, it is Shifra's mediocrity that saves her, since she is not capable of going to the lengths that Naomi, or Leah, or Tirtza do. Paradoxically, the more elaborate and imaginative the feminine strategy is, the more it results in the loss of a glorious self.

The destructiveness of feminine rage is a major theme in Dvorah Baron's story "Excision."[65] The barren woman Zlata, who was divorced by her husband at the urging of his family as well as almost the whole shtetl, because she could not give him children, attends the services in the synagogue. She suddenly sees her former husband's new wife entering the chapel, with a newborn baby in her arms. The woman bursts out in a hysterical cry that makes everyone question whether God conducts his world in justice. The terrible scream that comes from the bottom of the woman's heart in a moment of complete self-abandon, when she no longer cares to hide her misery from her neighbors, becomes a feminine cry for cosmic justice in the face of patriarchal tyranny. The woman's cry puts on trial the ultimate patriarch, God himself, who, by rewarding the treacherous husband with a fertile wife, has thus reinforced the oppressive tenets of patriarchy. After this event, Zlata refuses any help and turns down every job offered to her. She roams the streets hungry and disheveled, fading away, until she finally dies.

Many of the female protagonists we have examined do not resign themselves to their fate without some kind of reaction, be it fully or partly conscious. The less memorable characters succumb to circumstances and suppress their discontent, experiencing only a brief, short-lived flare-up of a bitter outburst that soon recedes. But most of the energies spent by the more outstanding women in contriving, manipulating, and creating imagined new worlds in place of an intolerable reality—from the biblical Rebecca and Leah to the modern Naomi and Tirtza—are seen as either greatly wasted or, worse yet, turning on the women and themselves and destroying them. Yet not all female tactics for survival end disastrously. The woman's ability to imagine and to create may sometimes be forced out of latency, and even flower in dire circumstances. A case in point is the figure of the woman-narrator in Dvorah Baron's writings, who undoubtedly represents the writer herself.[66] The teller of Baron's tales is a young girl, the daughter of the local rabbi in a small Lithuanian shtetl, who grows up to become a writer. Thus the tales are spun from a double perspective: that of the young girl who records the events as they happen, not al-

ways fully understanding the meaning of the events that she witnesses, and the older woman, writing from a chronological and
geographical distance that enables her to assess and evaluate in a more
mature way the shtetl material stored in her mind.

The young girl is especially alert to the subjection, and the mental
and social abuse, of the women around her, not in her own family,
but in the Jewish community at large. The home situation is unbearable for a different reason: the saintly father is a sickly man, whose
scholarship is not appreciated by his congregants, most of whom are
poor and ignorant, and some of whom are more affluent, but coarse
and arrogant. The beloved mother is too refined for the devastatingly
poor and ignorant community to which her husband brought her.
The consumptive father will later die, leaving a young widow and
small orphans. Against this background the sensitive young girl's
only escape is separating herself from her surroundings, not by aban-
doning them mentally, but rather by becoming the objective observer, committing every detail of the life around her to memory, so
that she will be able to reproduce it in her writings later on in her life.
The girl's alter ego becomes the detached and dispassionate recorder
of the small family dramas that unfold in her father's court, as well as
of the heartbreaking situation in her own family. Oppression from
within is exacerbated by oppression from without, as the girl witnesses instances of anti-Semitism or hears hostile innuendos. The
creation of another self that is not emotionally involved and therefore
does not suffer, a double that serves as the historian of the life around
her, allows the girl to retain in her memory scenes and fragments of
life, human faces and gestures, that will later supply the yarn with
which the adult writer will weave her tales. Thus while the girl-
observer identifies with the suffering women who come to her father's court, she also enjoys a degree of freedom that they lack, precisely because of her ability to lift herself out of the present situation
and view the scenes that she witnesses as stories, and the real people
as characters.

Baron also pays tribute to the memory of her charismatic, long-
suffering father, by recalling how he used to relate to her what he had
read and studied, simply because often there was no one else to listen
to him. The father thus filled his daughter's mind with ideas, par-
ables, and images. If Baron's stories convey an amount of bitterness
against the oppression of women, they are not saturated with hatred
of men. On the contrary, the figure of the kindly, humanistic, and
beloved father creates a positive patriarchal model that hovers over
many of her stories and turns the blame away from men, towards the

universal forces of oppression such as poverty, ignorance, and, in the particular Jewish experience, persecution.

By introducing his daughter to books and to the world of the imagination, the father figure in Baron's writings supplied his daughter with a weapon that would help her fight the possible claustrophobia that might have been induced by the sense of "no exit" that permeated the sorrowful existence of the Jews in the shtetl. Looking at life as material for the written word was the female strategy of liberation used by Baron, who thus converted a potentially shattering experience into a life of rich creativity. In a story by another woman writer, Lea Goldberg, who made her mark in modern Hebrew literature mainly as a poet, the father figure is an image of betrayal who, paradoxically, also becomes a possible source of creativity for his daughter. In this story "And It Is the Light" (1946),[67] Nora, the protagonist, returns to her home in a small Lithuanian town, from Berlin, where she is now a student, for the summer vacation. The time is the early to mid-thirties. On the train she shows extreme sensitivity when she is asked who her father is. Later we learn that Nora's father is incarcerated in a mental asylum and that his wife has recently obtained a divorce from him.

Nora is torn between pity for her father and resentment over his mental disease, which she regards as a weakness, a form of letting go, exercised by a man unwilling to summon the powers needed to fight the battle of life. It turns out that the father had been severely beaten and abused in a flare-up of anti-Semitic actions, from which he has never recovered mentally. Just as Nora is conflicted about her father, so is she divided in her feelings towards the Jewish people and her own Jewish heritage. Nora is a secular girl who left the small town to acquire a profession in the big city. She abhors the narrow parochial mold of her hometown, and the Jews' lack of culture, as well as of hygienic habits. Nevertheless, to find comfort from her intolerable family situation, she turns not to one of the European writers whom she is obviously studying at school, but rather to a poem by the medieval Spanish Hebrew poet Moses Ibn Ezra (c. 1055–post-1135). Ibn Ezra, who had to flee Granada to Christian Spain, and for most of his days led the life of a refugee, wrote both sensual love verses, as well as liturgical poetry. The Ibn Ezra verses that constantly run through Nora's mind describe a secret light with which the poet is endowed, that intensifies and increases as the poet grows older, giving him strength. For Nora, the light has a secular and personal meaning, signifying clarity of mind and sanity, in contradiction to her father's deranged mind. Nora clings to these verses just as she is fiercely determined not to succumb to the powers of madness, as her father did.

Yet the light is not only the absence of mental confusion, but also the light of creativity that followed the medieval poet in his exile and strengthened him, and that, Nora hopes, will permeate her, too. Thus the mental darkness of the father acts as a catalyst of light for Nora. In her longings for a paternal figure, however, Nora creates an alter ego for her father, embodied in her father's childhood friend, who has just come for a visit from America, where he has been living for many years. Nora sees in Arin, who arrived unexpectedly, a substitute for her father, and projects on him all the qualities that she found missing in her father. While the latter is egoistic, immersed in his own dark, mental cocoon, and incapable of satisfying his daughter's need for a father, Arin is a "man of the world" who broke out of the small town and created a life for himself in America; he also displays interest in Nora, converses with her, and takes her to the theatre. Subsequently, when Arin disappears as suddenly and mysteriously as he arrived, the puzzled Nora learns that he had experienced a mental breakdown in America, and came to his hometown to find some peace and quiet in his childhood scenes. When Arin began to feel that he was slipping back into insanity, he left Nora and her mother with no explanation, fearful of hurting Nora if she learned the truth.

Nora is a divided person, aware of two powers that are battling in her own psyche, that of her strong determination to retain her sanity and lead a life of lucidity, coherence, and emotional stability, on the one hand, and that of her paternal heredity, which might pull her towards madness, on the other. She projects that duality into the outside world, by creating a healthy male double for her sick father. Ultimately, Nora is betrayed by the whole male world, embodied in the two men, and she realizes that the "light," that source of mental strength, as well as the talent to see the wonder and beauty of life, must come from within her feminine psyche. At the close of the story, Nora seems more disillusioned with the world than at the beginning, yet at the same time, she is stronger, more determined not to yield to the powers of darkness, and committed to the pursuit of "light" in the spirit of Ibn Ezra's poem.

Interestingly, while in the works of the male writers that we have discussed, the female characters invent a sick, or even mad, double in an attempt to relieve the pain inflicted by life, in the writings of the two women who are contemporaries of these male writers, the double that is evoked by the female protagonists is the healthy, redeeming, and creative self. A possible reason for this difference between the male and female writers is that the two women writers project their own selves into their works, though they both give the young female protagonists names different from their own, in an effort to explore and clarify the wellsprings of their respective talents. Baron's tales and Lea Goldberg's novella reverberate with autobiographical, confessional notes, in which the authors attempt to come to terms with their unique position as women creating within a male literary tradition. They both see their creativity as somehow related to their own relationships with the male world, whether in a positive or negative way, and both evoke the male literary and poetic tradition as a source of inspiration.[68]

Retreat into the Feminine Sphere

From the biblical women to the modern female protagonists, the wish to gain freedom from the shackles of patriarchy, to break through the walls isolating the female sphere from the male domain and be able to control a world dominated by masculine rules, has been a motivating force in women's actions. The call for liberation from a narrowly enclosed female existence is enfolded in the very name of Amos Oz's protagonist in "Nomad and Viper" (1963).[69] Geula's name, which means 'redemption' in Hebrew, illuminates the three levels of meaning that exist in this powerful story—the national, the existential and the sexual. Like many of Oz's protagonists, both male and female, Geula is at odds with her kibbutz society and experiences a claustrophobic sense of living in a small, encircled area—the kibbutz and, by extension, modern Israel—threatened by enemies from within and from without.

The enemies from without are the mad jackal, the furtive nomad, and the murderous enemy soldier—the foes from the animal as well as the human world—that surround the civilized, sedentary community, intending to infect it with rabies, plunder it, and return it to primordial chaos. Though the beast and the savage are fenced out, fought off, and kept at a safe distance, they find their allies in the heavily guarded, seemingly secure settlement. The jackals unleash dormant primitive and irrational forces in man's best friend, the dog, as well as in man himself. Thus the police dogs, called to hunt down thieving nomads, suddenly betray their masters, and instead reveal their kinship to the jackals by uttering "a savage howl," and staring "foolishly ahead" (25). Similarly, the presence of the nomads brings out the barbarian in the young kibbutz members who hotheadedly suggest violent retaliation against the pilfering Bedouins. And Geula, believed to have a calming influence on the young man, responds to the savage rhythm with rapture (36).

On one level, Geula can be seen as a representative of the generation that realized the Zionist dream of secular redemption in the form of political independence. To this limited extent, Geula's urge to get out of the confining, artificial borders of the kibbutz, and her heightened awareness of the savage element that closes in reflect the modern Israeli's sense of entrapment in a constant state of siege. They also reveal the Israeli's mixed feelings in his assessment of the national endeavor as an imposition of the Western rational heritage on a terrain populated by nomads and savages, whose primitive, barbaric presence constantly challenges the validity and judiciousness of the Zionist enterprise. Geula's profound sense of loneliness also reverberates with existential motifs of man's estrangement in a hostile universe.

But the present story offers an added dimension to this familiar Oz theme, by focusing on a woman character. If Geula's father had national redemption in mind when he gave his daughter her name in the prestatehood years, Geula is now seen in pursuit of a different, more private, ego-centered kind of salvation. Her calm, civilized exterior belies an inner world of seething feminine desires that have not found release and relief.

Geula is not mentioned until the end of the second chapter of the story, and her voice is conveyed directly to us only in the fourth chapter. Thus the theme of the suppression of the individual within a supposedly unified community is reflected in the gradual, slow emergence of Geula's voice out of the oppressive, overwhelming voice of the whole community speaking as one. The story starts with the voice of the collective "we" of the kibbutz, currently confronted with the disturbing presence of a large population of nomads who have been driven by drought and famine to the kibbutz borders. A meeting is called for the evening to discuss the sensitive situation, to which the girl Geula is also invited. Out of the collective "we" emerges the "I" of the storyteller, a young man who tells us that Geula is twenty-nine, unmarried, and that the whole kibbutz recognizes her meritorious qualities as a cultured girl with poetic interests, who is also the best coffee brewer among them.

Geula herself is depicted with the aid of images that convey thwarted eroticism; in fact, it is possible to follow Geula's movements within the story exclusively through the imagery of sexual tension and release. When we first meet Geula in the hot and damp night, she tries several times to smash a bottle lying on the ground, but "she still failed to hear the shattering sound that she craved" (29). And later, in the fragrant orchard, she crushes plum after plum, until she feels dizzy. Geula's voice, an inward cry complaining "no relief" and insisting "must get out" (29), reveals her sense of imprisonment not only within the boundaries of the kibbutz, but in her humiliated, rejected femininity.

Geula's coffee-brewing, described in minute details, is emblematic of her unsuccessful attempts to suppress and deny her other, sexual self. Her function as the kibbutz's semiofficial coffee-maker gives Geula a social role, similar to her membership on the culture committee. Yet the brewing of coffee signifies Geula's second self, which is ridden with the unhealthy tension of unfulfillment; it becomes a substitute for the sexual relief that she never experiences: "She stood and counted the number of times the coffee boiled—seven successive boilings. . . . With pursed lips she counted as the black liquid rose and subsided, rose and subsided, bubbling fiercely as it reached its climax" (35). The facade that she puts up is that of the active community person, fully integrated within her cohesive society, self-possessed and rational. The self that Geula is forced to submerge is that of her feminine being, which has not been accepted or recognized by the kibbutz society. If the general consensus is that Geula is a worthy member of the kibbutz community, the unsaid implication is that she is unattractive as a woman, and will never find a mate in a small, immobile society that does not change much: "On hot days . . . the acne on her cheeks reddens, and she seems to have no hope" (28). In reality, the woman Geula feels ostracized by a collective masculine voice that has passed a cruel and fatal judgment on her femininity. She is both at the center of her society and yet completely alone: "She goes alone and she comes alone. Some of the youngsters come and ask me what she is looking for there, and they have a malicious snicker on their faces. I tell them that I don't know. And I really don't" (28).

The dialogue between Geula and the stealthy nomad, who surprises her in her lonely walk in the orchard, is comic in its incongruity between the sophisticated, cynical girl and the primitive man, and at the same time, it is laden with erotic associations and undertones. The nomad "bestows a long caress on the air" (30), and the girl suddenly fastens the top button of her blouse (31). Geula then accepts a cigarette from the nomad, and the moment of smoking together becomes saturated with heavy sexual tension. The girl finds the one-eyed Bedouin "repulsively handsome," and amusedly accepts his compliment that she is beautiful. In a twisted way, Geula and the Bedouin are alike in that both are outcasts, unattractive and unattached. When this moment of closeness is over, Geula rudely dismisses the nomad and then returns to the kibbutz, feeling nauseated.

She is frightened by her own loneliness that has made her wish the nomad's sexual advances, and upset at seeing in him—if for a brief moment only—a soul mate and a man. As she runs back to the kibbutz she falls down and vomits, disgusted with herself, and sickened with her frustrated desires. But neither vomiting nor showering in cold water gives her the longed-for release. In her confused, hysterical state, she envisions how she comes before the kibbutz secretary, telling him that the nomad tried to rape her, and urging him to action: "Yes, let the boys go right away tonight to their camp and smash their black bones because of what they did to me" (35).

Geula's present state of mind of fierce, irrational desire for revenge is paralleled by that of the hot-tempered young people who now decide to attack the Bedouin camp and retaliate for all the robberies and pilfering that the latter have committed. In the spirit of complete chaos and the loss of reason and good judgment that envelops the whole Kibbutz, Geula now finds herself lying outside and letting a snake, most probably of the venomous kind, bite her. The last scene in the story, marking the last minutes of Geula's life, is again saturated with eroticism, the images prevalent in this scene possessing primal sexual undertones. Geula now experiences sexual pleasure and the release of her long-suppressed erotic tension, when she blocks the snake's hole, thus provoking the frustrated animal into biting her. The snake, long associated with sexuality and often a phallic symbol,[70] becomes the male invader: "It stuck out a forked tongue, and its triangular head was cold and erect" (38). Geula feels his bite as "a thorn in her flesh" (38) and as a pleasant pain. Ironically, Geula does find redemption for her thwarted sexuality at the end of the story, but she also experiences the ultimate release—from life itself.

Geula's search for personal salvation thus ends in self-destruction. Her moment of abandon with the repulsive nomad has confronted her with her other self; while to the world she has always been the voice of calm and reason, Geula's raging desires surface and she becomes a stranger to herself. No longer able to suppress them nor quiet her humiliated sexuality, Geula welcomes death as the only possible release from that unwelcome self, as well as from her unbearably confining environment.

Geula sees in the physically revolting Bedouin her own double, and in his primitive existence, a mirror of her own raging, uncontrollable self. Her excited anticipation of his attack fills her with revulsion not only towards him but towards her own sexuality; and when his both dreaded and desired move never materializes, Geula feels doubly humiliated. She sees no other choice but to destroy herself, while at the same time allowing the spirit of chaos and anarchy to pervade her whole environment. In her last moments, Geula is finally at peace with herself; she not only becomes a harmonious and complete person again, but she is also elevated into an even more improved, better self: for the first time in her life, Geula's "face was very calm and almost beautiful" (38). In the course of the story, Geula has taken a trip into her buried sexual self, but unable to grapple with it, she must destroy her ego, which then, in the moment of ultimate release and annihilation, becomes an even better self, no more unattractive, tormented, and divided.[71]

In many ways, Geula's story is tied to that of the biblical Dinah, both through the theme of "going out" (the same verb is used both in the biblical tale of Dinah and in Oz's story), and through the theme of rape. In both cases, the woman's attempt at liberating herself from a narrowly confining existence ends in disaster. The ancient Dinah was physically raped, while Geula feels mentally raped. Both stories end with violence as the girls' compatriots (Dinah's brothers in the Bible and Geula's friends in our present story) go out to take revenge. The themes of the invasion of a land and the collision of diametrically opposite cultures are traditionally tied in literature with the rape of women—whether imagined or real. The reasons for this phenomenon are the close identification of the land with femininity in the male mind, as well as the historical experiences in which the invading enemy forces attacked the women of the defeated country. Oz's story echoes certain elements in E. M. Forster's *A Passage to India*,[72] where the British woman, bewildered when confronted with a strange culture, resorts to imaginings of rape as a way of exorcising her unwanted fascination with, and fear of, the man who represents that culture. The British woman's strategy of dealing with the unknown and alien in the world and in herself, and with her uneasy conscience that tells her that her own countrymen are "raping" a foreign land, is by inventing unwanted sexual advances on the part of the Indian man.

Similarly, Geula's feverish fabrication of a sexual attack is tied to both the national and the sexual levels of the story. In terms of the political undertones, the nomad's imagined attack eases a collective conscience that is not completely at peace with the seizing of a desert land and cultivating it. The nomads who close in are a reminder of the earlier, uncultivated, savage state of the land, and the fences are seen as artificial dividers, enhancing the nagging suspicion that perhaps an imposition of an enclave of rationality and culture on the desert terrain is not entirely right. The invented barbaric attack gives moral justification to revenge. Therefore, Geula, who was expected to dissuade the young kibbutzniks from violent action, now lets them go out and attack the nomads. On the sexual level, the imagined attack gives comfort to the girl's injured feminine pride.

One might also claim that in the imagined rape we see the man in Amos Oz the writer, claiming, as men have done since ancient times, that rape is a feminine fabrication. Yet Oz has given so much authenticity to Geula's inner life, that her heightened imagination at the end of the story is completely consistent with her nature. Geula's strategy of suppressing her sexual self, which ends with literal self-destruction, is a theme known to us from other works, thus tying the modern Israeli girl to her sisters in the East European Jewish realities.

*   *

The fragmentation of the feminine self into different entities, and the divorce of the woman from the real life around her culminate in the story of Hannah, heroine of Amos Oz's *My Michael* (1968).[73] The speaker in this novel is Hannah herself, who records, in 1960, the previous decade in her life, also giving us flashes into her early childhood. Hannah's story concentrates mainly on her married life with Michael Gonen, whom she had met ten years before, in an episode that starts her memoirs.

Hannah's life is quite peaceful, banal, and normal on the outside, yet tumultuous, fantastic, and adventurous inside. She is the mother of a boy and the wife of a successful, if somewhat mediocre, academic, who struggles and plods and is now on his way to a fine career at the Hebrew University in Jerusalem. The novel records Hannah's gradual mental departure from the world around her, as she sinks inwardly, into complete psychic disintegration and emotional chaos. Hannah feels imprisoned within an oppressive, hemmed-in existence, and the main pursuit of her inner life—gradually, her sole preoccupation—is devising strategies of escape and flight. And yet in terms of her relationship with her husband and her environment in general, it is hard to see in Hannah an exploited woman, or a woman whose spirit has been subdued by male figures of authority, or whose ambitions were discouraged. Hannah's husband is loving and not very demanding; had she wanted to go on with her studies, or pursue a career, he would not have stood in her way. In fact, Hannah discontinues her studies voluntarily when she marries Michael, and does not express any particular sense of regret. The question is, what are the forces in Hannah's reality that she finds oppressive and intolerable, and does she use the "traditional" female tactics—that is, those that the male writers have long attributed to their female protagonists—as a means of relieving her sense of oppression?

Very early in the novel, Hannah makes it clear that she is a woman who has always been at odds with her femininity. The explanation that Hannah offers is a reflection of her creator's masculine sensibility: Hannah, who was a tomboy, always wished that she would grow up to be a man, not a woman (8); she therefore played with boys and read boys' books, and "used to wrestle, kick, and climb" (8). Yet when Hannah describes how she used to play with boys, mainly with the Arab twins Halil and Aziz, the role that she played was invariably a feminine role, that of the princess who rules over her male subjects; furthermore, Hannah is feminine in her vanity and in her wish to be found attractive by men. Consequently, Hannah's discomfort with her femininity is not due to her strong masculine nature but rather to her inability to reconcile herself to the traditional role assigned to women in her society.[74] Affected by her father's adoration of scholars and literary men, Hannah envisions for herself, early in her life, a future in which she would play a subordinate role to a great scholar (41). Although Hannah later mocks at this vision, it is clear that her beloved father has encouraged his daughter to see herself in a subservient role to a male authority one day in the future. In reality Hannah's own aspirations were never on a collision course with her father's expectations of her. It is still obvious, though, that Hannah's early conception of her future role in life—influenced by her unimaginative and somewhat limited father—stands in opposition to her fantasy-rich inner world, in which she sees herself as the ruler of men's hearts and destinies, not as a servant to them.

Hannah's relationship with her parents provides another clue to the understanding of Hannah's mental problems. She has never felt either love or kinship towards her mother, an uneducated, none-too-bright woman, who never mastered the Hebrew language properly. When her mother comes to help after Hannah's first son is born, Hannah's language turns satirical. Hannah acts rudely towards her, and is relieved when her mother finally leaves; later she comments: "What a small place my mother occupied in my thoughts. She was father's wife. That was all. On the few occasions when she raised her voice against Father, I had hated her. Apart from that, I had made no room for her in my heart" (281). The lack of a love relationship between mother and daughter has been seen as one of the reasons for a woman's estrangement from her own femininity.[75] The culture barrier between the Israeli-born Hannah and her mother, who came from Eastern Europe, together with their differences in temperament and imagination, prevented Hannah from seeing in her mother a positive, strong, and admired female role model with whom she could identify. Therefore, with her independent spirits rebelling against a future life of subservience, and with the lack of a respected figure of an older woman, Hannah concluded early in her life: "I hated being a girl. I regarded grown up women with loathing and disgust" (28).

Hannah's father was greatly loved by his daughter, and yet the message that he left her was that of fear of life, and man's subordination to greater powers. In his own parochialism, ignorance, and small self-esteem—revealed especially in his comic admiration of the "world-famous" persons he came across—Hannah's late father has not served as a model of strength and self-assertion. Significantly, when Hannah's father talked about the dangers and pitfalls of life, he drew a picture of women exploited by men: "My late father warned me when I was thirteen against wicked men who seduce women with sweet words and then abandon them to their fate" (274). If life was tough, it was twice as hard for women. The emasculated father thus cultivated in his daughter an image of timidity, lack of daring, and submission to the rules of a world one cannot control, which Hannah adopted as her exterior self. Nevertheless, since Hannah's temperament was different, inviting danger and reveling in action and adventures, she allowed her real nature to roam free only in her inner world of fantasy, while on the outside she conformed to the traditional paradigm of femininity, consisting of docility, lack of ambition, and passiveness.

Hannah marries a man who is right for the self that she shows to the world; Michael is trustworthy and loyal, more ambitious than Hannah, and intent on creating for himself and his wife a decent, good life. Yet the "normalcy" of her married life, a routine dictated by term papers that Michael has to complete, semesters that he has to finish, and detailed plans for the future, clashes with Hannah's inner being that strives for a life not bound by commitments and obligations, and not dictated by the clock and calendar. Hannah begins to feel at odds with time, and regards it as her worst enemy (274). Time is associated with law and order: "Time is like a police van patrolling the streets at night" (114); it is a destructive mechanism, causing regression into nothing: "With firm, unerring fingers Time wears down inanimate objects. All things are at his mercy" (120). Hannah is sarcastic when Michael sees in time a medium of healing and progress: "Time and hard work will bring us everything, Hannah. You'll see. In time we may be able to travel to Europe. . . . In time, we may be able to afford a new car. In time you'll feel better" (264). The incongruity between Hannah's deep terror and suspicion of time, and Michael's faith that plodding and laboring within time will result in happiness, creates a chasm between the highly sensitive Hannah and her less profound husband.

Man's fear of time and its ravages is an archetypal human emotion, commemorated in poetry since early history; thus Hannah's particular circumstances as a woman with a rich inner world of fantasy, caught in a life of ordinary routine and strict conformity, intensify her antagonism towards time. As a woman who takes pride in her beauty, Hannah naturally sees in the passage of time a destructive force. Moreover, as an acutely sensitive person, Hannah, like many modern protagonists and antiheroes, views time, to use Hans Meyerhoff's words, as "a source of suffering and anxiety and a reason for despair."[76] Meyerhoff sees the disillusionment with time as symptomatic of the contemporary protagonist, and explains that with the collapse of the element of eternity and the loss of the nineteenth-century optimistic myth of progress, twentieth-century man has come to conceive of time as a medium indifferent, and even hostile, to him.

Moreover, time and history are weighted with a special significance in the context of modern Jerusalem, a city charged with past memories and looking towards renewal and change. In the particular geopolitical realities of Israel, time also means periodic wars and military flare-ups, in which the Israeli is called upon to sacrifice his life for a land that has been promised to him very early in history. Gershon Shaked is right in arguing that while *My Michael* is not a social novel, the historical and social circumstances that underlie it are an inextricable part of the very fabric of the novel.[77] Hannah's hostility towards time as the ultimate oppressor is imbued with social-political undertones as well. Hannah's childhood friends, the Arab twins, are now enemies, and therefore have become mythic figures, playing a major role in Hannah's fantasies. Jerusalem is a city surrounded by enemies, whose residents pretend to lead a normal life while in fact they are constantly threatened with wars and hostilities. The Jewish population of Jerusalem is itself divided in its view of Jerusalem's religious past and its role in the present life of its residents. In short, Jerusalem is a city where, perhaps more than in any other place in modern Israel, an impressionable person like Hannah might experience the oppression of history, the sense that the individual is called upon to harness his energies, and commit his whole life, to an idea rooted in history and transcending the individual's need for personal happiness.

Thus Hannah's obsessive preoccupation with time and her wish to defeat it stem from two sources. First, they represent her own personal idiosyncracies as an introverted person at odds with the normal world of work and responsibilities that flows in synchrony with the minutes and hours. Secondly, Hannah epitomizes the collective feeling of the burdensome predominance of history in this particular place and time, that, as a sensitive woman, she is more acutely aware of than are the others. Consequently, Hannah becomes hostile to those who seem to be ignorant of forces and processes that are beyond time and place, like her husband Michael, who appears content to lead his life within the boundaries of normal human time.

Hannah's main strategy for existing simultaneously in the world of the here and now, on the one hand, and in a romanticized sphere of total freedom and unbridled desires that knows no laws and constrictions, on the other, is by inventing for herself several alter egos that are the complete opposites of her own "public" self.[78] As Otto Rank explains, in the light of the Freudian theory of Narcissism, the double represents elements of morbid self-love; yet at the same time, the double can be the antidote to this element of self-love, bringing about destruction to the divided individual.[79] Thus the double embodies simultaneously both the self's wish for immortality, or for freedom from the shackles of time, and its suicidal tendencies.

Hannah's youngest double, the girl who is sometimes dressed in a blue coat, points to Hannah's strong infantile tendencies, and to her stunted mental growth, a characteristic common to many female literary characters.[80] The little girl appears in the midst of a domestic scene, when Hannah sits at the Sabbath table with her husband and son (168). The peaceful, idyllic family scene turns into a nightmare when Hannah is suddenly severed from her surroundings and sees herself mirrored in the little girl beating feebly and desperately on the window. At the end of the paragraph describing this scene, syntax and sentence disintegrate, as Hannah is now no longer able to construct fully coherent sentences. Otto Rank's comments on the paradoxical nature of the double are fully exemplified here. While the girl stands for the world of freedom and impunity, the experience itself is one of complete terror. Hannah both craves to become the little girl again, and yet knows that it is impossible, and thus the girl beats "feebly" on the window pane and gradually disappears. The alter ego's despair indicates both Hannah's disappointment at not being able to fully return to childhood's paradisal state, and at the same time her terror of regressing into mindless infantility, and into the state of feminine defenselessness of which her father warned her.

The imaginary little girl is intertwined with a children's tale that Hannah evokes, and that has at its center a little girl named Hannah and a charcoal-seller (98, 99). Little Hannah was given a new dress, white as snow, to greet the Sabbath. When she was playing outside, she saw an old man bowed under the burden of his sack of charcoal, and went to help him. She then realized that her white dress was covered with charcoal, and burst out crying. But the moon sent its beams down and turned every smudge into a golden flower, and every spot into a silvery star. Little Hannah's white dress epitomizes our Hannah's longings for the innocence and purity of childhood; the charcoal smudges are life's brutal experiences, and the moon, the mythic source of romance and magic, stands for the wondrous transformation of life's dreariness into a thing of beauty. Hannah's unhappiness with her everyday life and her longings to transmute the grayness of her reality into "great joy" are again revealed here.

The mythic charcoal-seller, who turns childhood innocence into nightmare, reappears in different versions throughout the novel. In a hallucinatory vision that Hannah experiences in the hospital after she has had her baby, a heinous old man with a sack on his back attempts to harm her (81–82). Frequently, Hannah evokes the partly real and partly demonic old men who roam the streets of Jerusalem. These are uncanny figures, grotesque and often sinister, representing "Old Father Time," Hannah's foe. These terrifying old men bring to mind similar figures of doom in *Anna Karenina* and *Madame Bovary*,[81] the two major nineteenth-century novels that revolve around unhappy female protagonists.[82] In each of these two novels, a mysterious old man meets the female protagonist, Anna and Emma respectively, initially at a crucial point in her life, and then one last time before the woman takes her own life. Anna Karenina first meets the old man at the railway station and then sees him once again before she throws herself under the oncoming train. Similarly, Hannah's old man is seen "making a little crack" that "widened and spread like a railway network" (81). Hannah is undoubtedly linked to these two famous female protagonists through the theme of feminine frustration that results in self-destruction, which our heroine commits not by physically killing herself, but by dividing herself into so many splinters of being, that the real Hannah is finally thinned out of existence.

Another projection of Hannah's inward self is Yvonne Azulai, the sensuous, hot-blooded Sephardic woman, usually appearing together with the handsome and masculine Rahamim, the Bokharian taxi driver, when Hannah is sick and is taking drugs. Yvonne personifies Hannah's libidinous, lustful nature, her seething eroticism and her wish to break down moral and sexual taboos (197–8). Within Hannah's prudish, puritan society, there is no possibility of violating accepted moral codes. Hannah lives in a predominantly Orthodox neighborhood, but even Hannah's husband and their few friends are somewhat inhibited sexually. Except for subtly attempting to arouse the religious youngster Yoram, Hannah rarely expresses her volcanic sexual self outwardly, and when she does, it is with her own husband. Yet she plays the role of the violator of social and ethical taboos in her own way, for instance when she expects her husband to buy groceries on the black market, and the latter adamantly refuses. In this case, too, the disagreement between Hannah and her husband points to a much deeper, more essential incompatibility.

Another phantasmic visitor from Hannah's inner self is the Princess who, unlike Yvonne, is not a figure from the contemporary Israeli landscape, but rather an exotic European image. The Princess allows Hannah to escape her temporal and geographical confinement, and journey through wide, open horizons to unknown places, to other times, and to different climates. In Hannah's hallucinations, the Princess belongs to the city of Danzig (198). Danzig is appropriate as the backdrop for the image of the Princess since it has been historically a divided city, where two nationalities, German and Polish, converged and sometimes clashed; and thus Danzig, the twofold city, reflects Hannah, the divided woman. The little girl is too feeble and, therefore, not enticing enough for Hannah to wish to merge fully with her, and Yvonne is too feminine, thus at the mercy of her desires. The Princess, however, in her spatial and temporal freedom, is a figure of complete strength, mastery, and self-control, releasing Hannah's frustrated wishes to control men, as well as the rapidly progressing time, and the fast-moving life and people around her.

Responding to the growing chasm between her tempestuous inner life and her seemingly untroubled outward existence, Hannah projects the duality of her being into the outside landscape, perceiving a twofold reality in the world around her. Hannah sees under every ordinary scene a certain hidden violence or tumult. A woman leaning out the window in order to close it seems "as if she were about to throw herself into the street" (27). This Orthodox woman, who piously covers her head and who stands for discipline and rigid adherence to the religious law, is suddenly converted, in Hannah's imagination, into a figure of rebellion and violence. The boys from the orphanage look submissive on the outside, but "behind their air of resignation I could sense a suppressed violence" (43). Even Michael's scientific research points to the twofoldness of nature: "Michael talked about geology. . . . These words relate to facts which have meaning for me, for me alone, like a message transmitted in a code. Beneath the surface of the earth, opposed endogenic and exogenic forces are perpetually at work. . . . Beneath the crust of hard rocks rages the blazing nucleus, the siderosphere" (16).

The Arab twins, who play the role of Hannah's wild playmates and lovers, also reflect the duality of Hannah's existence. Before her marriage Hannah has a premonitory dream where she walks with Michael in the Arab market, and is suddenly being carried away by the twins; the scene that ensues combines sexual fantasies with extreme violence. The twins are figures from Hannah's childhood, but in their status as the social "others," and in the savage and primitive image that they project in Hannah's fantasies, they embody the political as well as the personal dualism in Hannah's existence. Hannah gives Michael the romantic role of rescuer in this dream, and yet she is only half-hearted in her wish to rid herself of the Arab twins and the sexual ecstasy that they stand for: "The darkness wanted Michael to come and rescue me only at the end of the pain and the pleasure" (47).

Michael, in his balanced state of mind, was supposed to rescue Hannah from her turbulent inner self, but he has failed to do so, mainly because Hannah's inner being resisted giving itself up; and as it gradually took over, it painted the outside world as more drab, and Michael as duller and more ordinary, than either of them was. As Hannah becomes more estranged from her husband, the Arab twins appear with more intensity. They are the military terrorists, reflecting Israel's explosive geopolitical situation as well as Hannah's attraction to the cultural and political antinomian, and to the breaking of political as well as sexual taboos: "Hard things plot against me every night. The twins practice throwing hand grenades before dawn among the ravines of the Judean Desert southeast of Jericho" (105). But the twins are also forces responding to Hannah's volcanic inner self, and messengers from her furious nether land, awakening and sharpening her metempirical sensibilities: "Silently the pair of them float over the neighborhood at the end of the night. . . . They have been sent to wake me. Someone imagines I am asleep" (119).

But the ultimate double is undoubtedly the city Jerusalem itself, which becomes closely identified with Hannah the protagonist, and which, in its historical and political reality, contains a twofold existence.[83] In the 1950s, when Hannah's memoirs are being recorded, Jerusalem is still divided into the old city, occupied by the Arabs, and the new city, inhabited by the Israelis. During daytime, Jerusalem is no more than a small town, with new buildings being put up, and people going about their business; but to Hannah Jerusalem is "a landscape pregnant with suppressed violence" (18), and a town where madmen roam free, talking in biblical language (110). It is a new city, yet many of its streets have an ancient flavor, enhanced by their names, which are those of biblical prophets. When Hannah sits with her baby in the Jerusalem park and talks with the other young mother, Jerusalem seems like every other city in the world, where people live, have children, and talk about politics and domestic doings; yet, the Jerusalem landscape reveals also the Arab life that surrounds it and that, for Hannah, is not only a military menace but also a counterpart of her mysterious inner reality: "Sometimes I try to amuse them by telling them a political joke. . . . But when I turn my head I catch sight of the Arab village of Shaafat dozing beyond the border, bathed in blue light. Red are its rooftiles in the distance and in the nearby treetops birds in the morning sing songs in a language I cannot understand" (94).

Geographically, Jerusalem is a small place where people huddle together within its hostile borders; however, "there is no end to Jerusalem" (107). It is a city dominated by the hardness of rocks, stones, and iron, yet "whole districts seem to be hanging in the air" (110). Jerusalem is enigmatic, resisting any attempt to comprehend it with the aid of reason and human senses, thus resembling Hannah, who does not allow anyone into her inner reality: "Every quarter, every suburb harbors a hidden kernel surrounded by high walls . . . City of enclosed courtyards, her soul sealed up behind bleak walls. . . . There is no Jerusalem. Crumbs have been dropped deliberately to mislead innocent people. There are shells within shells and the kernel is forbidden" (110). The city has a clearly feminine nature, and the woman that it stands for is, like Hannah, fragile, vulnerable, and constantly aware of the alien reality that threatens to overpower her: "Villages and suburbs surround Jerusalem in a close circle, like curious bystanders surrounding a wounded woman lying in the road: Nabi Samwil, Shaafat, Sheikh Jarrah . . . If they clenched their fists the city would be crushed" (111).

As a place burdened with the weight of history and imbued with the sense of the past, Jerusalem itself stands for Time and is therefore often perceived by Hannah as an evil pursuer: "In the afterglow of sunset the Jerusalem hills seemed to be plotting some mischief" (32). Jerusalem intensifies Hannah's sense of the oppression of history, and therefore, when Hannah goes to visit her brother in his kibbutz in the Galilee, she feels relieved: "Jerusalem was far away and could not haunt me here. Perhaps she had been conquered in the meantime by the enemy who hemmed her in on three sides. Perhaps she had finally crumbled to dust. As she deserved. I did not love Jerusalem from the distance. She wished me ill. I wished her ill" (281). And yet when Hannah watches the sunrise early in the morning, the "coils of barbed wires" remind her that even this kibbutz, as distant as it is from Jerusalem, is as surrounded by enemy and as confined within its threatening borders as Jerusalem; the whole state of Israel is an enlarged version of the geopolitics of Jerusalem (282). In this scene

Hannah reveals that her state of mind is inextricably connected with the Israeli state-of-siege reality. She complains that "there is no escape from Jerusalem," that is, from the claustrophobic sense of enclosure that dominates the city as well as the whole country. If Hannah resembles the French Emma Bovary in her taste for sentimental novels and extravagant shopping, she is still inseparable from her particular historical moment and geographical location. Hannah's acute awareness of political as well as existential loneliness now prevents her from resisting the dangerous but alluring charm of her inner life that relieves her of the constrictive and confining nature of her exterior reality. When she returns to Jerusalem she is determined "to set free two twin brothers," in other words, to let loose her seething inner life.

Because of Hannah's subjectivity, the reader never gets an unprejudiced view of Michael. To Hannah, he is dull, unimaginative, and not very bright. However, we must remember that for our protagonist, any person who has no double and who is not made up of a duality of opposites is one-dimensional and mediocre. The polarity between Michael and Hannah is that between the ordinary man, who realizes his human limitations and has come to terms with them, and the unusually sensitive person who has withdrawn into herself and plays a marginal role only in the everyday life of work, commitments, and accomplishments. If we see Michael mainly as a person devoted to his work, and at peace with time, Hannah is *homo ludens* par excellence, exempting herself from life and retreating to the world of play. As the Dutch philosopher Johan Huizinga tells us, the play is an archetypal practice that underlies all human activities, since every area of civilization, language, technology, and art, has been permeated with the element of play from its very inception.[84] Play activity fulfills a very basic human need to act freely and without impunity. It offers a relief from many everyday anxieties by providing the player with a sphere where he can emulate life in terms of competition, success, and failure, without being subject to the serious consequences of real life. While the ordinary person realizes that the ludic element has a marginal function in life and can never encompass the totality of the human existence, a person like Hannah allows the ludic sphere to pervade almost her whole being. The ludic sphere frees Hannah from the oppression of time and history by enveloping her in the timeless moment or the eternal present. While for Michael the game, like collecting stamps, is a temporary and therapeutic retreat from the burdens of life, for Hannah the play is the only valid sphere of existence, which she eventually enters fully and completely.

The play world allows Hannah to assume different roles and break through the temporal and spatial barriers that constrain her movements. As she sinks further into the ludic sphere and severs contact with the world, Hannah loses her vocal cords and experiences difficulties in talking. The loss of voice indicates her relinquishing communication with the world. The memoirs would finalize her departure, since by putting everything in writing, she in a sense exhausts her language reservoir and is now ready for the life of wild instinct, characteristic of the savage Arab twins, who use body language rather than verbal expression in order to communicate.

Twice in the novel Hannah uses the image of the "bell jar" under which she finds herself and which epitomizes her sense of separation from the world: "As I sewed I asked myself, what is this impenetrable glass dome which has fallen on us to separate our lives from objects, places, people, opinions? Of course, Michael, there are friends, visitors . . . But when they are sitting in our living room . . . their words are always indistinct because of the glass, which is not even transparent. It is only from their expressions that I manage to guess something of their meaning" (220). Thus Hannah is not only losing her voice, but also her hearing, and, in fact, her sight: "Sometimes their shapes dissolve: vague masses without outlines" (220). The "glass dome," which in Hebrew is the "glass bell,"[85] is equivalent to the glass bell jar that descends on Esther, the protagonist of Sylvia Plath's *The Bell Jar.*[86] Like Hannah, Esther Greenwood descends into madness out of a sense of female powerlessness, and in an attempt to reject or overcome this state. Phyllis Chesler's insight into Sylvia Plath's predicament applies to Oz's protagonist as well: "Madness and asylums generally function as mirror images of female experience, and as penalties for being female, as well as for desiring and daring not to be."[87] We have to remember that Esther Greenwood is the talented alter ego of Sylvia Plath, the writer and poet, while Hannah's talents are minimal, and she certainly lacks the drive and ambition of Esther. Still, in the image of the bell jar, as well as in the use of mirror images and alter egos, Oz is forcing us to see an analogy between his own female protagonist and that of Sylvia Plath's. The existence under a "bell jar" and the withdrawal into the chaotic self thus become universal feminine experiences that tie together female protagonists of different backgrounds and cultural heritages.

Furthermore, like Esther, who at the end of the novel is freed of the bell jar, Hannah, for whom the bell jar is not being lifted, wishes for it to be at least transparent. In other words, though Hannah craves the separation from the world, she wants the ability to function under the glass jar and outside it at one and the same time, and to be able to move freely between the two worlds. She wants to be able to see her alter egos when she is outside the glass barrier, and to see the "public" Hannah when she is inside the glass jar; but this is impossible. Towards the end of the novel she still asks for the glass to be transparent, so she could see the outside world as well as what is inside the bell jar: "I don't make excessive demands: only that the glass should remain transparent. A clever, pretty girl in a blue coat. A shriveled kindergarten teacher with varicose veins spreading on the thighs. In between, Yvonne Azulai drifts on a sea which has no shores. That the glass should be transparent. Nothing more" (246).

Other images also illuminate Hannah's mental "state of siege." Oz juxtaposes images of entrapment and restriction, such as the small apartment and the window with its heavy iron shutters, with images of movement and flight, such as the imaginary travels through the Russian steppes or the city of Danzig, and the two submarines Dragon and Tigris, or the sledge with the "furiously galloping horses" (23). On the level of everyday life, Hannah lets the world around her progress and change while she remains in a static position of inaction; Michael and his friends finish their degrees, get jobs, and are promoted, but Hannah achieves nothing, and takes only a small part in raising her own child. Yet in her fantasies Hannah is in a constant state of mobility. She is afraid of the passage of time, and welcomes motion only in the timeless moment of her playing sphere. She sees herself and Michael as "two travelers consigned by fate to adjacent seats on a long railway journey" (67). But this is an intolerable journey both because Michael is an uninteresting partner and because it is a movement that will only lead to death: "Days passed without leaving a trace. I owe myself a solemn duty to record in this journal the passing of every day . . . for the days flash past like hills seen from the train on the way to Jerusalem. I shall die Michael will die . . . and there will be a strange train full of strange people and they like us will stand at the window . . ." (103). Hannah craves another kind of journey which will be a journey against time, led by Hannah herself, and not bound by the rules of time: "If I could overpower the engine and be the princess of the train, manipulate two lissom twins as if they were extensions of me, left hand and right hand" (103). Hannah's imaginary adventures consist of such travels in which time is conquered and does not move forward; yet Hannah still experiences the sensation of movement in a mythic sphere, in the "snowbound Russian steppes," or in search of the submarines "Nautilus" and "Dragon" (104).

As Hannah divorces herself from the life around her, she views the external world as traveling away from her. She is now like a person riding on a fast-moving train who thinks that the outside scenery is in motion, while she is sitting still. She is rapidly moving away from the ordinary life of Michael and her son, and so she sees Michael as driving away from her. Yet if Hannah retreats now into the timeless moment of the game world where things will never change and die, then it is true that Michael is the one who is traveling, within time, while she stays fixed in an immobile, static pose, turning inward, and averting her sight from reality: "Farewell, Michael. I shall stand at the window and trace shapes with my finger on the misty pane. You may suppose, if you like, that I am waving to you. I shall not disillusion you. I am not with you. . . . Fare you well" (285).

Thus Hannah's strategy of coexistence in two realities ends in her final separation from the world of family, time, and history. While she pleads for an easy mobility between the two spheres, she eventually finds herself being catapulted into the world of inner chaos. If Michael continues in his deliberate, measured steps forward, and progresses in synchrony with the watch and the calendar, Hannah's journey takes an opposite direction and is marked by a rapid, uncontrollable pace, as she is spiraling into the subconscious where language, time, and civilization are rendered obsolete.

If Hannah shuttles violently between the world of every day and the realm of fantasy, between the time of the watch and the timeless moment of the inner self, Hannah's creator preserves the chronological structure of the novel, and maintains a firm hold on the logical movement of events. If Hannah seems confused, the author and his reader are never at a loss as to where and when reality is reflected, and when Hannah's fantasies take over and carry her to a sphere that abides by different rules. It is as if the author, from a position outside the novel, has taken over Hannah's confessional diary and, while preserving its subjectivity, rearranged some of its parts to make it more coherent to the reader. On the other hand, in Amalia Kahana-Karmon's *And the Moon in the Valley of Ajalon* (1971),[88] the time element that prevails in the heroine's existence as well as in the novel itself is vertical and not horizontal. The spatial and temporal discontinuity is unexpected, yet frequent, and points to the interior schisms in the woman protagonist. If Oz's novel progresses towards a denouement, Karmon's novel has forsaken the linear movement and offers a series of multiple moments that are not necessarily causally connected. In Karmon's novel the presence of an author, however distant, who imposes order on chaos, is no longer felt, and the female protagonist's discontinuous, unsorted thoughts and perceptions are recorded in the most immediate manner. The novel thus becomes a patchwork of impressions, images, and fragmented glimpses that mirror the protagonist's state of mind.

The resemblance of Karmon's work to Virginia Woolf's two novels that also revolve around women protagonists, *Mrs Dalloway* and *To the Lighthouse,* has already been noticed.[89] In fact, Karmon's novel shares many elements in common with other modern works, those that Leon Edel has called, the "subjective" or the "psychological" novels.[90] Karmon, however, sees the acute awareness of the flow of consciousness that takes over the regular time sequence and the linear progression of events as characteristic mainly of the woman's experience. The protagonist of her novel, No'a Talmor, lives in an idealistic past, a reality that perhaps has always existed only in her imagination. Her husband Asher's feet are securely anchored in the here and now; he is a successful businessman who constantly looks for new projects and advantageous connections. By contrast, when No'a's eyes are turned outward, it is only to see in other characters a new illumination, or alter egos, of her inner being. The new business associate that enters No'a's and Asher's life is considered "a good professional" by Asher, but is seen as a "messenger from regions of brightness" by his wife (119), who quotes a verse from Matthew Arnold to express her conception of Philip. When conversation turns on a woman named Yemima, Asher thinks it is the name of a corporation, while for No'a the ailing Yemima reflects her own ailing soul.

The novel starts in a semirealistic scene when No'a appears in her husband's office asking for some cash from his secretary, who is in charge of the office while Asher is abroad. No'a feels like a stranger in her husband's world, and her aging father, who works for her husband and is also made to feel unneeded, enhances her sense of alienation from Asher's existence. In Philip, No'a sees a man who would understand her sensitivities, but no real closeness is ever achieved between the two. Philip is a hope of salvation that, by definition, can never materialize. No'a tells Philip that they will never climb the "Shalom" tower, the highest building in Tel Aviv, together (156), implying that they will never share a heightened moment of awareness.

When episodes and scenes from the past intrude into the present, they are not conveyed in a "flashback" manner, but rather become the present moment of the narrative. In one such instance, we see the two young students, No'a and Asher, falling in love with each other, in prestatehood Jerusalem. Asher, it is gradually understood, is involved with the underground, and is responsible for placing explosives in an Arab market (76). If the youthful Asher is shrouded with a heroic, mysterious, and romantic halo, which seems to envelop No'a's complete existence at the time, the adult Asher is no

longer a dashing idealist, but a pragmatist whose life focuses on material success. Asher complains to his daughter that her mother is
no longer alive but has remained in a state of arrested childhood,
and that therefore he has to treat her like a child (158). At the end of
the novel No'a reads the unpublished manuscript of an acquaintance,
Mr. Hiram, and sees in it the story of her own life. The manuscript
starts with the "mask of death," which is a new game played in the
circus, and which becomes analogous to No'a's death-in-life reality.
The protagonists that Mr. Hiram claims to deal with are those people
who have been forced into a passive, repressed state of being, who
have had a moment of brief rebellion, after which they resign to the
compromises of life (200). Thus the novel's last chapter ends not with
its protagonist, No'a, but with a reflection of her life in someone
else's script. This ties up with No'a's feeling that she is being "torn
out of herself" (185).

In her constant sense of being cruelly fragmented, especially because she is expected by Asher to alienate herself from her inner core,
No'a projects her divided soul into the outside world. Unlike Hannah's feminine alter egos, who are all figments of the protagonist's
imagination, Yemima and Beruria are real characters whose travails
are seen by No'a as mirroring her own predicament, reminiscent
of the manner in which Clarissa Dalloway appropriates Septimus as
her alter ego, in Woolf's *Mrs. Dalloway*. No'a claims many times:
"Yemima, you are me, Beruria, you are me" (160). Beruria has lost
her mind, and thus reflects No'a's fears of losing her grip on reality;
Yemima, on the other hand, has gone through a hysterectomy, thus
giving a physical actuality to No'a's rejection as a woman by her husband, and her consequent fears that she is losing her femininity. Another second self is the parrot, who flees his cage when Philip appears
on the scene, reflecting No'a's hopes of escape through this man, and
whose return coincides with Philip's departure from the country. The
colored, transparent mobiles that No'a designs, and that her husband
tries to translate into commercial success, are another metaphor of
her existence. The thin mobiles indicate the protagonist's sense of
the flimsy and insubstantial nature of reality, and in the game of shadows that they play on the wall (157) they reflect No'a's own escape
from the external reality to the subjective images flickering in her
consciousness.

But it is No'a's sense of her feminine self, transmitted through
Karmon's modernistic style, that lends the novel its uniqueness. The
many quotes from the Bible and the other ancient documents, integrated into the language often in an ironic manner that reverses the
words' original meanings, indicate No'a's long memory, her mind

that is steeped in the rich tradition of Judaic letters, as well as her regret over the incongruity between the ancient sources and the modern reality, all accumulated into an intense sense of total existential estrangement. The disruption of chronology, the novel as a series of moments and glimpses that never become a coherent whole, is another emblem of the feminine being. The image of the woman as possessing an acute intuition, and as the keeper of the absolute truth that is constantly being compromised and trampled upon by modern life, is enhanced by the elliptical style, the suggested yet unsaid words, and the language that simultaneously records real events and inner images, exterior landscapes and inner impressions. Mainly, the shifting of the narrative voice mirrors the sense of the relativity of existence and its lack of harmony and coherence. The narrative may shift from the third person to the first person almost in the same breath. But the many angles do not offer a multiplicity of views; they are all different vantage points taken by the narrator-protagonist herself as she tries to convey the many-layered nature of her heightened consciousness, and the inner rifts that she constantly experiences. Often, the third-person narrator appears no longer human but rather like the eye of the camera, conveying the scene with photographic precision and detachment, free of any human emotions. This happens, for instance, when No'a describes how she retreats to her workshop in the attic, where she designs new colors and shapes for her creations. Suddenly, the narration becomes extremely objective, as if not conveyed by a human being: "Someone, named No'a Talmor, climbs upstairs, sits in her workshop, frozen" (159). Later there is a shift in tone, and now the teller becomes the person behind the camera, not the eye of the camera itself: "One day she took a stick. Angrily she hurtled her mobiles on the floor" (159). Frequently, the reader is not sure whether the colors and shapes that No'a is cataloguing are descriptions of outer scenes, or inner, subjective impressions.

The novel's language, which is full of archaic words and grammatical structures, reveals the narrator's painful sense of the loss of glorious times. More than in Oz's novel, the woman protagonist's anguish at the diminished reality that surrounds her, and that encroaches on her almost mystical, private sphere, is a pervasive element in Karmon's work. In her rebellion against the "male" world, Karmon's narrator defeats the reader's expectations of a coherent, logical sequence of events, or of syntactically complete sentences, which she associates with the masculine perception of the world. Shaked is right in suggesting that Karmon is the legitimate heir of a male writer, S. Yizhar, an earlier novelist who employed the stream-

of-consciousness method.[91] But in her incomplete sentences, elliptical technique, and the method of simultaneity, whereby the narrative is at one and the same time situated in different landscapes and
different times, Karmon expresses her notion of the feminine experience of the world and the most appropriate language for the portrayal
of that experience.

The woman's retreat from the coherent grammar of everyday communication into new linguistic creations, where the word is enjoyed
for the subjective magic that it holds for her, is a technique used by
Kahana-Karmon's protagonist in the short story "Impoverishment."[92]
The age-old male tradition of associating the city with the woman is
here employed by the female protagonist, Osnat, as she recounts an
unhappy meeting with a former lover on a rainy day in the city of Tel
Aviv. The spirit of the Book of Lamentations permeates the narrative,
and enhances the woman's mourning over the treacherous man, whom
she still loves. The Book of Lamentations likens the city of Jerusalem,
abandoned by God and ransacked by the enemy, to a widow. In
Kahana-Karmon's story the protagonist sees in the dreary and shabby
scenes of the city a projection of her own faded youth and lost vitality. The city of Tel Aviv is relatively new, and its name implies
spring and renewal, but Osnat's eyes soak in only bleak, depressing
sights of a city in decline, which mirror her own state of mind and
present self-image.

Returning home from a painful encounter with the now indifferent
man, still full of the city's rainy dreariness, the protagonist finds solace in her current occupation, which is preparing indexes for scholarly books. The last part of the story abandons sentence and syntax,
offering instead a long list of ancient titles. Although the list in itself
carries no meaning to the reader or to the protagonist, the almost
mystical flavor of the archaic titles, the names of old cities where the
books were published, and of the long-gone scholars and rabbis who
wrote them become a source of comfort for the woman. The titles
and places retain the glory of bygone years and past scholarship, and
tie the heroine with the long, noble tradition of Hebrew learning.
The present moment is forgotten as Osnat immerses herself in the
charm of the ancient words and savors their esoteric sounds. The city
and its everyday reality now recede to the background as the "masculine" sphere, where people compete and are engaged in power
struggles. The old titles, though a testimony to male scholarship, become the new reality of the heroine, who now feels revitalized and
"purified."

Osnat retreats from syntax and from the present into a list of ancient
titles and manuscripts, and No'a arrives at such a sense of alienation at

the end of the novel that she no longer feels part of the real world but sees herself as the protagonist of an obscure manuscript that will never be published. Another modern female protagonist, Aviva, in Rachel Eytan's *Pleasures of Man* (1974),[93] also sails away from the modern city and its noisy, oppressive, male-dominated ambience. Eytan's novel does not resort to innovative styles and techniques in order to reveal the feminine predicament, yet in the experience of estrangement and in the juxtaposition between the male and female modes of relating to the world, Eytan's protagonist is somewhat reminiscent of Karmon's. The novel satirically portrays the life of the glittering circles of Tel Aviv society, where Aviva, the wife of the successful Amnon, is victimized by her ruthless, unscrupulous husband. Eytan's landscapes are mainly exterior; if Karmon's No'a escapes to archaic language and lets scenes from the past take over, Aviva runs away to France with her French lover, but then returns home. She seems to be extremely dependent on her husband, especially sexually; yet on the other hand, she has no illusions about his character and his intentions to continue to hurt her. If her escape to another geographical landscape proves futile, Aviva also flees to a different mode of reality: she constantly uses terms and concepts from Jewish mystical literature to convey her feminine frailty. Like the Shekinah in the Zohar, Aviva sees herself as lacking in immanent light, and needing the emanation of light from the masculine element. She also views herself as an empty vessel that needs the masculine sphere to give fullness and substance to her life (70).

At the end of the novel Aviva feels victimized and defeated; she attempts to write a play, but her predominant sense is that of traveling away from her reality. She senses that she is taking a trip "into herself, into a dark hole . . . another universe, completely different, where the sounds there will seem like the quiet drop of a tooth" (298).

Hannah, No'a, and Aviva all opt for sailing away into the inner self, leaving husband and sanity behind, and expressing in their departure their wish for self-annihilation. As we have seen, in Oz's novel the oppressor is neither the man nor the masculine realm. In the works of the two women writers, however, the males enfold in their being the sum total of the world's imperfections and its attempts to defeat the sensitive, frail, and idealistic woman. Although some of the male protagonists in Karmon's short stories are as introspective and oppressed by life as her female protagonists, the majority of Karmon's works are seen from the woman's point of view and identify the male world as the oppressor. In Karmon's and Eytan's novels, the ills of the modern city and life are inextricably tied to the flawed, callous nature of the male of the species, who revels in the corrupt nature of modern reality. The man rejects and banishes the woman, whose sight is sharper and more critical, because she assumes the role of his nagging moral conscience, which he tries to ignore. By contrast, Oz's Hannah is neither idealistic nor moral, and in her animosity towards reality she transcends the modern man-woman confrontation. Therefore Hannah, as well as Geula and other of Oz's female protagonists, is transported into an archetypal image of the antinomian in all of us, while Karmon's and Eytan's women remain within the male-female opposition.

The "Jewess" and Outside Oppression

Oppression from within Hebraic tradition represented a small part of the woman's predicament. Throughout Jewish history, the woman participated with the man in the image of the persecuted, and shared with him the status of the pariah and the unwanted stranger among people who only reluctantly allowed him to dwell in their midst.

In the ancient documents, the Hebrew woman is seen as fearless and often ferocious in her fervent dedication to her people. Deborah and Judith are strong women, who, in their resourcefulness and charisma, save their people from brutal tyrants. Yet these two women's inner strength stems from the firm confidence of people who dwell on their own land, and are called upon to protect their territory from a foreign intruder. But as the fate of the Jewish people changes and their existence becomes more precarious, the feminine strategy for survival is no longer spirited militancy, but passive, yet tenacious endurance. In one incident (recounted in several versions and set in different periods), a courageous mother watches how her seven sons are being brutally tortured by the Greek tyrant Antiochus, for refusing to "taste swine's flesh" (II Macc. 7).[94] Though this Hebrew woman is still found on her own land, and the Greek ruler is the foreign invader, she exhibits a strategy that would later become a common Jewish experience: death for the sake of the Sanctification of the Name (*Kiddush HaShem*).

While martyrdom now becomes an experience shared by both men and women, the literary documents give ample evidence of strategies that are uniquely feminine and that grow out of the woman's nature and her own particular situation. The Midrash tells us of Rabbi Hanina ben Tardion, one of the "ten martyrs," and Beruria's father, who was condemned to die by fire because he defied the Romans and continued to instruct the Torah and spread its teachings. His wife was also sentenced to death, while his other daughter, Beruria's sister, was forcibly placed in a whorehouse. Beruria asked her husband, Rabbi Meir, to try to save her sister from this shameful situation. Rabbi Meir decided to test the woman and see whether she had been "defiled" already. He believed that if she stayed pure, a miracle could still happen that would bring about her salvation. Clearly, Rabbi Meir's position, expecting the young woman to keep her chastity under impossible circumstances, seems quite rigid and unrealistic. Yet the reader's curiosity is now raised in anticipation of whether the woman managed to live up to the high standards required of her by her compatriots, and how she succeeded in doing it. Rabbi Meir disguised himself as a Roman trooper and asked for the woman's services. The woman began to stall him; first she claimed that she was menstruating, and when her "client" said he would wait, she encouraged him to choose another girl, pointing out that many of the other prostitutes were much prettier than she was. Rabbi Meir became convinced that his sister-in-law had not been dishonored; he therefore bribed the guard and the young woman was set free.[95] If it seems too farfetched that Beruria's sister could get away with this kind of deception all the time, the point that the Midrash is making is quite clear: even in the most dire circumstances, the Jewish woman kept her chastity and used all the subterfuges available to her in order to outwit her enemy.

While the medieval documents record occasions of *Kiddush HaShem*, where women and men alike sacrificed their lives, and sometimes even killed their own children rather than betray their faith, it is interesting to see how the modern poets recreated prevalent folk tales, often originating in the Middle Ages, about the Jewish woman's confrontation with a Gentile man intent on defiling her.[96] A popular theme with modern poets is the young girl's resistance to the temptations set by the powerful, awesome Gentile pursuer; often, the girl is the rabbi's daughter, who thus becomes an emblem of the Jewish woman.[97] In a poem by Y. L. Gordon, "In the Depths of the Sea,"[98] set during the expulsion of the Jews from Spain in 1492, a group of Jewish exiles find themselves on a ship sailing towards an unknown destination, completely at the mercy of a ruthless crew and its captain. The captain spots the beautiful rabbi's daughter and sends a messenger to her, offering her a chance to come under his wings and become his mistress. The captain threatens that if the girl does not comply, he will strand his passengers on a deserted island, where they will surely meet with a bitter end. The young girl sends a positive reply, asking for her compatriots to be brought to a safe shore, before she becomes the captain's lover. When the Jews land safely on a friendly shore, the young rabbi's daughter and her mother throw themselves into the sea and drown.

While Gordon's narrative poem is lengthy and verbose, replete with long tirades about Jewish fate and divine injustice, Tchernichovsky's three poems about "the rabbi's daughter" capture the drama of the Jewish girl's attempts to stave off her non-Jewish suitor through the tightly-knit ballad form and tension-filled dialogues. The most intricate is the poem entitled "The Rabbi's Daughter" (1924),[99] set against the aftermath of the Khmelnitski massacres (1648–49), when Haidamaks, gangs of Cossacks and peasants who saw themselves as the heirs of the Khmelnitski movement in Poland, periodically attacked and robbed Jewish communities.[100]

The poem starts after a pogrom in one of the Jewish towns, when the drunk Haidamaks divide the loot among themselves. Their chief, a young Haidamak, scorns all the gold and silver that his men have robbed from their Jewish victims; instead, he goes to see the rabbi's daughter, whose beauty, so the young man feels, far surpasses that of all material things. He confesses to her that he has loved her for a long time already, and that he joined the riots only in order to gain access to her. While Gordon's captain is heartless, brutal, and lecherous, callously demanding that the young girl become his mistress, Tchernichovsky's Gentile is depicted in a more favorable light, thus making the girl's dilemma more poignant. He is young, and even the girl addresses him as *na'ar,* 'lad'; furthermore, he speaks about his great love, not lust, for the rabbi's daughter.

The young Haidamak presses his suit first by declaring his love for the girl, and then by further flattering her, confessing that his only motive for joining in the action was his overwhelming need to see her. When the girl apparently does not respond, the man resorts to a veiled threat, telling her that if it were not for him, she would have been taken to the camp, like all her sisters. He continues to persuade the girl by offering to marry her that very night, after she converts to Christianity, and describing the beautiful gown that she will wear and the lavish party that will be thrown in their honor. In a poem that contains ten stanzas, the girl's voice is heard only in the sixth; thus the dialogue up to this moment is, in effect, a one-sided affair, with the young man continuing to press his case and the girl's silence speaking more than words.

When the young man has completed his pleas, threats, and flattery, however, it is the girl's turn to talk. We can assume that while the man was talking, she has been only half listening to him, looking for a way to rid herself of him. Unlike in Gordon's poem, where both the girl and her suitor are stereotypes, in Tchernichovsky's ballad, the young man transcends his stereotypical origins as the villainous Gentile, and becomes possessed of individual qualities. While he displays no qualms about the killings in which he has just participated, his youth, his sincere love for the girl, and his recognition of her gentleness and beauty make this ballad more than just a generic situation. Furthermore, the dialogue form, which transmits the actors' words, but does not allow for an omniscient speaker to divulge inner motives and feelings, intensifies the dramatic suspense of the confrontation between the girl and the young man.

The girl apparently understands that she would not be able to use excuses based on religious convictions; the Haidamak would neither understand nor accept such explanations. But she is probably convinced that his tender feelings for her are genuine, and that he is not entirely heartless. She therefore appeals directly to his emotions, saying that since she has just lost her parents and friends, she is not ready for the festivities of a wedding. The young man, frustrated but sympathetic, answers that he will come back for her in two weeks, adding his hope that he will be able to evade the Poles' bullets and return to her alive. The girl now sees her opportunity. She tells the ignorant and probably superstitious young peasant that she knows of a spell that would protect him from his enemies' bullets. When the man expresses his doubts, the girl tells him to test the effectiveness of the spell by firing a shot at her. The young man is hesitant, but he finally relents and shoots the girl. When she dies, he still will not admit that she used a ruse, tricking him into killing her. We are left with the young man wondering whether the spell was not effective enough, or whether the girl pronounced it wrongly. Although he is curious to know if there is another explanation to this mystery, his pride does not let him articulate it.

The girl's tactic utilizes her suitor's ignorance and his suspicion, deeply rooted in his people's consciousness, that the Jew in general, but more so the rabbi's daughter, possesses witchcraft and supernatural powers. While the reader is in suspense, waiting for the girl's ruse to be revealed, the girl devises a clever, though desperate scheme, and succeeds in fooling the young man completely.

Tchernichovsky's ballad "The Rabbi's Beautiful Daughter" (1942) [101] is set in the medieval German city of Worms. [102] Here the dialogue is between two knights, who have come to rob the rabbi's home, and the sexton, who opens the door to let them in. The knights ask for the rabbi and are told that he has died; they then ask for his beautiful daughter, and are told that she disappeared when she went to bury her father. The knights proceed to demand access to the rabbi's treasures. When they can find nothing in the house, they order the sexton to open the rabbi's grave, where they unearth no material treasures, but discover the rabbi's real treasure, his beautiful daughter, lying alongside her father. Here the Jewish woman and her persecutors are stereotypical, and the girl's tactic, killing herself to avoid being found by the brutal enemy, thus becomes the only strategy left to the woman who cherishes her feminine honor more than her life. In Tchernichovsky's ballads, the young girl is fully within the Judaic heritage and regards the patriarchal figure, the absent, dead father, as a potent symbol of her heritage. If he is physically powerless, leaving his daughter with a message of death and martyrdom, he inspires his daughter to devise schemes to outwit the enemy, if only through death.

In the poem entitled "The Rabbi's Daughter and Her Mother" (1942)[103], also in the group "Ballads of Worms," the poet avoids any narration and records directly the suspenseful, explosive dialogue between the girl and her mother. The poem is structured as a series of couplets, representing the girl's arguments and her mother's answers. The lines are short, terse, and pointed; their dramatic quality is enhanced by the girl's tentative, groping words and the mother's tone of absolute certainty and unequivocal conviction. The girl tells her mother about the knight who has been courting her and arguing that the Jews are the world's pariahs, "damned in this world and the next." The girl betrays her sympathy towards the man, who has been unable to "eat and drink" since he has come under the Jewess' "spell." The young girl does not understand that she is actually sealing her own doom when she proudly repeats the knight's claim that she "bewitched" him. When the young man implied that he had come under the Jewess' "spell," drawing on the prevalent myth of the Jewess as sorceress, he did not necessarily mean to flatter the young girl. There is a veiled condemnation in his words, which might evolve into a reason for persecution, that the inexperienced girl does not fully comprehend, but that does not escape her mother's ears.[104] When the girl continues to argue that the knight promised her "a gold necklace and beautiful attire," the mother's answer, unexpected in its harshness and graphic nature, seems like a cruel blow to the girl's romantic dreams. She tells her daughter that the Gentile suitor himself will be lavishly dressed when he watches how the young Jewish girl is thrown "into the pyre." The polarity between the young girl, who is naive, flattered by her conquest, and curious about the stranger, and the mother who is cynical, disillusioned, and adamant in her position, heightens the drama of the two feminine experiences reflected here.[105]

In the works of Aharon Appelfeld, known as a "Holocaust writer," women, like men, are seen in the grips of a nightmare, the laws of which they are unable to comprehend. As a rule, Appelfeld refrains from dealing directly with the actual horrors of the period and the explosive reality of the death camps. The monstrous event known as the Holocaust is a forbidden territory in this writer's canon; it is viewed from a chronological and geographical distance: the anguished anticipation before it occurs and the crippling impact it leaves behind. But the "heart of darkness" itself is never touched in a realistic, graphic style. In those stories that occur before the deportations and the gas chambers, people are engaged in self-deception, purposely avoiding the menacing signs of an approaching catastrophe. In *Badenheim 1939,*[106] it is only the chronic invalid Trude who senses something terrible in the air, but it is attributed to her feminine excitability and ailing condition. In other stories, the terrors of the past cast a gigantic shadow, and the protagonists, both men and women, are seen as social and mental misfits, forever haunted by an inexplicable sense of guilt and terror. In those stories that occur not before or after the Holocaust, but during the event itself, the protagonist is usually an escapee, a wanderer, who somehow manages to stay outside the actual horrors, and who is not fully aware of his own identity.[107]

While the Holocaust left a crippling effect on both men and women, Appelfeld has written a few works in which it is the woman's particular experience that is explored, and in which it is the protagonist's femininity that is a major factor in her demise or survival. Two works revolving around young girls, the short story "Kitty,"[108] and the novella *Tzili,*[109] are of special interest.

Kitty, a young girl on the threshold of adolescence, is placed with nuns in a monastery for safety. She has to learn a new language and a new set of prayers and cultural symbols, as well as come to terms with her own pubescent body, now in a process of change and growth. The nuns epitomize repressed femininity, an acquiescence with the negation of their gender and sexual being. Kitty senses intuitively that she herself has to hide and submerge aspects of her being, yet she has no clear idea what they are. She is not fully conscious that it is her Jewishness that has to be negated, since she is not entirely aware of her national-religious identity; and she cannot repress her femininity before she has come to grips with it. Thus, while the nuns attempt to integrate Kitty into their sphere of existence, the young girl's Jewishness, as well as her budding, insistent sexuality will inevitably defeat them.

While Kitty lives physically in the sheltered, isolated monastery, she prefers to see the distant horizons and the open landscapes (220). The religious artifacts lose their theological meanings and are converted by Kitty's subjective imagination into images of flight and joyous movements; thus she envisions the angels actually flying and even dancing (222). The dance, of course, is fabricated by Kitty's imagination, and stands in opposition to the nuns' sedentary, static, and serene existence. Into the immobile, solid stone statue, Kitty projects flow and streaming, sensed only by her.

Yet the feeling—however vague—that something in her is being repressed pervades Kitty's being. Therefore, when the furniture is being moved in preparation for the visit of the abbess, Kitty interprets the creaking of the closets and the sounds of scrubbing as indicating that some "chained being" is lurking behind the heavy furniture, and that whenever one tries to move it, it screams (222). The "screaming being" is both Kitty's Jewishness and her blossoming femininity that crave freedom and escape, and that are anathema to the fervently pious, enclosed monastery life. Thus Kitty's Jewishness and sexuality are intertwined in her predicament. The nuns refuse to talk about her physical reality as well as about her family background and her race. Both Kitty's national and sexual identities are now associated, in Kitty's mind, with sinfulness. When the abbess comes for a second visit, Kitty feels imprisoned by "her secret" (235), which is, in effect, a twofold secret, that of her body and that of her soul.

While Kitty's body develops and her sexuality bursts out, she herself remains in a state of mental freeze, unable to master the French language and express herself with words. With the arrival of spring and then summer, nature's bloom finally affects Kitty's near-muted existence, and she explodes with speech. Yet the speech is more an eruption of Kitty's imprisoned, overflowing young soul than meaningful words and sentences (228). For the nuns, Kitty seems to be mentally handicapped; they are convinced that she has some "defect" which is not only verbal, but envelops her whole personality (228). Kitty's "defect" is, again, the girl's feminine nature and her origins, both opposed to the very spirit and essence of the monastery, and both considered a "sin" in the monastery reality.

Kitty's muted existence seems a matter of choice rather than a physical or mental defect; it is a stubborn withdrawal into her own world. The nuns notice her inquisitive, attentive looks, yet they cannot make her speak (228). Kitty's voluntary muteness ties her with other Holocaust protagonists, especially youngsters, who lose their speech temporarily as a result of the trauma of separation from their family and the horrors that they have witnessed.[110] Kitty's speechlessness serves also as a comment on the bankruptcy of language in modern times, enhanced especially by the prostitution of language in Nazi propaganda, that helped deepen modern man's disillusionment with verbal expression as a tool of humanistic progress.[111] Through Kitty's inability to express herself with words and sentences, Appelfeld himself comments indirectly on the question of the validity and effectiveness of the word after the Holocaust. In spite of Adorno's famous statement that after the Holocaust it is no longer possible to write poetry,[112] which implies that the incommunicability of this nightmarish experience renders language inadequate, poor, and untrustworthy, Appelfeld himself obviously feels that the Holocaust experience does belong within the verbal-artistic domain, and that his attempt to convey this experience with the aid of language does not minimize the enormity of the event. But through Kitty's retreat to the world of silence, that stands in contrast to her vivacity, her growing body, and her will to live and gratify her senses, Appelfeld conveys his mistrust of language. In Kitty's refusal to ingratiate herself with the nuns and start talking, her creator reflects the girl's strength and her subconscious protest against the reality that she finds herself in, as well as its language. In addition to her refusal to master the language, Kitty displays a "rebellious" turn of the shoulder (236).

Kitty's attention is claimed by two women: Maria the nun, an austere figure whose repressed sexuality, so Appelfeld explains, did not result in "grace," and the maidservant Peppi, a promiscuous and ignorant peasant woman who welcomes the Germans as potentially new lovers. When Maria leaves the monastery unexpectedly, Kitty is again deserted by someone close to her. Earlier, the nuns note that when they speak to the girl about the Holy Father, Mother and Son, "a tremor of joy" lights the girl's eyes (226). In thinking that the girl is attracted to the religious symbols, the nuns fail to see her yearning to be with the family that she lost. With the departure of Maria, who for a while substituted for the girl's absent family, Kitty further withdraws into herself. Peppi comes with the news that the Germans are coming, and asks Kitty to join her in looting the monastery, and then "having fun" with the soldiers. When Kitty refuses, Peppi ominously calls her "a dirty Jew" and promises that the soldiers will come to take her (240). Kitty's only escape from this menacing situation is the mystery of her feminine body, which she considers with wonder and delight. When the nuns hide Kitty in the cellar, the images of the juicy apple, the fermentation in the jars, and the stirring that Kitty thinks she sees in the jar of beets convey the girl's withdrawal into her budding feminine body. Kitty's immersion in her blossoming femininity prevents her from realizing that she is being taken to her execution. At the moment of death, she finds the ultimate freedom: "How marvellous it all seemed—like floating in space" (246).

Both Kitty's femininity and her Jewishness are seen as the cause of her tragic end, as well as her salvation. In her last days in the cellar, when Kitty has mentally departed from her surroundings, she finally articulates to herself that she is Jewish, and she also senses her femininity in the most intensified way. In her final assertion of her racial and feminine identities, Kitty finds a haven from pain and misery and goes to her death without fear and anguish.

Unlike Kitty, Tzili, the protagonist of the novella by this name, is a real survivor. What saves her is a combination of her slow wits as well as her femininity. As a youngster, Tzili feels like a pariah in her own family, where she is the only dim-witted child among her bright and ambitious siblings. But her position as the outcast at home prepares her for her later predicament, when the family disperses, and Tzili is left to fend for herself. If Tzili is described as dull-witted and dumb by her family, she possesses the tenacity of the "wise fool" who endures and survives while his betters perish.[113] In her wanderings through the European hinterland, avoiding the Nazis, exploited and brutalized by the local peasants, Tzili epitomizes the totality of the Holocaust experience, and, as the persecuted outcast she, in fact, reenacts the entire Jewish history. By presenting the Holocaust experience through the eyes of the feeble-minded woman, Appelfeld provides an unexpected, unusual angle to the horrendous event. If it would appear that the Holocaust tragedy is best epitomized in the great waste of human genius and energy, Appelfeld creates the sense of horror precisely through the frail, defenseless, and seemingly less-than-human protagonist.

When Tzili starts her wanderings through the small towns and woods, she is persecuted as a woman and not as a Jewess. She presents herself as the daughter of a famous prostitute, Maria, and thus no one suspects her Jewishness. Yet she is constantly harassed by lusty, callous peasants. The first person who breaks her loneliness and talks with her at length, a blind old man, eventually attacks her and tries to rape her. After this incident, Tzili begins to see her budding feminine body as the real oppressor (21). Her next stop, with the ailing former prostitute Katerina, proves equally disastrous. Tzili slaves for Katerina and even begins to call her "mother," but she has to escape when Katerina offers her young body to a peasant. She finds shelter with an old couple, where she works hard and is being beaten regularly by the old woman; yet she has to leave again when the old man will not leave her alone.

Tzili is now reduced to the animal level; both her noncerebral former nature and her disillusionment with the human community, which includes not only the cruel peasants but her own oppressive family (48), help her adjust easily to the new reality. Although she is cold and her body is sore, she feels content, like an animal "whose neck has been freed from its yoke at last" (57). She is now attuned to the cycle of nature and feels at one with the open spaces. Later, she is joined by a Jewish man who escaped from a concentration camp, where he left his wife and two children. In the winter, the man digs a bunker which now becomes a love-nest for the two. Tzili tries to resist the man's advances, but to no avail. When Tzili's lover, Mark, has had enough of her, he disappears, never to be seen again. Tzili later ventures out of the bunker and becomes a servant to a peasant woman, who tells her that she, Tzili, is pregnant. Fleeing the woman's brutality, Tzili joins a group of refugees, dimly realizing that the war is over. Tzili gives birth to a stillborn baby, and at the end we see her on a ship sailing to Palestine.

The story does not end with a note of elation and rebirth, but nor does it leave us with despair. Tzili is seen as emerging from the image of a hunted animal to the stature of a woman who possesses strength, is able to express herself, and can even gain the loyalty of other people. When the peasant woman asks her who impregnated her, Tzili answers defiantly, "a good man" (117). When she first meets the partisans, she repeats the words she learned from Mark, insisting that she is not afraid of death (120); she refuses to join them, feeling secure enough to go her own way (121).

Tzili's strategy for survival is her easy adaptability to new situations and realities. Mark commends her for having so cleverly and successfully adopted the Gentile identity that even he, a Jew, could not at first tell her origins (76). At Mark's urging and encouragement, Tzili ventures into the town and comes back with food and cigarettes. She learns how to bargain and be firm with the peasants. When Mark abandons her, she is left with no bitter feelings. His phantasmic image rises up before her in difficult situations and helps her make a decision. Although she attributes her newfound strength and cunning to Mark's apparition, it is her own untapped inner resources that Tzili draws on. Significantly, her only bad feelings are towards her oppressive family, whom, she says, she will never forgive. In Mark she has found love and even respect for her abilities to survive and, therefore, Mark's abandonment of her does not discredit him in her eyes.

Interestingly, the chaos of the Holocaust triggers and enhances Tzili's journey towards the discovery of her feminine nature and strength. While the Holocaust era moves on with terrifying persistence, Tzili's private existence, running parallel to it, is a period of growth and self-knowledge. Tzili is persecuted as a sex object, not as a Jew, and she finally arrives at a modicum of self-respect through her feminine experiences: her awakened sexuality, her anticipation of the birth of her baby, and her disappointment at losing it. While her contacts with other people prove invariably disappointing, it is Tzili's femininity that provides her with the sensations of pleasure, love, and maternal feelings that preserve her human image and even strengthen it. Again, Appelfeld has used his protagonist's feminine joys and sorrows as analogous to the Holocaust turbulence, and, at the same time, he has anchored the woman's ability to survive in her feminine tenacity.

Notes

[1] Nehama Leibowitz, *Studies in the Weekly Sidra*, Series 4/5718 (Jerusalem: The Jewish Agency, 1957).

[2] For an analysis of the "bed trick" motif in the Bible, the Midrash, and world literature, see Zvi Jagendorf, "'In the Morning, It Was Leah': Genesis and the Reversal of Sexual Knowledge," in David H. Hirsch and Nehama Aschkenasy, eds., *Biblical Patterns in Modern Literature* (Chico, Calif.: Scholars Press, 1984), 51–60.

[3] See Genesis Rabbah 70. For the various midrashim revolving around Jacob and Leah's wedding see Louis Ginzberg, *The Legends of the Jews*, vol. 1 (Philadelphia: Jewish Publication Society, 1909–28), 355–61.

[4] See the commentators Ralbag and Metsudat David on Judg. 4:4.

[5] Ralbag gives both interpretations, while Radak mentions the possibility that Deborah is alluding not to herself but to Jael, and rejects it.

[6] Both Radak and Ralbag comment on the peculiar use of the verb in Judg. 5:1. Radak says that the verb appears in the third person feminine singular because Deborah is the pivot of this story; Ralbag believes that Deborah herself composed this ode, but that it is a common biblical practice to include in the syntactical subject the listeners, or those who join in the reciting of a victory ode, while the verb itself appears in the singular.

[7] While to the modern reader Deborah's sitting under the palm tree might indicate a relative freedom contrasting with the restrictive lives of her female contemporaries, the commentary of Metsudat David sees in Deborah's conducting her court in the open space a sign of modesty, since it was not considered proper for a woman to meet with men in the privacy of her home.

[8] The "strange woman" episode and its link to the "fear of women" syndrome is discussed in detail in Chapter Two. The Haskalah poet Micah Joseph Lebensohn, in his poem "Jael and Sisra," gives voice to the element of "fear of women" that is submerged in the biblical story. He describes Deborah as a ferocious, awe-inspiring woman warrior and Jael as her opposite, a gentle, domestic soul, whose sensitive conscience does not allow her to commit murder; when she finally kills Sisera, she feels like the prototypical killer Cain. Jael comes to terms with the killing of Sisera only when she hears Deborah's approval of her deed and the prophetess' assurances that she, Jael, has fulfilled a divine wish. It is still doubtful, however, where the heart of the young, romantic poet lay. Lebensohn is much more convincing in his portrayal of Deborah's awesome stature and Jael's emotional and moral dilemma, than in the pat conclusion to the poem—in which Jael is finally reconciled to having committed murder—that seems to have been added artificially to conform to the biblical spirit. See *The Collected Poems of Micah Joseph Lebensohn,* in Hebrew (Tel Aviv: Devir, 1956), 20–23.

[9] In his discussion of Judg. 5:27, the commentator Radak cites an ancient midrash (which he dismisses), that says that Sisera had intercourse with Jael seven times.

[10] *The Fear of Women,* op. cit., 127.

[11] The lack of solidarity among women has been seen as characteristic of female groups depicted in literature. For a discussion of female communities in literature, see Nina Auerbach, *Communities of Women: An Idea in Fiction* (Cambridge, Mass.: Harvard University Press, 1978).

[12] *The Second Sex* (New York: Knopf, 1953).

[13] Women waiting for men to give meaning to their lives constitute a central motif in much later literature, too. Nina Auerbach, in *Communities of Women,* discusses the theme of "waiting" as emblematic of the feminine situation in nineteenth-century English and American fiction, especially in times of war. Imagery of enclosure is prevalent in the works of female writers; see Sandra M. Gilbert and Susan Gubar, *The Madwoman in the Attic: The Woman Writer and the Nineteenth-Century Literary Imagination* (New Haven: Yale University Press, 1979), 85 et passim.

[14] See Chapter One, n. 11.

[15] For a literary analysis of this tale, see Zvi Adar, *The Biblical Tale,* in Hebrew (Jerusalem: Jewish Agency, 1957), 22–46.

[16] This is how the Anchor Bible translates 1 Sam. 25:3. See: P. Kyle McCarter, ed., *1 Samuel,* the Anchor Bible series (Garden City, N.Y.: Doubleday, 1980), 389.

[17] For a discussion of these comic types, see Northrop Frye, *Anatomy of Criticism* (Princeton, N.J.: Princeton University Press, 1957), 172–75, 226–28. These distinctions between extreme and moderate human types, with regard to truth and to pleasure (amusement), are derived from Aristotle's *Ethics.*

[18] See *1 Samuel,* the Anchor Bible, 392.

[19] See the Anchor Bible, ibid., 400–402.

[20] The Hebrew of II Sam. 20:20 is not entirely coherent, but this is the accepted meaning of the woman's arguments.

[21] *Communities of Women,* op. cit., 13 et passim. The Midrash recognized polygyny as an evil leading to feminine rivalry when it said: "When there are two women in the household, there is constant fighting" (Tanḥuma, Tetse).

[22] Pesaḥhim 62b. In this context it is interesting to mention a biblical woman who has been endowed with a mythic dimension by the Midrash sages and portrayed as the "wise woman" par excellence: Seraḥ, the daughter of Asher. Seraḥ's wisdom is tied to her supernatural powers; she knew that Joseph was alive when his father Jacob thought that he was dead, and she was also the keeper of "the secret of redemption." According to the Midrash, Seraḥ became immortal. See Joseph Heinemann, *Aggadah and Its Development,* in Hebrew (Jerusalem: Keter, 1974), 56–63. Genesis Rabbah 94 identifies Seraḥ with the "wise woman' who saved the city Abel from Joab. While the Midrash labels Seraḥ as "a wise woman," it does not identify either Beruria or Yalta as "wise women," although it elaborates on their knowledge. The reason for this has to do with the other side of feminine wisdom that Beruria and Yalta display, that of fury and lack of contentment. Another possible reason is that the Midrash sages believed that the tradition of wise women ended after biblical times.

[23] Midrash on Prov. 31.

[24] Eruvin 53, 54.

[25] Beruria lived in the middle years of the second century C.E., approximately between 110–169 C.E. Her father, R. Haninah ben Tardion, was executed among the ten martyrs during the Roman persecutions following the Bar Kokhba revolt of 135 C.E. The tales about Beruria are found in the Babylonian Talmud, which was completed in the fifth century C.E. However, the Midrash on Proverbs, from which the tale of Beruria and the death of her sons is cited (see n. 23), was completed in the ninth-century C.E.

[26] See Abot 1:5.

[27] Berakhot 51b.

[28] Shabbat 77b.

[29] Ḥulin 109b.

[30] On the origins of the Lilith myth and its development, see Joseph Dan, "Samael, Lilith, and the Concept of Evil in Early Kabbalah," *Association for Jewish Studies Review* 5 (1980): 17–40. The tale of Lilith discussed here is cited in this essay.

[31] For a study of feminine fury and madness and their transformation into monstrosity in nineteenth-century women's writings, see *The Madwoman,* op. cit., 35 et passim.

[32] See Dan's essay, op. cit., 22n.

[33] Dan, 22.

[34] Ibid., 22.

[35] Ibid., 22f.

[36] Patai, *The Hebrew Goddess,* op. cit., 186–206. See also Yishayahu Tishbi, ed., *Mishnat Ha-Zohar* (Jerusalem: Mosad Bialik, 1949), as well as Tishbi's

study of the paradoxical nature of the Shekinah in his introduction to the chapter "Shekinah," vol. 1, 220–30.

[37] Patai, 205.

[38] Tishbi, op. cit., 222–25.

[39] See Scholem, *Major Trends*, op. cit., 286, 305. The tales of Reb Nahman exemplify the merging of the theme of the national and cosmological quest for redemption with the personal-psychological search. See Joseph Dan's preface to Arnold J. Band, ed., *Nahman of Bratslav: The Tales* (New York: Paulist Press, 1978). Furthermore, it seems that Reb Nahman was especially receptive to the Zohar's portrayal of the Shekinah as fierce and harsh out of personal reasons—his own problematic relationship with women. See Arthur Green, *The Tormented Master: The Life of Rabbi Nahman of Bratslav* (New York: Schocken, 1981), 353.

[40] This parable is cited in Joseph Dan, *The Hebrew Tale in the Middle Ages: A Study of Its Development*, in Hebrew (Jerusalem: Keter, 1974), 207–17.

[41] Feminine rage in its comic aspect appears also in a medieval *maqama*, a form of poetic fiction, by Joseph ibn Zabara (1140–1200), titled *The Book Of Delight*. It tells of Socrates, who once, walking with his disciples, was attacked inexplicably by a woman washing clothes in the river: "She cried out upon him, and cursed him, and reviled him, and heaped him with abuse; then she threw of the water upon him and drenched him. He said, Surely she cast her lightning and hurled her thunder, and now she bringeth forth rain." See Curt Leviant, ed., *Masterpieces of Hebrew Literature* (New York: Ktav, 1969), 405. Interestingly, there is no attempt to understand the reasons for the woman's rage; feminine fury is viewed as a natural catastrophe that a man has to live with and endure.

Ibn Zabara's *maqama* also offers a reversal of the biblical motif of feminine wisdom in a story in which a wise king exposes the folly and treachery of women. See Leviant, 401–4.

[42] See *For the Sake of Heaven*, op. cit., 158–61; also Martin Buber, *Tales of the Hasidim: The Later Masters* (New York: Schocken, 1948), 226.

[43] See Chapter Two.

[44] *For the Sake of Heaven*, 161.

[45] *The Later Masters*, 226.

[46] In *The Collected Works*, in Hebrew (Tel Aviv: Am Oved, 1951), 197–205. For biographical details and a bibliographical list on Berdichewscky and his critics, see Dan Miron's edition of Berdichewscky's "Miriam," in Hebrew (Tel Aviv: Yahdav, 1971), with a lengthy introduction by Dan Miron, and a bibliography.

[47] For this aspect in Berdichewscky's works, see Gershon Shaked, *Dead End*, in Hebrew (Tel Aviv: Hakibbutz Hameuchad, 1973), 15–32. See also Shaked's study of this story in *On Four Stories: Studies in the Elements of the Short Story*, in Hebrew (Jerusalem: Jewish Agency 1963), 66–92.

[48] For Shaked's discussion of Nathan's dibbuk as the source of Klonimus' rebellious eruption, see *Dead End*, 25. "Klonimus and Naomi" is not the only instance where a woman is seen as the transmitter of madness, however.

In Berdichewscky's story "Miriam," op. cit., the girl Miriam drives a hunch-backed boy to madness without even being aware of her influence on him.

[49] Simon Halkin has shown how the Haskalah writers condemned the ghetto Jew for his lack of sensitivity towards nature, music, and beauty. In this respect, Naomi is indeed a different type of a shtetl girl. See *Modern Hebrew Literature* (New York: Schocken, 1970; first published 1950), 40–41.

[50] Trans. Gabriel Levin. In *Eight Great Hebrew Short Novels,* op. cit., 167–216. Page references are to this edition. The Hebrew text consulted is the Schocken edition of 1971.

[51] See *Essays on Agnon's Stories,* in Hebrew (Tel Aviv: Schocken, 1963), 46–49.

[52] Lea Goldberg, who knew Agnon personally, tells us that he was very fond of Adelbert von Chamisso's story "Peter Schlemihls Wundersame Geschichte." See "S. Y. Agnon: The Writer and His Protagonist," in Hebrew, in *LeAgnon Shai* (Jerusalem, 1959), 52, 53. The story revolves around a shadow which has an independent mobility, and is sold by its original owner.

[53] In *Nostalgia and Nightmare* (Berkeley: The University of California Press, 1968), 115.

[54] Agnon frequently tells a story in a language appropriate to a teller other than the writer himself, even when that teller is not a character in the story. See Lea Goldberg's study of this technique in "The Writer and His Protagonist," op. cit., 47–61.

[55] The phrase translated as "he forgot the ways of the world" ("In the Prime," 167) carries subtle sexual connotations in the Hebrew.

[56] A study of stories in which a man departs from his shadow either willingly or unwillingly can be found in Otto Rank, *The Double,* translated by Harry Tucker (Chapel Hill: University of North Carolina Press, 1971). Otto Rank's first study of the subject appeared in an article published in 1919. Rank tells us that shadow superstition is related to the "double" phenomenon.

[57] Kurzweil studied the significance of the dog as a primal sexual symbol in a number of Agnon's works, most significantly in the novel *Temol Shilshom;* see *Essays on Agnon,* op. cit., 104–15 et passim.

[58] The translator opted for "a deep sigh." I believe, however, that the "heart" is important here, since it brings Tirtza closer to her mother, who suffered from a heart ailment.

[59] For the other aspects of this story see Chapters One and Three.

[60] For a different reading of the ending of the story, see Arnold Band, op. cit., 242, 243.

[61] For more on feminine fury and its eruption in madness either as a voluntary escape or as lack of control, both in life and in fiction, see Phyllis Chesler, *Women and Madness* (Garden City, N.Y.: Doubleday, 1972), 5–31, and *The Madwoman in the Attic,* op. cit.

[62] For a fuller analysis of this story, see Chapter Four.

[63] In *The Collected Works,* in Hebrew, op. cit., 79–93.

[64] The concept of the "severed" or "uprooted," inspired by Berkowitz's

story, has become an emblem for a whole generation of protagonists who found themselves at a dead-end situation in the shtetl, in the early years of the twentieth century. On Berkowitz's "severed heroes," see Avraham Holtz, *Isaac Dov Berkowitz, Voice of the Uprooted,* op. cit., 50–64 et passim. Holtz also offers a translation of Berkowitz's "Severed," 123–48.

[65] In Hebrew, in *The Collected Stories,* op. cit., 79–93.

[66] I am referring here to the girl-narrator or the girl-observer, who appears in the stories collected in *The Thorny Path,* op. cit., and in the Hebrew collection *Parashiot,* op. cit.

[67] "And It Is the Light," in Lea Goldberg, *Prose,* in Hebrew, (Tel Aviv: Poalim, 1972), 11–94; the story was first published in 1946.

[68] For other uses of the double in women's writings, see *The Madwoman in the Attic,* op. cit.

[69] In *Where the Jackals Howl* (New York: Harcourt Brace Jovanovich, 1981), 21–38. The story was written in 1963 and revised in 1975. The Hebrew version consulted is the Am Oved edition, 1977.

For an analysis of the story, see Hillel Barzel's introduction in Hillel Barzel, ed., *Six Writers,* in Hebrew (Jerusalem: Yahdav, 1977), 207–15. For general insights on Oz's works, see Gershon Shaked, *A New Wave in Hebrew Literature* (Tel Aviv: Poalim, 1971), 180–203; see also Robert Alter's "Afterword: a problem of horizons" in Elliot Anderson, ed., *Contemporary Israeli Literature* (Philadelphia: Jewish Publication Society, 1977), 329–32.

[70] Lederer, *The Fear of Women,* op. cit., 22, 48, 122, and Erich Neumann, *The Great Mother,* op. cit., 185, 186.

[71] I have not used the Freudian jargon of id, ego, and superego, so as to avoid wandering into the psychoanalyst's domain. A case can be made here, however, that during her encounter with the Bedouin, Geula takes a trip into her id, while in the last moment of the story, which is an ironic state of total peace, her superego finally emerges.

[72] *A Passage to India* was written in 1924.

[73] Trans. Nicholas de Lange in collaboration with the author (New York: Knopf, 1972). The Hebrew version consulted is the Am Oved edition, 1976; first published in 1968.

[74] On women who are defiantly at odds with the female role, see Chesler, *Women and Madness,* op. cit., 15 et passim.

[75] On mothers and daughters, see Chesler, 17–25.

[76] *Time in Literature* (Berkeley: University of California Press, 1960), 104.

[77] Shaked, *A New Wave,* 195–96.

[78] I use the term "second self" in the way Otto Rank refers to it. For Rank, the shadow, the mirror image, and the subjective projections of the self, even if they do not become independent persons, are also considered as "doubles." On the other hand, C. F. Keppler, in *The Literature of the Second Self* (Tucson: University of Arizona Press, 1972), believes that the "second self" must be an independent figure, not just a subjective projection of the character.

[79] See Rank, *The Double,* op. cit.

[80] See Gilbert and Gubar, *The Madwoman,* 518 et passim.

[81] Gustave Flaubert published *Madame Bovary* in 1857. Tolstoy completed

Anna Karenina in 1877. Both are novels written by a man and focusing on a female protagonist, and in this respect they have something in common with Oz's novel. Images of confinement, the hideous old man as a messenger of death and doom, and the protagonist's journey towards self-destruction are themes common to all three novels.

[82] Shaked in *A New Wave*, 13, mentions Hannah's resemblance to Emma Bovary in her retreat to a false world of romantic fantasy, fueled by cheap romantic novels, and rightfully points out that Hannah's adultery is committed in her imagination only, while Emma's adulterous affairs are real. Beyond that, Emma Bovary seeks physical and social fulfillment, while Hannah's fantasies are oriented towards the inner self, since Hannah completely lacks any social aspirations.

[83] On the identification between Hannah and Jerusalem, see Shaked, *A New Wave*, 189–90.

[84] See *Homo Ludens*, translated by R. F. C. Hull (Boston: Beacon Press, 1955).

[85] See the Hebrew text of *My Michael*, op. cit., 151.

[86] *The Bell Jar* was first published in London in 1963. Scorn for the mother figure is another trait that Hannah and Esther share.

[87] *Women and Madness*, 15, 16.

[88] Amalia Kahana-Karmon, *And Moon in the Valley of Ajalon* (Tel Aviv: Hakibbutz Hameuchad, 1971).

[89] Shaked in *A New Wave*, 223, points out No'a's resemblance especially to Mrs. Dalloway.

[90] See Leon Edel, *The Modern Psychological Novel* (New York: Grosset and Dunlap, 1964).

[91] Shaked, op. cit., 222.

[92] In Kahana-Karmon's collection of stories in Hebrew, *Bikfifah Ahat* (Tel Aviv: Poalim, 1966).

[93] Rachel Eytan, *Pleasures of Man;* in Hebrew, *Shidah veShidot* (Tel Aviv: Am Oved, 1974).

[94] On the different versions of this tale, see Gerson D. Cohen, "Hannah and Her Seven Sons," *Jubilee Book in Honor of Mordechai Kaplan* (New York: Jewish Theological Seminary, 1953), 109–22.

[95] Abodah Zarah, 18b.

[96] Some examples of martyrdom where the woman's ordeal is particularly highlighted in the medieval records are the piece, by an anonymous poet, on the Martyrs of Mainz, in Carmi, *Hebrew Verse*, op. cit., 372–73; and the poem on the murder of Bellet and Hannah, Carmi, 387–88.

[97] A related topic that will not be discussed in the present study, but that waits to be explored in Hebrew, Yiddish, and American-Jewish literatures is that of the actual relationship of the Jewish woman and the non-Jewish man.

[98] In *The Collected Poems*, in Hebrew, op. cit., 165–75.

[99] In *Poems*, op. cit., 438–41.

[100] See H. H. Ben Sasson, ed., *A History of the Jewish People* (Cambridge, Mass.: Harvard University Press, 1976), 752.

[101] In *Poems*, 737–39, from a group of poems entitled "Ballads of Worms."

[102] For the history of Jews in Central Europe in this period, see H. H. Ben Sasson, ed., *A History of the Jewish People,* op. cit., 593–611.

[103] In *Poems,* 736–37.

[104] The Jews in the city of Worms knew periods of intense persecution, especially during the plague of the Black Death in the fourteenth century, when they were accused of polluting the water. In 1349, the whole Jewish community of Worms, numbering three hundred people, set fire to their homes and went up in flames.

[105] The polarity between the older Jewish woman, representing tradition and acceptance of authority, and the young woman, whose rebellious drives lead her to join a failed uprising in Russia, resulting in her arrest, is depicted in Tchernichovsky's longer poem, "Dumplings" (in *Poems,* 133–44). The poem describes in minute detail how the old woman Gittel makes dumplings in her kitchen. The process of kneading the dough, smoothing it with the rolling pin, pressing it together, molding evenly shaped dumplings, and dropping them in boiling water, is analogous to her granddaughter Reizele's experience of oppression in Czarist Russia's school system, and the final eruption of her repressed self in the form of political action.

[106] Trans. Dalya Bilu (Boston: David R. Godine, 1980).

[107] On Appelfeld's works see Shaked, 149–67; see also Hillel Barzel, ed., *Six Writers,* in Hebrew (Tel Aviv: Yahdav, 1977), 11–23. Obviously, I do not attempt here to offer a comprehensive assessment of this very important contemporary writer, but only to focus on two female characters. Appelfeld's adolescent boys, who are the protagonists of some of his Holocaust stories (see, for instance, the stories collected in Barzel), have many experiences in common with the adolescent girls. However, the woman's coming to terms with her sexuality, against the Holocaust background, and the fusion of the shame and guilt associated with the girl's new feminine experiences and her Jewishness are, of course, unique to the two works discussed here.

[108] Trans. Tirza Zandbank in *Modern Hebrew Stories,* ed. Ezra Spicehandler, (A Bantam Dual Language Book; New York: Bantam, 1971), 221–47. Page references are to this edition.

[109] Trans. Dalya Bilu (New York: Dutton, 1983), first serialized in *Molad* (Israel), in 1982. All page references are to the Dutton edition.

[110] See, for instance, Jerzy Kosinski, *The Painted Bird* (1976), which describes the ordeal of a child and his retreat into silence. Interestingly, the flight from language as a protest against the world, resulting from a war experience, is exemplified in Agnon's Reb Hayim, a minor character in *A Guest for the Night* (1939), whose suffering during World War I causes his inability, or unwillingness, to talk when he returns home.

[111] On the theme of the modern revolt against verbal discourse, see Ihab Hassan, *The Literature of Silence* (New York: Knopf, 1967) and George Steiner, *Language and Silence* (London: Faber, 1967).

[112] Theodor W. Adorno, *Noten zur Literatur,* vol. 3 (Frankfurt am Main, 1965), 125.

[113] The "divine simpleton" is a figure who roamed Christian Europe, and

even entered into Hasidic literature; see Martin Buber, *Or HaGanuz* (Jerusalem, 1967), 30. He was usually a madman or a half-wit who, because of his extreme suffering and isolation from society, came to be seen as possessing divine knowledge or as being under the protection of God. It seems that Tzili's ability to survive, partly due to her reduced mental abilities, ties her to this folk character of mythic dimensions.

Epilogue

The two literary pieces cited in the opening to Chapter Five juxtapose two feminine strategies which serve, in their diametrical polarity, as a comment on the evolution of the females' spheres of being and of the landscapes of their movements. The first excerpt is from the biblical Book of Ruth, a document that belongs to the beginnings of the Hebraic civilization. Ruth will become the ancestress of King David, the most illustrious and memorable figure in Israelite history, and the glorious founder of an expanded, strong kingdom. Dalia Ravikovitch's poem, written in 1959, is the product of the modern Hebrew woman, dwelling in the reborn land and reflecting a secular, modern sensibility. This modern sensibility is often saturated with the memory of the long historical road that has stretched out before the Israelite nation since the times of Ruth, yet this historical memory is not particularly in evidence in Ravikovitch's present poem.

If the anonymous masses of the ancient women seem to project a placid, acted-upon collective figure, Ruth emerges as quite different. She resorts to a subterfuge laden with sexual innuendos in order to awaken the man's sense of familial obligation, which he seems to have neglected. While the sexual ruse might offend the modern feminist sensibility, it is conveyed euphemistically and circuitously, the narrator being careful not to cross the barrier into bad taste. By employing the feminine tactic of instilling a sense of sexual guilt in the man, the woman Ruth, the Moabite foreigner, carves out for herself a niche in the history of the nation with which she has chosen to share her destiny. She is also rewarded for her efforts by being given a place of honor in the biblical canon, and having a separate document named after her. Ruth is resourceful, aggressive, and fearless. When she addresses Boaz, she speaks in the name of time-honored social and religious laws that ought to alert the historical memory and responsibility of the man. She reminds him of a tradition that underlies his own culture, and that was founded at the inception of his own civilization. But Ruth relies not only on the past; by marrying the man and bearing a child who would carry her dead husband's name, she secures the future perpetuation of a family. And when we remember that Ruth's descendant would become the king of Israel and the carrier of its Messianic dreams, we see that Ruth has put herself at a juncture where the historical memory of past traditions and cultural values converges with an eschatological vision of a destiny the horizons of which transcend time and place.

On the other hand, the landscape of the speaker in Dalia Ravikovitch's poem is an interior one, that of the hallucinatory inner self of the woman who has sunk into the dark recesses of her mind to explore her feminine condition, and can only frame it in a nightmarish, almost surrealistic vision. There is no time and place here, but the timeless moment of the dream and the spectral topography of the disturbed self. The first-person speaker is the dehumanized woman who has turned into a windup doll, and performs to the dictates of an outside manipulator. The sonnet starts with an unexpected show of rebellion that is not free of hysteria, when the doll suddenly frees herself from the laws of mechanics to which she is bound, and runs amuck, whirling in all directions. The doll is punished for this moment of transgression, and although now, more than ever, she conforms to the image of docile beauty and phlegmatic behavior expected of her, she is no longer wanted.

From the fearless ancient woman who breaks her way into a nation's memory and its recorded history, to the paranoid, frantic, modern woman who forsakes time and place to embark on an ego-centered trip, descending into her own turbulent self, women have always sought ways of self-expression and self-assertion. Since the majority of ancient women were locked into silence, we have no way of knowing whether they attempted to explore their own feminine and human identity. But when the ancient women spring out of their speechless existence, they are not seen as engaged in introspection, but as laboring to redeem themselves from their nameless status and put their own imprint on their nation's destiny. Ruth marries into an illustrious Israelite family and becomes the progenitor of the nation's leader; Rebecca attempts to manipulate her husband, and indeed God himself, into conforming to her conception of the identity of the person who will become the third patriarch; and Abigail cleverly engineers her union with the future king of Israel.

In the modern texts, where women's long silence is finally broken, and their foiled creative energies are released, the woman's strategy is no longer that of becoming integrated into the exterior landscapes, but is rather a search that turns inward. If in the Hasidic literature the man is seen as a seeker, forever on a quest to repair the faulty human time and solve the enigma of existence, the modern feminine protagonist is on a quest, too, but on one in which she has to abandon time and history in order to explore the very essence of her being. Often the trip into the self takes the woman, like Oz's Hannah, into the realm beyond language and the verbal expression, where the self is fragmented and divided. But the search can also result in new linguistic formulations of the feminine horizons, as reflected in Karmon's works and in Ravikovich's poem.

Eve's odyssey also charts the journey of the male writer who has progressed from his early tendency to relegate the female character to a subordinate literary function, to a new conception of the heroine as an emblem of the entire human condition. In the works of Amos Oz, the woman becomes a paradigm of the Israeli's alienation within his geopolitical environment and of modern man's otherness in a hostile universe. If Oz's female characters are outcasts, not partaking of the collective sense of shared destiny, so are his male protagonists: the kibbutz pariah, planning revenge on the establishment, the disillusioned inventor, finding himself at the end of his life estranged from his family and caged in a futile existence; and the doomed, poetry-loving paratrooper, at odds with his chosen military career. Furthermore, Oz's most powerful feminine character, Hannah, is akin to so many antiheroes and fools who populate the modern novel. Hannah's despair of time and history, her escape into the fool's illusory sphere of eternal game, her renunciation of language and speech, and her final journey into a no-man's-land where civilization and its verbal symbols are rendered obsolete are familiar to the modern reader. They remind us of the darkly comic sagas of such diverse modern protagonists as Samuel Beckett's iconoclastic clowns and Julio Cortazar's anguished seekers, waiting for a moment of illumination in the labyrinthine maze of meaningless everyday existence.

But the attempts of the enlightened, modern male writer to redeem the female character from her marginal, secondary literary role are not without dialectical tension. Often the veneer of modernity fails to cover completely the submerged early female prototypes. The contemporary writer's tribute to the early sources results, many times, in his inability to free himself of ancient female images and paradigms. For instance, though for Oz the woman's otherness is not exclusively feminine but part of the collective human condition, nevertheless, he often resorts to early male conceptions when he attributes demonic powers to the woman and views her as the chaotic antinomian. Indeed, some of the most memorable female characters since Haskalah, those who have been promoted by the male writer to a central position in the literary work, such as Berdichewscky's Naomi, Agnon's Tehilah, Gemula, and the legendary mother in "The Kerchief," as well as Yehoshua's Ziva, and Oz's Hannah, Geula, and Lily, are all endowed with mysterious energies that transcend the here and now. Some are transmitters or carriers of madness and psychic chaos, such as Naomi, Geula, Lily, and Ziva. Some possess potent magic talents of healing and redemption, such as the larger-than-life mother in Agnon's "The Kerchief" and the ageless Tehilah, the modern reincarnation of the "wise woman," who enfolds in her being the eternal beauty and indestructibility of the city that she embodies, Jerusalem. These female characters still retain the early feminine attributes, the diabolic powers of destruction, on the one hand, or the ability to transcend the laws of human life and become immune to the world's exigencies, on the other. Though they frequently seem to belong to authentic, recognizable realities, these female protagonists are still mythic images, ahistorical figures who either retard the male's progress in time, or are able to rise above human history, but they are not completely part of the male world and destiny.

A different form of paradox exists within the orbit of female writers. While in life the woman has traveled from oppression to relative equality, and from a segregated existence into the mainstream, especially in a society where women are drafted into the army just like men, the works of the women writers that we have examined reflect a conception of feminine destiny that is still not synonymous with the human destiny, and a sense of powerlessness vis-à-vis the male sphere.

In earlier Judaic sources, produced by the male mind, the woman shuttled between total insignificance and lack of power, on the one hand, and the mythic status of a subversive force, capable of effecting cosmic and psychic catastrophes, on the other. As the woman writer attempts to rid her female creation of both extremes and assimilate her into the mainstream, she also has to divest the woman of her metaphysical and metahistorical potency and redefine her existential and literary self in terms reflecting the woman's claim for equality. Consequently, the new female protagonist may feel atrophied and depleted, having been exiled from her mythic sphere but not yet become fully integrated in the common human experience. Significantly, Agnon creates a strong identification between his exalted Tehilah and the idealized Jerusalem, the most mythic of all earthly cities. For a younger writer such as Oz, too, the woman's affinity with the awe-inspiring city of Jerusalem implies her tremendous powers to create and destroy worlds, albeit imaginary ones. Yet Amalia Kahana-Karmon's vulnerable woman protagonist sees herself mirrored in Tel Aviv, a new city, lacking in mythic memory and historical character, and quickly descending into shabby urban bleakness.

The tendency to elevate the female protagonist to a mythic force is also evident in A. B. Yehoshua's novels. It is true that Yehoshua's characters, male and female alike, are given a realistic, everyday authenticity both as individuals immersed in private concerns such as money, love, and sex, and as prototypes representing a cross-section of contemporary Israeli society. Yet the more memorable of his female protagonists are endowed with imposing larger-than-life qualities, converting them into symbols of momentous cultural and historical processes. The indestructible, ageless Veducha in *The Lover*, miraculously awakening from a comatose sleep, is no less than historic Zionism itself, lulled into apathy and then jolted into a renewed sense of awareness in the aftermath of war. And Naomi, the schizophrenic matriarch of Yehoshua's Faulknerian novel *A Late Divorce*, not only infects her whole family with insanity, but is revealed as the mental seismograph of a society in the grips of collective hysteria. The mad woman removes the thin veneer of sanity from each of the novel's protagonists and uncovers the submerged spiritual and emotional instability of the individuals as well as of the total culture.

Against this background, a recent novel by a woman writer, Shulamit Lapid's *Gei 'Oni* ("Valley of My Strength," 1982), is of particular significance. It portrays a female protagonist whose sanity and healthy earthiness stand in contradistinction to both the mental fragility of the females in the works of the modern women writers and the seer's madness of some of the female protagonists created by the male writers. Fanya, the novel's central character, is placed in a historical context as a woman who came to Palestine in the wave that later became known as the "First *Aliya*." The woman is seen as stronger than the men, enduring horrors in her native Russia which drove her brother insane, and hardships in the uncultivated land of Palestine that killed her husband. Nevertheless, Lapid avoids both aggrandizing her female character and romanticizing the era, thus producing a realistically-drawn protagonist within the framework of historical fiction.

One route in Eve's odyssey may be depicted as an evolutionary line that leads from the reticent early woman, silenced by her culture as well as by her literary creator, to the expressive modern female who challenges a sexist tradition and uses the male texts to assert her own feminine self. Yet this neat, optimistic formula is much too simple to account for the variety of female experiences that we have followed. The literary documents reflect a tortuous and circuitous female course, in which every progress is counterpointed by retreat, and the opportunity to break out of the prison of silence often results in withdrawal into self-imposed segregation. Nevertheless, as Eve's journey continues to unfold, the female character will no doubt escape from the position of either less than human or more than human, in which she has been locked in the past, and her power will be transferred to new spheres. At the same time, the tension between earlier myths and new realities becomes the challenge that awaits both the male and the female writer, as well as the source of new invigoration for the literary work.

A Selected Bibliography

All the works were consulted in their Hebrew editions. However, where the author knows of an English translation, only the English edition is listed here. Biblical books and Midrash sources were consulted in the original and are not included in the present bibliography.

Works Cited

Agnon, S. Y. "Vehaya He'Aqov Lemishor" ("And the Crooked Shall Be Made Straight"). In Hebrew. *The Collected Works*, vol. 2, 61–127. Jerusalem and Tel Aviv: Schocken, 1971.
———. "In the Prime of Her Life." *Eight Great Hebrew Short Novels*, 165–216. Ed. Alan Lelchuk and Gershon Shaked. New York: New American Library, 1983.
———. *Sippur Pashut (A Simple Story)*. In Hebrew. *The Collected Works*, vol. 3, 55–172. Jerusalem and Tel Aviv: Schocken, 1971.
———. "Tehilah." Trans. Walter Lever. In *Israeli Stories*, ed. Joel Blocker, 22–64. New York: Schocken, 1970.
———. *Temol Shilshom. (Only Yesterday)*. In Hebrew. Jerusalem and Tel Aviv: Schocken, 1953.
———. *Twenty-One Stories*. Ed. Nahum N. Glatzer. New York: Schocken, 1970. Stories discussed here: "Agunot," "The Doctor's Divorce," "The Kerchief," "The Lady and the Pedlar," "The Tale of the Scribe."
———. *Two Tales*. Trans. Walter Lever. New York: Schocken, 1966.
Amichai, Yehuda. *Not of This Time, Not of This Place*. Trans. Shlomo Katz. New York: Harper and Row, 1948.
Appelfeld, Aharon. "Kitty." Trans. Tirtza Zandbank. *Modern Hebrew Stories*. Ed. Ezra Spicehandler. A Bantam Dual Language Book. New York: Bantam, 1971, 220–46.

————. *Tzili.* Trans. Dalya Bilu. New York: Dutton, 1983.

Baron, Dvorah. *The Thorny Path.* Trans. Joseph Shachter. Jerusalem: Israel University Press, 1969.

————. *Parashiot.* In Hebrew. Jerusalem: Mosad Bialik, 1951.

Berdichewscky, Micah Yosef. "Klonimus and Naomi." In *The Collected Works.* In Hebrew. Tel Aviv: Am Oved, 1951.

————. *Miriam.* In Hebrew. Edited, with an Introduction, Dan Miron. Tel Aviv: Yahdav, 1971.

Berkowitz, I. D. *The Collected Works of I. D. Berkowitz.* In Hebrew. Tel Aviv: Devir, 1959. Stories cited: "Cucumbers," "Grandchild," "Mariashka," "Severed," "The Letter."

Bialik, Chaim Nachman. "My Mother of Blessed Memory," and "My Song." In *Selected Poems, Bilingual Edition,* sel. and trans. Ruth Nevo. Tel Aviv: Dvir, 1981.

Buber, Martin. *For the Sake of Heaven.* Trans. Ludwig Lewisohn. Philadelphia: Jewish Publication Society, 1953.

————. *Tales of the Hasidim: The Early Masters.* Trans. Olga Marx. New York: Schocken, 1948.

————. *Tales of the Hasidim: The Later Masters.* Trans. Olga Marx. New York: Schocken, 1948.

Burla, Yehudah. *'Ishto haSenu'ah (His Hated Wife).* In Hebrew. Tel Aviv: Massada, 1920.

Eytan, Rachel. *Shidah VeShidot (Pleasures of Man).* Tel Aviv: Am Oved, 1974.

Fogel, David. "Facing the Sea." Trans. Daniel Silverstone. In *Eight Great Hebrew Short Novels,* ed. Alan Lelchuk and Gershon Shaked, 217–68. New York: New American Library, 1983.

Goldberg, Lea. "Vehu' Ha-Or" ("And It Is the Light"). In Hebrew. *Prose,* 11–94. Tel Aviv: Poalim, 1972.

Gordon, Y. L. "The Love of David and Michal." In *The Collected Poems.* In Hebrew. Peterberg, 1884.

————. *The Collected Poems.* In Hebrew. Vilna: Raam, 1898.

Kahana-Karmon, Amalia. *And Moon in the Valley of Ajalon.* In Hebrew. Tel Aviv: Hakibbutz Hameuchad, 1971.

————. *Bikfifah Ahat.* Tel Aviv: Poalim, 1966.

Lebensohn, Micah Joseph. "Jael and Sisera." In Hebrew. The *Collected Poems,* 20–23. Tel Aviv: Dvir, 1956.

Leviant, Curt, ed. *Masterpieces of Hebrew Literature.* New York: Ktav, 1969.

Neubauer, Abraham and Moshe Shteinshneider. *Shebah Ha-Nashim uGenutan.* Ed. A. M. Habberman. Jerusalem: Ben Uri, 1968.

Oz, Amos. *My Michael.* Trans. Nicholas de Lange with the writer's collaboration. New York: Knopf, 1972.

————. "The Hill of Evil Counsel." In *Eight Great Hebrew Short Novels,* ed. Alan Lelchuk and Gershon Shaked, 269–317. New York: New American Library, 1983.

————. *Where the Jackals Howl.* Trans. Nicholas de Lange. New York: Harcourt, 1981. Stories from this collection discussed here: "Nomad and Viper," 21–38; "Strange Fire," 107–35.

Schirmann, Hayim, ed. *Saḥut Bediḥuta deKiddushin.* Jerusalem: Tarshish, 1946.

Tchernichovsky, Saul. *The Collected Poems.* In Hebrew. Jerusalem and Tel Aviv: Schocken, 1950. Poems discussed here are: "Dumplings," 133–44; "The Dinah Affair," 571–76; "The Rabbi's Beautiful Daughter," 737–39; "The Rabbi's Daughter," 438–41; "The Rabbi's Daughter and Her Mother," 736–37.

Yehoshua, A. B. "The Evening Journey of Yatir." In Hebrew. *'Ad Ḥoref,* 9–57. Tel Aviv: Hakibbutz Hameuchad, 1975.

Literary Criticism, Women's Studies and Judaic Studies

Adar, Zvi. *The Biblical Tale.* In Hebrew. Jerusalem: Jewish Agency, 1957.

Alter, Robert. *The Art of Biblical Narrative.* New York: Basic Books, 1981.

Aschkenasy, Nehama. "A Non-Sexist Reading of the Bible." *Midstream* 27, no. 6 (1981): 51–55.

———. "Biblical Females in a Joycean Episode." *Modern Language Studies* 15, no. 5 (1985): 28–39.

———. "Biblical Substructures in the Tragic Form: Hardy, *The Mayor of Casterbridge;* Agnon, "And the Crooked Shall be Made Straight." In *Biblical Patterns in Modern Literature,* 85–94. Ed. David Hirsch and N. Aschkenasy. Chico, Calif. Scholars Press, 1984.

Auerbach, Nina. *Communities of Women: An Idea in Fiction.* Cambridge, Mass.: Harvard University Press, 1978.

———. *Woman and the Demon: The Life of a Victorian Myth.* Cambridge, Mass.: Harvard University Press, 1982.

Bailey, J. S. "Initiation and the Primal Woman in Gilgamesh and Genesis 2–3." *Journal of Biblical Literature* 89 (1970): 137–50.

Band, Arnold. *Nostalgia and Nightmare.* Los Angeles: University of California Press, 1968.

Barzel, Hillel. *Agnon's Love Stories.* In Hebrew. Ramat Gan, Israel: Bar Ilan University, 1975.

———, ed. *Six Writers.* In Hebrew. Jerusalem: Yahdav, 1977.

Baum, Charlotte, Paula Hyman, and Sonya Michel. *The Jewish Woman in America.* New York: Dial Press, 1976.

Ben Sasson, H. H., ed. *A History of the Jewish People.* Cambridge, Mass.: Harvard University Press, 1976.

Biale, Rachel. *Women and Jewish Law: An Exploration of Women's Issues in Halakhic Sources.* New York: Schocken, 1984.

Campbell, Edward F., ed. *Ruth.* A New Translation with Introduction and Commentary. The Anchor Bible. New York: Doubleday, 1975.

Cassuto, Umberto. *A Commentary on the Book of Genesis.* Trans. Israel Abrahams. Jerusalem: Magnes, 1972.

Chesler, Phyllis. *Women and Madness.* Garden City, N.Y.: Doubleday, 1972.

Cohen, Gerson D. "Hannah and her Seven Sons." In *Jubilee Book in Honor of Mordechai Kaplan,* 109–22. New York: Jewish Theological Seminary, 1953.

Dan, Joseph. *The Hasidic Tale.* In Hebrew. Jerusalem: Keter, 1975.

————. *The Hebrew Tale in the Middle Ages: A Study of Its Development.* In Hebrew. Jerusalem: Keter, 1974.

————. "Samael, Lilith, and the Concept of Evil in Early Kabbalah." *Association for Jewish Studies Review,* 5 (1980): 17–40.

Davidson, Terry. *Conjugal Crime: Understanding and Changing Wifebeating Pattern.* New York: Hawthorne Books, 1978.

de Beauvoir, Simone. *The Second Sex.* New York: Knopf, 1953.

de Vaux, Roland. *Ancient Israel: Its Life and Institutions.* Trans. John McHugh. Toronto: McGraw-Hill of Canada, 1961.

Edel, Leon. *The Modern Psychological Novel.* New York: Grosset and Dunlap, 1964.

Erikson, Erik H. *Identity: Youth and Crisis.* New York: Norton, 1968.

Ferrante, Joan M. *Woman as Image in Medieval Literature.* New York: Columbia University Press, 1975.

Fisch, Harold. "Ruth and the Structure of Covenant History." *Vetus Testamentum* 32, no. 4 (1982): 425–37.

————. *The Dual Image: The Figure of the Jew in English and American Literature.* New York: Ktav, 1971.

Fraenkel, Jonah. *Studies in the Spiritual World of the Aggadic Tale.* In Hebrew. Tel Aviv: Hakibbutz Hameuchad, 1981.

Freud, Sigmund. *Three Essays on the Theory of Sexuality* (1905). In *The Standard Edition of the Complete Psychological Works,* vol. 7. Ed. and trans. James Strachey. London: Hogarth Press, 1964.

Fromm, Erich. *The Art of Loving.* New York: Harper and Row, 1974.

Frye, Northrop. *Anatomy of Criticism.* Princeton, N.J.: Princeton University Press, 1957.

Gilbert, Sandra M. and Susan Gubar. *The Madwoman in the Attic: The Woman Writer and the Nineteenth-Century Literary Imagination.* New Haven: Yale University Press, 1979.

Ginzberg, Louis. *The Legends of the Jews.* Philadelphia: Jewish Publication Society, 1909–28.

Goldberg, Lea. "S. Y. Agnon: The Writer and His Protagonist." In Hebrew. *LeAgnon Shai,* 47–61. Jerusalem: 1959.

Green, Arthur. *The Tormented Master: The Life of Rabbi Nahman of Bratslav.* New York: Schocken, 1981.

Greenberg, Blu. *On Woman and Judaism: A View from Tradition.* Philadelphia: Jewish Publication Society, 1981.

Halkin, Simon. *Modern Hebrew Literature: Trends and Values.* New York: Schocken, 1970.

Hassan, Ihab. *The Literature of Silence.* New York: Knopf, 1967.

Hazleton, Lesley. *Israeli Women: The Reality Behind the Myth.* New York: Simon and Schuster, 1977.

Heilbrun, Carolyn. *Towards a Recognition of Androgyny.* New York: Knopf, 1973.

Heinemann, Joseph. *Aggadah and Its Development.* In Hebrew. Jerusalem: Keter, 1974.

Holtz, Avraham. *I. D. Berkowitz: Voice of the Uprooted.* Ithaca, N.Y.: Cornell University Press, 1973.

Huizinga, Johan. *Homo Ludens: A Study of the Play-Element in Culture.* Trans. R. F. C. Hull. Boston: Beacon, 1955.

Jackson, Livia Bitton. *Madonna or Courtesan: The Jewish Woman in Christian Literature.* New York: Seabury Press, 1982.

Jagendorf, Zvi. "'In the Morning, Behold, It Was Leah': Genesis and the Reversal of Sexual Knowledge." In *Biblical Patterns in Modern Literature,* 51–60, ed. David H. Hirsch and Nehama Aschkenasy. Chico, Calif. Scholars Press, 1984.

Keppler, C. F. *The Literature of the Second Self.* Tucson: University of Arizona Press, 1972.

Kurzweil, Baruch. *Bialik and Tchernichovsky.* In Hebrew. Jerusalem: Schocken, 1971.

———. *Essays on Agnon's Stories.* Tel Aviv: Schocken, 1963.

Lederer, Wolfgang. *The Fear of Women.* New York: Harcourt, 1968.

Leibowitz, Nehama. *Studies in the Weekly Sidra.* Series 4/5718. Jerusalem: Jewish Agency, 1957.

Maccoby, Hyam. "The Delectable Daughter." *Midstream* 16, no. 9 (1970): 50–60.

McCarter, Kyle, ed. *1 Samuel.* A New Translation with Introduction. The Anchor Bible. Garden City, N.Y.: Doubleday, 1980.

Meyerhoff, Hans. *Time in Literature.* Berkeley: University of California Press, 1960.

Millet, Kate. *Sexual Politics.* Garden City, N.Y.: Doubleday, 1970.

Nacht, Jacob. *Simlei 'Ishah. The Symbolism of the Woman.* In Hebrew. Tel Aviv: Hotsa'at Va'ad talmidav va-ḥanikhay shel ha-meḥaber, 1959.

Neumann, Erich. *The Great Mother: An Analysis of the Archetype.* Trans. Ralph Manheim. Princeton, N.J.: Princeton University Press, 1970.

Otwell, John H. *And Sarah Laughed: The Status of Women in the Old Testament.* Philadelphia: Westminster Press, 1977.

Patai, Raphael. *Sex and Family in the Bible and the Middle East.* Garden City, N.Y.: Doubleday, 1959.

———. *The Hebrew Goddess.* New York: Ktav, 1967.

Rank, Otto. *The Double.* Trans. Harry Tucker. Chapel Hill: University of North Carolina Press, 1971.

Rauber, D. F. "Literary Values in the Bible: The Book of Ruth." *Journal of Biblical Literature* 89 (1970): 27–37.

Rieff, Philip. *Freud, the Mind of a Moralist.* New York: Viking, 1959.

Rogers, Katharine M. *The Troublesome Helpmate: A History of Misogyny in Literature.* Seattle: University of Washington Press, 1973.

Ruether, Rosemary, ed. *Religion and Sexism.* New York: Simon and Schuster, 1974.

———. *Sexism and God Talk: Towards a Feminist Theology.* Boston: Beacon Press, 1983.

Russell, Letty M., ed. *Feminist Interpretation of the Bible.* Philadelphia: Westminster Press, 1985.

Sarna, Nahum M. "The Ravishing of Dinah: A Commentary on Genesis, Chapter 34." In *Studies in Jewish Education*. Ed. A. Shapiro and B. Cohen. New York: Ktav, 1984, 143–56.

Scholem, Gershom G. *Kabbalah*. New York: Quadrangle, 1974.

———. *Major Trends in Jewish Mysticism*. New York: Schocken, 1974.

———. "Martin Buber's Interpretation of Hasidism." In *The Jewish Expression, 397–418*. Ed. Judah Goldin. New Haven: Yale University Press, 1976.

Shaked, Gershon. *A New Wave in Israeli Writings*. In Hebrew. Tel Aviv: Poalim, 1974.

———. *Dead End*. In Hebrew. Tel Aviv: Hakibbutz Hameuchad, 1973.

———. *On Four Stories: Studies on the Elements of the Short Story*. In Hebrew. Jerusalem: Jewish Agency, 1963.

Speiser, E. S., ed. *Genesis*. A New Translation with Introduction and Commentary. The Anchor Bible. Garden City, N.Y.: Doubleday, 1982.

Steiner, George. *Language and Silence*. London: Faber, 1967.

Sternberg, Meir. "A Delicate Balance in the Rape of Dinah." In Hebrew. *Ha-Sifrut* 4, no. 2 (1973): 193–231.

Tishbi, Yishayahu. *Mishnat Ha-Zohar*. Jerusalem: Mossad Bialik, 1949.

Trenchard, Warren C. *Ben Sira's View of Women: A Literary Analysis*. Chico, Calif.: Scholars Press, 1982.

Trible, Phyllis. "Depatriarchalizing in Biblical Interpretation." *Journal of American Academy of Religion* 41, no. 1 (1973); rpt. in *The Jewish Woman: New Perspectives*, ed. Elizabeth Koltun, 217–40. New York: Schocken Books, 1976.

———. *God and the Rhetoric of Sexuality*. Philadelphia: Fortress Press, 1978.

———. *Texts of Terror*. Philadelphia: Fortress Press, 1984.

Vos, Clarence J. *Women in Old Testament Worship*. Delft: Judels and Brinkman, n.d.

Woolf, Virginia. *A Room of One's Own*. New York and London: Harcourt Brace Jovanovich, 1929.

Index

Biblical characters are listed by name. Biblical books are not included here. Modern protagonists are not listed separately. Modern works are listed only under authors' names.

Midrash, portrayal of women in,
11–15, 43–45, 48–50, 84,
101, 111–12, 119–20, 129–
31, 144–45, 145–46, 164, 170,
179–85, 231–32, 243 n.22
Milk, as sexual symbol, 171
Milton, *Paradise Lost* (Adam and
Eve), 39, 42
Miron, Dan, 35 n.29
Misogyny, 8–9, 14, 18, 84, 103.
See also Essenes; Fear of
women; Lilith; "Strange
woman"; Duplicity, female
Moderation, women and. *See* Wise
women
Moses: and Zelofhad's daughters,
110–11; and the Shekinah, 150
Mother (Motherhood), 77–
105, 143–44. *See also* Leah;
Peninah
Mother and son, 85–103
Mother and daughter, 148–49,
214–15, 235–36
Mysticism, Jewish: attitude to
women in, 15–17, 77, 79, 101,
107, 120, 150, 185–86. *See
also* Lilith; Shekinah

Nacht, Jacob, *Symbolism of the
Woman*, 75 n.25, 76 nn.43, 44
Neumann, Erich, 71, 77, 79–81,
86, 100, 101, 102. *See also*
Great Mother; Terrible Mother
Nonsexist attitudes, in Bible, 11–
12, 174
Novel as genre, women and, 27–
28, 225–30

Old man, as symbol of feminine
fate, 217–18
Otherness, of women, 3–35. *See
also* Agnon; Burla; Duplicity,
female; Eve; Eytan; Kahana-
Karmon; Holocaust literature;
Lilith; Madness: of women;
Oz; Satan; "Sitra Aḥra";
"Strange Woman"
Oz, Amos, "The Hill of Evil
Counsel," 88–94; *My Michael*,
31, 70, 213–25, 230–31, 253;
"Nomad and Viper," 31, 208–

13, 230–31, 254; "Strange
Fire," 68–71, 254

Patai, Raphael, 16, 186
Patriarchy, women and, 109–30,
147–50, 164–65. *See also* Fa-
ther; Jacob
Peninah, 84
Peretz, I. L., "The Miracle That
Failed," 57; "Three Gifts," 6
Pinter, Harold, *The Homecoming*,
104 n.29
Plath, Sylvia, *The Bell Jar*, 223
Polygyny, 21, 84, 85, 121, 122,
123, 128, 145, 179, 243 n.21

Queen of Sheba, 69

Rabbi Akiba: and seduction, 48–
49; daughter of, 49; wife of, 146
Rabbi Meir, 48, 94, 145–46, 232
Rabbinic authority, women and,
15, 113–19, 120–21, 150–53,
187–88, 204–6
Rachel, the matriarch, 81, 82, 84,
92, 121, 123, 125, 162
Rachel, the poetess, 26
Rank, Otto, *The Double*, 217
Rape, 123, 173; of Dinah, 125–33;
of Tamar, 138–140, 154; in
Fogel's novella, 154–55; imaginings of rape as female
strategy, 211–13
Ravikovitch, Dalia, 30, 251–52
Rebecca, the matriarch, 81, 123,
162–65
Redemption: woman as obstacle to
national and cosmic, 51–57.
See also Eve; Lilith
female redemption through self-
destruction, 208–13
woman redeeming (son's) action,
99. *See also* Light
Responsa literature: on women
15, 19
Rizpah, 92
Rogers, Katharine M., *The Troublesome Helpmate*, 8, 74 n.2,
75 n.12
Ruth, 85, 87–88, 89, 91, 112,
251–52